WITHDRAWN

*A Clerk of Oxenford*

# A Clerk of Oxenford

ESSAYS ON LITERATURE AND LIFE

*Gilbert Highet*

*New York / OXFORD UNIVERSITY PRESS / 1954*

A clerk ther was of Oxenford also,
That unto logik hadde long y–go . . .
[And] him was lever have at his beddes heed
Twenty bookes, clad in blak or reed,
Of Aristotle and his philosophye,
Than robes riche, or fithele, or gay sautrye.

—Geoffrey Chaucer, *Prologue to the Canterbury Tales,* 285–96

O R

Here now is one of Oxford's graduates
Who spent three* terms on 'Mods' and seven on 'Greats' . . .
And he would rather have, at his bed's head,
Twenty good books, bound in black or red,
Of poetry, or of philosophy,
Than a silk shirt, or a wide-screen TV.

* It should have been five, but I had time off for diphtheria.

*Preface*

————————————————

THIS IS A COLLECTION of essays on life and literature, written during the past two years.

Early in 1952, on the invitation of the President of the Oxford University Press in New York, I began to give weekly talks on literature over a small local radio station. Starting very quietly, the talks evoked an unexpectedly warm response from the reading public. With the usual interval in the summer, they have been continued regularly ever since; but they are now heard in many different parts of the United States, have been re-broadcast in Canada, and are about to be put on the air in Australia.

A selection of essays based on the first series of these talks was issued in 1953, as *People, Places, and Books*. This also was quite unexpectedly successful. Many readers and listeners wrote to me, expressing their friendly interest in them, and suggesting that another collection of such essays should be published. This volume is the response to their interest.

I hope, therefore, that it will be considered on its own merits as a book of essays, and not as a mere transcription of radio talks. Those who have read *People, Places, and Books* will observe that the range of this collection is considerably wider, and that it goes more deeply into analysis of literary method and substance. Letters from numerous correspondents have convinced me that there is a strong demand in the United States for this type of aesthetic discussion and criticism. I feel sure they are right: hence this book.

As before, my gratitude is due, first of all, to my wife, Helen MacInnes, who listened to every single essay (immediately after it was written) and criticized them all with her own inimitable tact and delicacy; then to those three indispensables, the sponsor (Oxford University Press, New York, represented chiefly by Mr. Fon W. Boardman), the agent (Mr. Andrew Stewart, of Denhard and Stewart), and the technician (Mr. Stanley Bumbly, of Nola Studios, Steinway Hall, New York); and finally to all my kindly listeners and gentle readers.

*New York*                                                          G. H.
*May* 1954

# Acknowledgments

I SHOULD LIKE to express my thanks to a number of persons and firms who have been kind enough to grant me permission to reprint illustrative passages from works in which they hold copyright:

Arkham House, Sauk City, Wisconsin, from *Dark Carnival* by Ray Bradbury;

Edward Arnold, from *Abinger Harvest* by E. M. Forster;

Dodd, Mead & Company, from *A Bed of Neuroses* and *Death in the Rumble Seat* by Wolcott Gibbs;

Faber and Faber Ltd., from *Poems* by Stephen Spender; from *Adamastor* by Roy Campbell by permission of Curtis Brown Ltd.;

Harcourt, Brace and Company, Inc., from *Such, Such Were the Joys* by George Orwell, *The Wasteland* by T. S. Eliot, and *Abinger Harvest* by E. M. Forster;

Harper & Bros., from *Quo Vadimus* by E. B. White and *The Middle-Aged Man on the Flying Trapeze* by James Thurber;

Henry Holt and Company, Inc., from *A Shropshire Lad, Last Poems,* and *More Poems* by A. E. Housman;

Houghton Mifflin Company, from *Collected Poems 1917–1952* by Archibald MacLeish;

John Lane The Bodley Head Ltd., from *Collected Poems 1917–1952* by Archibald MacLeish;

J. B. Lippincott Company, from *High Conquest* by James Ramsey Ullman;

The Macmillan Company, from *Collected Poems* by William Butler Yeats and the Dundee edition of the McGonagall poems;

William Morrow & Company, Inc., from *Désirée* by Annemarie Selinko;

New Directions, from *Selected Poems* by Ezra Pound, and to the Committee of Ezra Pound, London;

W. W. Norton & Company, Inc., from *The Valley of Flowers* by F. S. Smythe;

Odhams Press, Ltd., from *From London to Ladysmith via Praetoria* by Winston S. Churchill;

S. J. Perelman, from *The Dream Department*;

Punch, reproduced by permission of the Proprietors;

Random House, Inc., from *Collected Poems* by John M. Synge and *Poems* by Stephen Spender;

St. Martin's Press, from *Collected Poems* by James Stephens;

James Thurber, from *The Middle-Aged Man on the Flying Trapeze*;

*Time*, from 'The Jaskpurt of Naustrent' (copyright 1952 by Time, Inc.);

The Viking Press, Inc., from *Finnegans Wake* by James Joyce;

E. B. White, from *Quo Vadimus*;

and to any others who may inadvertently have been overlooked.

# Contents

---

## IMAGINATION AND REALITY

# The Arts of Prose

*Perchance To Dream*

---

ONCE upon a time.

Wonderful words. Not always pleasant; but exciting.

Once upon a time a man called Spallner had an accident. He was crossing the street when a car ran into him and knocked him down. A crowd gathered. As he lay there, waiting for the ambulance, he heard them talking about him. 'Is he going to die?' they were asking one another—as though he couldn't hear them, almost as though he weren't there. He felt there was something badly wrong with them . . . And then the ambulance arrived. Even in the ambulance, with his eyes shut, he could still see their faces staring at him, greedily.

It took Spallner some time, but he got better. One of the things that worried him while he was in hospital was the crowd. There had been *something* about their faces; certainly there was something terribly strange about the speed with which they had appeared, out of nowhere, so quickly, as though——

After Spallner left hospital, he went back to work. On his first day in the office, he heard a noise outside, and looked down. A collision: a body lying in the street; a crowd gathering, quickly, quickly. He ran down and pushed his way in, just in time to see a red-haired woman and a little boy with a freckled face. And he remembered both these two from the day of his own accident. They had been there, looking down at him. They had been there.

A man can't go round waiting for accidents to happen. But there are news reports, and photographs. So Spallner hired a clipping service to get him photographs of all the bad accidents over a ten-year period—street crashes, and fires, and explosions. In every one of them he found the freckle-faced boy, and the woman with red hair. Over ten years, the woman had never changed her hair or her dress, and the boy had not grown an inch. But they were in every picture, looking down at the body, or bodies.

The photographs reached Spallner's office one day after lunch. Spallner went over them in amazement; then he put them in his brief case and—well, what would you do? He started to drive down town to the central police station. But before he reached it, a truck smashed into his car. He lay on the pavement, helpless. As he lay, he heard them coming. The crowd. Their faces bent over him, breathing his air. There was the woman with red hair, still in the same dress, still with the same intent expression. There was the freckled boy. Two of the men bent over him. Their faces too, he knew their faces, they had been in every crowd. 'Don't move me, don't move me!' he cried; but they bent lower, and moved him. They tidied him up. They straightened him, and he bled more easily, more copiously. Then they stood back, watching him.

He heard a siren in the distance. The ambulance. But he knew now it was useless; so did they. He said his last words: 'I'll be joining you now. I'll be a member of your group.' Then he closed his eyes, and waited for the coroner.

That is a summary of a short story by the young Californian writer, Ray Bradbury. I have taken the liberty of retelling it, partly because it is a splendid story, partly because Ray Bradbury is an exceptionally good author who deserves to be better known, and partly because I want to take back something I wrote in an earlier book.*

Discussing the Anglo-Irish writer C. S. Lewis, I said that most 'science-fiction' seemed to me to be trash—merely childish fairy tales without moral or intellectual content. This evoked many letters (most of them quite polite), pointing out that I was wrong, and recommending writers of 'science-fiction' with whom I ought to acquaint myself. Since then, I have read a large number of genuine 'science-fiction' romances and short stories. Thinking them over, I must say that most of them *are* trash, on the same level as cowboy tales, cheap ghost stories, and 'lost world' exploration fantasies, poorly imagined and vulgarly written. But a surprising number of them are good, far better conceived and more interestingly written than many of the dull realistic novels and machine-made historical romances that pour off the printing presses.

However, we have been describing these stories wrongly, and therefore defining them wrongly. In most of the best of them, there is not much real science. There is only dreaming. For instance, in an admirable fantasy called *Childhood's End*, by Arthur Clarke, there are space ships, and there is an invasion of our world by inhabitants of another part of the uni-

* 'From World to World,' *People, Places, and Books* (Oxford University Press, 1953). The story is Ray Bradbury's 'The Crowd,' from his collection, *Dark Carnival*.

verse; but the construction and propulsion of the ships and the science of the strangers are utterly beyond the understanding of any human being. They are therefore not human science, but something much more like magic. And so, too, is the astonishing climax of the story—not science at all, but a mystical experience, spiritual and even religious in character. The Ray Bradbury tale retold above is a variant of the ghost story; and the ghost story is many thousands of years old. One of the earliest of the human race's many fears was the fear of the dead who return, to infect the living with their death. Others of Ray Bradbury's fantasies are highly skilled, and even humorous, or macabre, variations on the theme of the living-dead, the vampires. Such stories are not 'science-fiction'; they are not a new departure at all, nor are they necessarily vulgar and literarily negligible. On the contrary, they have a long and noble ancestry.

They should really be called tales of fantasy. In the United States, they were first brought into literature by one of our most distinguished writers. If you have once read his stories, you can never forget them. He himself called them *Tales of the Grotesque and Arabesque*. Here is one of them.

A lonely traveler, sailing eastward from Java, was caught in a typhoon. Dismasted, his ship collided with another vessel, in the thick darkness of an unnatural night, and hurled him aboard the stranger. He was carried away into the unknown.

The new ship was black, immensely large, with vast ropes and tree-like masts that towered upward into the ebony sky. The traveler was terrified. He hid, concealing himself in the womb of the mysterious apparition. Only slowly and timorously did he come out, and walk among the crew. They did not see him. They were dressed in strange clothes—more like memories of the past than regular sailors' gear. They moved ponderously, speaking in low harsh tones, like the wind groaning and the waves grumbling. They seemed old. They seemed infinitely old. The traveler lived among these weird and hideous forms for days, for weeks. All that time they never sighted another sail. The ship sped onward day after day, night after night.

Then, to his horror, he saw that she was caught in a tremendous ocean current, setting faster and faster due south, toward an unknown terminus. She could neither stop, nor veer, nor turn back. It was agonizing to be carried on so helplessly, in the power of a force so hungry and so resistless.

Then, with horrible suddenness, there appeared ahead of the ship a gigantic whirlpool, a huge chasm in the very floor of the ocean, through which, like a multitude of Niagaras, the stupendous current was pouring swiftly and ceaselessly. The traveler had only a few moments to write his last words and seal them up:

The ship is quivering—oh God! and—going down!

That magnificent story you will have recognized. It is the 'Manuscript Found in a Bottle,' by Edgar Allan Poe. Like many of the best fantasy-tales, it is rather a dream (or a collection of dreams) than an account of everyday reality. You know how often we dream of being carried helplessly forward toward an unknown but perilous destination. You probably remember one of the strange ideas which sometimes beset long-distance travelers, the feeling that the journey is infinitely long, out of this world. You certainly recognize the main theme: the famous myth of the Flying Dutchman, the haunted ship which must sail on and on to eternity. And you recall that death has often been represented, in dream and in myth, as a dark ship: the ferryboat of Charon, transporting the dead across the river Styx to the underworld; the dusky barge

Dark as a funeral scarf from stem to stern

in which the dying King Arthur sailed away to Avelion; the

mysterious boat in Böcklin's picture, 'The Isle of the Dead';
and, strangest of all, the black ship which appeared in a dream,
the night before his death, to President Lincoln, and seemed
to carry him away into unknown darkness.

These fantastic tales spring from different sources and are
fed by different streams from the fictional stories we usually
read. A novel tries to tell of what has happened in the external
world. It is pretending to be real. It is successful in proportion
to its power to seem lifelike and to be checked and verified by
everyday experience. A fantastic tale (even though it may
*seem* to be a description of events in the external world) really
tells of adventures experienced internally; and its chief appeal
is in creating memorable symbols for such adventures of the
soul. The novel is history. The fantastic tale is myth; folk tale;
magic; dreams; mysticism. We live in two worlds: the external
world with which we have rational connections, the realm of
law and society and business; and the world of our desires and
imagination, much of our creative effort, and most of our
emotions, love and hatred and pride and fear. Both of these
worlds can be reflected in literature: and it is chiefly through
poetry and fantasy that the second, the internal world, is converted into art.

Once we have seen this, we can recall the splendid ancestry
of such fantasies. In poetry we remember Coleridge's 'Ancient
Mariner,' Shakespeare's *Tempest*, and Homer's *Odyssey*. In
prose, there is Poe, and his immediate ancestor, who wrote
the *Tales of Hoffmann*. In our own time, there is John Collier,
a varied and wonderful writer; and A. E. Coppard, one of the
world's finest short-story writers; and Lord Dunsany, the Irish
mystic surrounded by goblins and leprechauns. Not long ago
there was Algernon Blackwood; and a little before him that
formidable San Franciscan, Ambrose Bierce (do you think he
might still exist, in some nightmare town in northern Mex-

ico, inhabited by the living dead?). Rudyard Kipling wrote several superb fantasy stories, including at least two scientific forecasts. Stevenson revealed a profound psychological secret in 'Dr. Jekyll and Mr. Hyde,' and the great realist Balzac exposed another in the 'The Shagreen Skin.' A few years earlier, one of the most powerful demons of our world of imagination was created by a girl of twenty-one, the wife of the poet Shelley: as part of a friendly competition she evoked the terrible figures of Frankenstein and his monster. Behind her again there is Swift, with that odd blend of realism and fantastic horror, *Gulliver's Travels*; and Rabelais; and *The Arabian Nights*, and so far back into an earlier age of myth.

Thinking over these names, we can see why so much modern fantasy-fiction is contemptible, or, at best, tedious. It is not because its themes are silly. It is because its authors cannot write. Their style is commonplace, or cheap, or sometimes (like that of H. P. Lovecraft) turgid. Yet Ray Bradbury has a fine style: laconic, sensitive, sometimes poetic; so, in some books at least, has Arthur Clarke; and so has Theodore Sturgeon. It is one of the paradoxes of literature that good stylists are far more rare than good ideas.

After all, what are the four chief themes of fantasy-fiction? They are all dreams: one is a nightmare. The nightmare is that other beings may challenge our mastery of the world, and treat us as we treat animals. The dreams are that we may travel into the past or into the future, that we may visit the planets and the stars, and that we may talk with the dead and the immortal. Is this escape literature? Surely not. These themes are rooted deep in the human soul. The nightmare comes from our half-realized knowledge that we are cruel, and that we ought to be humble. The rest, the dreams, are our inextinguishable hopes that somehow we may conquer time, and space, and mortality.

Ray Bradbury, *Dark Carnival* (Arkham House, 1947).

Ray Bradbury, *The Martian Chronicles* (Doubleday, 1950).

Ray Bradbury, *The Illustrated Man* (Doubleday, 1951).

Ray Bradbury, *The Golden Apples of the Sun* (Doubleday, 1953).

Ray Bradbury, *Fahrenheit 451* (Ballantine, 1953).

Arthur Clarke, *Childhood's End* (Ballantine, 1953).

Robert A. Heinlein, *The Puppet Masters* (Signet, 1951).

Theodore Sturgeon, *E Pluribus Unicorn* (Abelard Press, 1953).

Theodore Sturgeon, *More Than Human* (Farrar, Straus & Young, 1953).

*One Smith in a Billion*

---

PROBABLY you have noticed how some people—even when you have never met them—seem very attractive, almost seem to be friends of yours already. You remember their good qualities and forget their bad. You would recognize their faces if you met them. You can almost hear the tones in which they speak. The style of their talk and writing penetrates your mind. You enjoy thinking about them, and meeting them indirectly—even if they are far removed from you in time or space. You know them through a painting, or a diary, or a symphony, or a group of poems. It is impossible not to think with affection of Schubert, or Frans Hals, or Chaucer. They must have been delightful companions.

I have three or four friends like that—friends whom I know quite well although I have never heard them talk, and have met them only through their portraits and their writings. One of them was a big burly fellow with a round, ripe voice. His name was Smith. He died over a century ago.

Almost everybody liked Smith. He was terribly popular. Even the coldest, hardest intellectuals, even the loftiest type of English snob, all liked Smith. Supreme tribute, his own family liked him. He married his young wife when he had no money and practically no prospects, only his own innate resources of health, vigor, and humor. Just after the wedding he collected his only capital, six small silver teaspoons, rushed up to his bride, and threw them into her lap, saying, 'There, you lucky girl, I give you all my fortune!' She thought he was a little crazy, but she knew he was talented, she lived happily with him for forty-five years, and after he died she wrote a charming tribute to him addressed to her grandchildren:

> Such a mind, such versatility of talents, such a bold and fearless love of truth, such an ardent love of human happiness . . . must eventually break through all obstacles and gain for itself honor and distinction.

And then, in double-sized characters, underlined, she added:

AND SO IT DID!

Vive Smith!

His first name was Sydney. He was a liberal English clergyman, and there is good reason to believe that he was the funniest man who ever breathed. Certainly he was the funniest man called Smith—and that covers a good deal of the human race, including Red and H. Allen. Sydney Smith was born in 1771 of a rich but wildly eccentric father, who educated him to the age of twenty and then did no more for him, except to pester him with threatening and begging letters—a character who would have fitted beautifully into a Dickens novel. Sydney went to one of the best schools in England, Winchester, and to one of the best colleges at Oxford, New College. Nowadays these two have the reputation of producing rather quiet, correct, tight-lipped, rolled-umbrella characters. Either they have changed, or Sydney was a bold exception.

His career after leaving college was difficult. He had talent and education, but no money. His father wouldn't give him any. There were three classes in England at that time: the working class, the commercial and manufacturing middle class, and the aristocracy; and Sydney belonged to none of them. There are plenty of careers nowadays, both here and in Britain, open to college-trained youths without capital, but there were very few then. He thought of going in for the law, where he would have been brilliant; but it was insecure and sometimes rather degrading: he chose the Church. That was not degrading, but it was a hard discipline. He succeeded in it. He started in 1794 as a poor curate. He ended in 1845 as a rich dignitary, Canon of St. Paul's Cathedral. Still, his success reached him late. The years which ought to have been his most productive— from his early thirties to his middle fifties—were spent in country parsonages almost as remote as a village in the Ozarks would be to us today. Much ambition he had to repress in himself, much energy he had to expend on making his lonely family happy and healthy. It was hard, but he did it: one of his friends said Smith's wife and children used to be kept in shouts of laughter two or three hours every day by his unequaled high spirits. He made excellent jokes about his poverty. Once a visiting lady asked him why he had no deer in his grounds (deer! like a duke!): so he took his two pet donkeys and fitted antlers on their heads. The fact that The Reverend Sydney Smith's stags used to say 'hee-haw' at intervals was, he explained, a result of their special breeding. He also wired oranges onto trees in his garden, to give it an atmosphere of hothouse luxury.

Meanwhile he wrote a good deal. He criticized books regularly for the newly founded *Edinburgh Review,* which paid him satisfactorily and helped to keep his mind active; he published a splendid series of anonymous letters defending the principle of tolerance toward the Roman Catholics in England; and he made one or two famous and extraordinarily effective speeches on the Whig, or liberal, side in politics.

But all that was only the ground bass. The melody playing above it, that was the important thing. Sydney Smith was a rare humorist. He was every kind of funny man—the wit who makes epigrams, the fantast who throws out wild imaginings, the verbal juggler, the clown and the mimic and the parodist and the caricaturist. He was almost irresistible. The famous tragedy queen, Sarah Siddons, who was always ineffably distant and dignified in society, was overcome by Sydney Smith's gaiety at their first meeting, got the hiccups from laughing, and had to be helped into the next room to recover. A solemn Scottish lawyer-philosopher, Sir James Mackintosh, was caught in a shower of Smith's comical imaginations, caved in under it, and finally rolled on the floor, helplessly crowing and hooting. Smith could quite often stop a party dead because all the guests were laughing so hard that nobody could say anything, and the servants were leaning against the wall guffawing and wiping their eyes. Both Abraham Lincoln and Queen Victoria used to collect his sayings, and they wished they could have met him: so do I, so do we all. The only trouble is that when Sydney Smith really got going nobody would remember even a quarter of the best things he said, so that all we have now is fragments of a rich feast. Still, they are delicious.

It is impossible to classify his jokes without mutilating them all and killing some of them; but many of them started with a logical idea, prolonged into the superlogical realm of the absurd. Once somebody mentioned a young man who was going to marry a fat elderly widow. Sydney Smith cried out:

Marry her! Impossible! You mean part of her; he could

not marry her all himself. It would be a case not of bigamy, but of trigamy. The magistrates should interfere. There is enough of her to furnish wives for a whole parish. One man marry her!—it is monstrous. You might people a colony with her; or give an assembly with her; or perhaps take your morning's walk round her, always provided there were frequent resting-places and you were in rude health. Or you might read the Riot Act and disperse her; in short, you might do anything with her but marry her.

It isn't really cruel, it is simply nonsense. When someone else spoke of a very smart and chic lady in her middle thirties, Smith remarked:

Whenever she appears, even although there is no garrison within twelve miles, the horizon is immediately clouded with majors.

He defined marriage as like a pair of shears—so joined that they cannot be separated, often moving in opposite directions, yet always punishing anyone who comes between them. He also talked very well about food and diet—for the English of that day almost all overate. The doctor told him that he ought to take a walk every day on an empty stomach. Smith said 'Very well: on whose?' Once when he was being kept on a very meager invalid diet, he said he wished he might have 'the wing of a roasted butterfly.' And he said some funny but wise things about rich food, like this:

My friend sups late; he eats some strong soup, then a lobster, then some tart, and he dilutes these esculent varieties with wine. The next day I call on him. He is going to sell his house in London and retire into the country. He is alarmed for his eldest daughter's health. His expenses are hourly increasing, and nothing but a timely retreat can save him from ruin. All this is the lobster. [After it is digested] the daughter recovers, the finances are in good order, and every rural idea . . . excluded. In the same manner old friendships are destroyed by toasted cheese, and hard salted meat has led to suicide.

Sydney Smith was witty about foreign countries. When a missionary bishop went out to New Zealand among the savage Maoris, Sydney advised him to entertain the cannibal chiefs at his residence, saying, 'I deeply regret to have nothing on my own table suited to your tastes, but you will find plenty of cold curate and roasted clergyman on the sideboard.' He added, if the cannibals finished off by eating the bishop himself, 'Well, I sincerely hope he will disagree with them.'

In his youth he spent some time in Scotland, and some of his best friends were Scotsmen. It was he who first said that it required a surgical operation to get a joke into a Scotsman's head, and he observed what you and I will still find to be true if we go to Scotland and mention the cold damp weather.

No nation has so large a stock of benevolence of heart as the Scotch. Their temper stands anything but an attack on their climate. They would even have you believe they can ripen fruit; and, to be candid, I must own that in remarkably warm summers I have tasted peaches that made most excellent pickles; and it is upon record that at the Siege of Perth . . . their nectarines made admirable cannonballs.

And he also noticed something which otherwise I know only from J. M. Barrie:

You will find that they usually arrange their dishes at dinner by the points of the compass: 'Sandy, put the gigot of mutton to the south, and move the singet sheep's head a wee bit to the nor-wast.'

Sydney Smith was just as wise and funny about the English:

There is nothing which an Englishman enjoys more than the pleasure of sulkiness . . . It is not so much that Mr. Bull disdains to talk, as that Mr. Bull has nothing to say. His forefathers have been out of spirits for six or seven hundred years, and, seeing nothing but fog . . . he is out of spirits too; and when there is no selling or buying, or no business to settle, he prefers being alone and looking at the fire.

And on women he was gallant and perceptive:

Women cannot face danger accompanied with noise, and smoke and hallooing; but in all kinds of . . . quiet horrors they have infinitely more philosophical endurance than men.—Put a woman in a boat in a boisterous sea, let six or seven people make as much noise as they can, and she is in a state of inconceivable agony; ask the same women in a serene summer's evening, when all nature is at rest, to drink a cup of poison for some good which would accrue from it to her husband and children, and she will swallow it like green tea.

Once, in London, Smith heard two women leaning out of windows on opposite sides of the street, and abusing each other. He said, 'They will never agree, for they are arguing from different premises.'

He could make jokes on even the gravest subjects, such as violent death. Once he engaged in a campaign to compel the railways to leave the carriage doors unlocked in case of an accident followed by a fire; he won; but he said that if the directors had not given way,

I should have described them gazing with satisfaction on the burnt train . . .: 1st carriage—a stewed Duke; 2nd —two bishops done in their own gravy; 3rd—three ladies of quality browned. 4th—lawyers . . . stewed in their own briefs à la Maintenon. 5th—a grammar school returning home, legs out of window like a pigeon pie. 6th—a fat woman much overdone. 7th—two Scotchmen dead but raw, sulphuric acid perceptible.

Sydney Smith was for many years most famous because of one image, a single paragraph in a speech he made on the liberal side when the bill to reform Parliament was being opposed by the House of Lords. He said the attempt to stop reform reminded him of the great storm which attacked the Devonshire town of Sidmouth.

> The tide rose to an incredible height—the waves rushed in upon the houses—and everything was threatened with destruction. In the midst of this sublime and terrible storm, Dame Partington, who lived upon the beach, was seen at the door of her house . . . trundling her mop, squeezing out the sea-water, and vigorously pushing away the Atlantic Ocean . . . I need not tell you that the contest was unequal. The Atlantic beat Mrs. Partington. She was excellent at a slop or a puddle, but she should not have meddled with a tempest.

Fifty years later an eyewitness still remembered Sydney Smith pretending to be the old lady sweeping back the waves with a large mop and a frown of angry determination. The meeting broke out into inextinguishable laughter, which changed into delighted cheers.

Smith's letters have recently been re-edited and issued in two large volumes. They give an interesting picture of his life, and of Britain in the early nineteenth century; but they are much more sober than one would expect, and often they show his soft heart—as when he tells his friend Jeffrey:

> The haunts of Happiness are varied, and rather unaccountable; but I have more often seen her among little children, and home firesides, and in country houses, than anywhere else.

In many ways Sydney Smith reminds me of three other clergymen, all brilliantly witty: one was the Austrian priest, Abraham a Sancta Clara, who put more jokes into his sermons than would be possible anywhere except in Vienna; one was Laurence Sterne; and one was the dean who wrote baby talk and thought high politics, Jonathan Swift. No doubt the four of them are all talking their heads off at this moment, in a specially built annex to heaven. I can imagine them—hard, dry jokes from Swift, a flood of Viennese gaiety from Abraham, spouts of unfinished merriment from Sterne, and overarching them all, sparkling and splashing like a Niagara of champagne, the torrential wit of Sydney Smith.

G. Bullett, *Sydney Smith* (Joseph, London, 1951).
H. Pearson, *The Smith of Smiths* (Hamilton, London, 1934).
G. W. E. Russell, *Sydney Smith* (Macmillan, London, 1905).
N. C. Smith, *The Letters of Sydney Smith* (Oxford, 1953).

*Ice and Fire*

---

IT TAKES courage to settle a new land: to abandon one's home, to risk poverty and starvation, to struggle with a strange climate, to fight the natives, or, if there are none, to wrestle with other incomers desperate and ruthless. As well as courage, it takes wisdom. New institutions have to be devised, if the land is to be permanently settled. Laws and schools, social and intellectual structures have to be created. It is not enough for such a settler to be a farmer or a fisherman: he must also become something of a statesman, his wife something of a doctor and a teacher, and both of them inventors. Not all settlements are fully successful. Some new countries still remain empty, or half peopled. But it is always moving and uplifting to read the story of a successful settlement, and see how the new country created new people to inhabit it.

Such were the Pilgrims, and the Virginia settlers. Yet there is an earlier tale of such adventure which is less famous through the world, but has produced better literature. This is the history of Iceland. A remote place it is—a lava island, larger than Ireland, full of volcanoes, far in the northern Atlantic. The Norsemen discovered it about 850. (That was the beginning of their great period, when they roamed as far as Constantinople in the east and Massachusetts in the west, conquered Ireland, harried Scotland, settled down in England, and took over Normandy.) Just about a thousand years ago, Iceland was well populated and was growing into one of the earliest Western republics. The main stream of immigrants was Norwegian; but there were Celts, too, from the Scottish islands and from Ireland. It was a hard life; but it was uncommonly interesting. It produced some tough men; some brave women; some fine books.

There are many kinds of Icelandic books—poetry, myth, history. The best of them all, the rarest and most memorable, are the sagas. A saga is simply a tale—not a piece of fiction, but a true story about a famous man, or a powerful family, or a dramatic event. Soon after the death of a hero, the Icelandic storytellers began to collect the chief incidents of his career and to weave them into a continuous story; then they would tell it from memory at parties, just like the Gaelic talesmiths and the Homeric poets. About A.D. 1200 these stories began to be written down. Thirty or forty of them have been preserved to our time. They give us a rich, a fascinating, picture of the settlers' life, with its violent passions, its savage cruelties, its tremendous gallantry and determination, and (most interesting of all) its gradual progress into culture, from anarchy to order, from brute force into law, from paganism to Christianity, from the boyish bravado of rovers and pirates into the steady energy of thoughtful men: indeed, one might almost say from the sheer lunacy of primitive savages into the sanity of the civilized.

The Icelandic sagas fill two large bookshelves. I have not read them all: few have, except specialists, such as the charming old Cambridge professor in C. P. Snow's *The Masters,* who has them all in his head and has built a huge relief map of Iceland on which to trace their heroes' exploits. But I have read some of them, including the best, and I like rereading them. They are usually well translated, for their language (apart from the esoteric bits of poetry) is simple and quite close to ours, and their stories are straightforward. My two favorites are the story of a formidable outlaw, *Grettir the Strong,* and the story of a wise and gentle statesman, *Burnt Nial*—so called because he was burned to death in his own house by an enemy.

Nothing will give a better idea of the style of the sagas, and of the straight-spoken courage of the men and women who inspired them, than a quotation of one of their greatest scenes. Nial and his family have been surrounded in his lonely farmhouse. Failing to break in, his enemies have set fire to the doors and the roof. Flosi, their chief, allows the women and children and servants to escape, and then calls to Nial himself.

> Flosi said, 'I will offer thee, master Nial, leave to go out, for it is unworthy that thou shouldst burn indoors.'
>
> 'I will not go out,' said Nial, 'for I am an old man, and little fitted to avenge my sons, but I will not live in shame.'
>
> Then Flosi said to [Nial's wife] Bergthora, 'Come thou out, housewife, for I will for no sake burn thee indoors.'
>
> 'I was given away to Nial young,' said Bergthora, 'and I have promised him this, that we would both share the same fate.'
>
> After that they both went back into the house.
>
> 'What counsel shall we now take?' said Bergthora.
>
> 'We will go to our bed,' says Nial, 'and lay us down; I have long been eager for rest.'

Then she said to the boy Thord, 'Thee will I take out, and thou shalt not burn in here.'

'Thou hast promised me this, grandmother,' says the boy, 'that we should never part so long as I wished to be with thee; but methinks it is much better to die with thee and Nial than to live after you.'

Then she bore the boy to her bed, and Nial spoke to his steward and said, 'Now thou shalt see where we lay us down, and how I lay us out, for I mean not to stir an inch hence, whether reek or burning smart me, and so thou wilt be able to guess where to look for our bones.' . . .

Skarphedinn saw how his father laid him down, and how he laid himself out, and then he said, 'Our father goes early to bed, and that is what was to be looked for, for he is an old man.'

When you read any of the sagas for the first time, one thing is likely to disconcert you a little—and, oddly enough, it is a quality in them that the Icelanders themselves love. This is that they are full of genealogy. It is like visiting one of the Southern states, where everyone is related to everyone else and people can trace their relationships even unto the ninth and tenth generation. So also, the people in the sagas were the First Families of Iceland. Their descendants love hearing about them and following their movements, their marriages and feuds and exiles and adventures; so sometimes you have to wade through many chapters of family chronicle to strike the main stream of the story. This is a bit boring; but it does give a strong impression of sincerity.

The next thing you notice is the extraordinary will power and courage of the people, both men and women. Very few cowards came to Iceland across the gray North Atlantic, and not many were born there. The men were both pioneers and pirates—for sometimes they would farm for a few seasons, and then take to their viking ships to loot the coasts of Europe, returning rich and refreshed, or else dying in battle and leaving their skins to decorate an English church door. There are many stories that show them taking an oath or making a silent resolution, and then keeping it through years of fierce opposition and suffering. Everyone has some courage at some moments. The saga people admired the courage that is needed for a long, grim struggle against fearful odds, and most of all the courage a man can show even when he knows he is outnumbered and finished. Some of the finest incidents in the sagas show a brave man facing death with a crisp epigram, or with a controlled and powerful gesture that shows his stout heart still unbroken and unbreakable. One young viking on a long voyage got a boil on the side of his foot. When he disembarked, and was taken in to be presented to the powerful Earl Eric, he would not limp, though the boil oozed blood and pus at every step. The Earl asked him what was wrong. Gunnlaug said he had a boil under his foot. 'Yet you do not limp,' said the Earl. The young man replied, 'I shall not go lame while both my legs are the same length.' By this action and this bold utterance, he showed himself as good a man as anyone there, tacitly challenged the Earl, and dominated himself.

As you read on in the sagas, you will also be impressed by the silence of their people. In Iceland, the greater a man or woman is, the less he or she talks. (This is the reverse of our own system.) They brood for long periods; then, at a crucial moment, they say something powerful and final, words which they have for many months been distilling and storing, or a sentence which is slow, quiet, but filled with implosive energy. Once a group of the hero Gunnar's enemies surrounded his house. One of them climbed the roof to discover a way in. Gunnar stabbed him through the window, and he fell down. His friends said, 'Is Gunnar at home?' He answered, 'Find out for yourselves: I know his blade is at home,' and so he died. Sometimes at crises the men remain utterly silent, which is even more forcible. (As Grettir said, 'No man is a fool if he keeps silence.') When Hvitserk heard of the cruel death of his father in a pit full of snakes, he was playing a game like chess. He said nothing, but squeezed a piece he was holding so tightly that the blood burst out under his fingernails. Listening to these grim phrases or watching these grimmer silences, we remember that Iceland is a country where the winters are long and the mountain snows are endless, but the volcanoes smoke from time to time, and then, with long-pent-up violence, erupt.

Another good thing about the people of the sagas is their bodily strength and beauty. The stories are full of tremendous physical energy, feats we should hardly believe if we could not parallel them from the lives of other primitives like the Zulus and the American Indians. The men were terrific wrestlers, swimmers, runners, weight-lifters. Both the men and the women were notable for their good looks. A wind of health blows from the sagas.

The stories themselves are long, complex, episodic. Usually they not only tell a tale but describe many different characters, pose a number of problems for meditation, and vivify a complete sector of social history. They are not epics, because they are in prose and lack the superb marching rhythms and dazzling imagery of Homer or Milton. They are closest to the modern historical novel, the objectively told stories like *Ivanhoe* and *Salammbô*. They are solid books, full of solid virtues and vices. If I were a lonely man, or a despondent man, believing this was a terrifying age of hitherto unparalleled anxiety and danger, or if I were a young man who thought I lacked courage and wanted to train for it, I should read half a dozen of the Icelandic stories, beginning with *Grettir the Strong* and *Burnt Nial*.

They can still inspire living authors. In the last generation or so, new stories have been written in the manner of the sagas, and some of them are well worth reading. Two of their authors are Scandinavian; both women, and both Nobel Prize winners. The other two are British—one English and one Scots, both of Norse ancestry.

The Swedish writer, Selma Lagerlöf, in 1891 produced *Gösta Berling's Story,* a cycle of wildly romantic short stories set in modern Sweden, rather resembling Isak Dinesen's *Seven Gothic Tales.* They are handsomely told but are scarcely saga-like, apart from their arrangement and their occasional violence. The Norwegian Sigrid Undset has two long, complex historical novels about thirteenth-century Scandinavia: *The Master of Hestviken* and *Kristin Lavransdatter.* They seem to me to have all the disadvantages of the saga style without all its advantages, for they are intricate without being energetic; but the atmosphere is beautifully sustained and separate incidents are sometimes strong and memorable.

These two women really wrote romantic saga-novels. But two men tried to produce tales which—if discovered in manuscript—might be pronounced genuine Icelandic works. Eric Linklater, in *The Men of Ness,* re-created the life of the vikings, centering on the sea. It reminds us that in stirring periods of history it is only safe and quiet people who live in towns, while the men who become the masters of events inhabit plain and desert and sea. His vikings look something like modern fighters of the air. I cannot recommend his book wholeheartedly, because, like the salt fish the vikings ate, it is a little too hard and crisp for everyone's taste; but it is full of vitamins.

The most exciting modern saga of the old North is *Eric Brighteyes,* by Henry Rider Haggard. Many readers know *King Solomon's Mines* and *She,* and the Allan Quatermain books, but *Eric Brighteyes* is neglected, partly because readers do not know how to approach it. It is a stirring Icelandic tale combining elements from many of the sagas, together with much Norse mythology. Its hero Eric is brave and handsome, but unlucky. Two women love him—which is all the more ill luck. He is poor and has powerful enemies. His heroism does not mean success: it means loneliness and defeat; but it ends in glory. The tale is filled with daring and uncanny adventures. Below is a Wagnerian moment from its very end, the night before Eric's last battle, when he sits with his only friend waiting for the dawn. The two men see the aurora borealis, the northern lights, above the peak of Mount Hecla: but this is what appears to them.

> In the rosy glow there sat three giant forms of fire, and their shapes were the shapes of women. Before them was a loom of blackness that stretched from earth to sky, and they wove at it with threads of flame. They were splendid and terrible to see. Their hair streamed behind them like meteor flames, their eyes shone like lightning, and their breasts gleamed like the polished bucklers of the gods. They wove fiercely at the loom of blackness, and as they wove they sang. The voice of the one was as the wind whistling through the pines; the voice of the other was as the sound of rain hissing on deep waters; and the voice of the third was as the moan of the sea. They wove fearfully and they sang loudly, but what they sang might not be known. Now the web grew and the woof grew, and a picture came upon the loom— a great picture written in fire. Behold! it was the semblance of a storm-awakened sea, and a giant ship fled before the gale—a dragon of war, and in the ship were piled the corses of men, and on these lay another corse, as one lies upon a bed. They looked and the face of the corse grew bright. It was the face of Eric, and his head rested upon the dead heart of [his friend] Skallagrim.

*Eric Brighteyes* is a fine book. It does not, of course, supersede the ancient sagas: it is to them as Scott's novels are to the ballads and chronicles, more detailed and less primitive, more artistic and better balanced but less original, still a modern assertion of trust in permanent ideals of courage and nobility: it is a bridge between our own fugitive present and bold unknown moments of the past, a rainbow path along which heroes can come to challenge us, and beautiful women, to make our youths aspire to that love which is won only through suffering and resolution.

*The Story of Burnt Nial* (tr. G. W. Dasent, Everyman's Library 558).

*The Saga of Grettir the Strong* (tr. G. A. Hight, Everyman's Library 699).

*Four Icelandic Sagas* (tr. Gwyn Jones, American-Scandinavian Foundation, 1935).

*Three Icelandic Sagas* (tr. M. H. Scargill and M. Schlauch, American-Scandinavian Foundation, 1950).

*Laxdaela Saga* (tr. Thorstein Veblen, Huebsch, 1925).

*The Saga of the Volsungs* (tr. M. Schlauch, Norton, 1930).

H. R. Haggard, *Eric Brighteyes* (in *Lost Civilizations*, Dover, 1953).

Selma Lagerlöf, *Gösta Berling's Story* (tr. P. B. Flach, Doubleday, Post, 1917).

E. Linklater, *The Men of Ness* (British Book Center, 1951).

Sigrid Undset, *The Master of Hestviken* (tr. A. G. Chater, Knopf, 1934).

Sigrid Undset, *Kristin Lavransdatter* (tr. C. Archer and J. S. Scott, Knopf, 1934).

# Looking Back on Today

---

IN MOST Western countries, we read a great deal of prose fiction. In magazines and newspapers and bound books, short stories and romances and fantasies and realistic novels keep rolling off the presses. Some of the people and many of the scenes we read about become compellingly real to us, and seem to be parts of our own lives. Modern fiction has many distinguished talents, several undoubted geniuses, and many unassuming but vigorous craftsmen. Everyone loves a good story.

I happen to have a fairly large library of modern fiction in several languages. The other day I was looking over it, when an odd idea struck me. My profession is to teach the appreciation of the best books written in the Greek and Latin languages. This means (among other things) sorting out the gold from the rubbish, trying to determine what is permanently valuable among the books written, say, in the first century before Christ, and what, although popular then, now has only antiquarian interest. I began to wonder what our own descendants, far in the future, would think of the stories we read today.

Now, there are two different ways of putting this question. One is to ask which novels they will still think worth reading and which they will have discarded: a terribly hard question, almost impossible to answer. The other is to inquire what a sensible man, living in the year 3000 or so, would think of our novels, and what picture he would form of us from the evidence they provide. Would he admire them, or think most of them trash? And would he think they corresponded closely to the realities of our life (as he knew it through historical documents, photographs, and other evidence), or conclude that our prose fiction—even when it claimed to be realistic—was pretty far removed from hard fact? This second question is rather hard too, but we can answer it a little more easily than the first. Let us stand back, well back, and look at the novels of the last forty or fifty years. Comparing them with our own experience and knowledge of the world, what do we see?

The first thing we see, and the first thing our descendants will notice, is that truth is far larger and more complex than fiction. Dozens of things have happened to every one of us which have never been put into stories. Nearly all of us know men and women who have led strange exciting lives full of distress or of success, but we have never read a story that describes any character, or career, or motives like theirs. Can you discover yourself in any novel? You can find other people —sometimes nearly as interesting, sometimes more vital and more eloquent—but you can scarcely find yourself. And surely this is one of the worst things about the vast quantity of machine-made fiction that pours out and serves as stuffing to keep the advertisements in the big magazines from running into each other. The authors rely so much on pattern and formula that they are afraid to observe real persons. Instead, they give us stereotypes: tall and attractively ugly husbands called Clyde, sensitive and understanding wives called Karen and Marcia; or sometimes, in a real triumph of the obvious, an exquisite Mary deeply in love with . . . John.

On the other hand, our descendants will admire some of our best fiction as a clue to social history—that is, assuming that they can still read. They will know it is not complete, but they will appreciate what it does give them. Many modern novels are full of vital information about social customs, about class structures and tensions, about family and neighborhood groups, and ways of getting an education, formal and informal. In this, they are far more factual and historically valuable than our movies, which so seldom show us a real house, a credible family, a genuine office or factory or town. Perhaps there will be tremendous quarrels between two groups of historians, one asserting that social life back in the mid-twentieth century can best be interpreted through our novels, the other declaring that the movies must be more truthful, since they show real objects and living people. And possibly—horrors— a third school will arise to maintain the essential truth of 'Noble Wife' and 'Forgotten Child' and the rest of the soap operas which pollute the daytime ether like perfumed smog.

The readers of the future will also enjoy many of our novels because they can hear us talking in them. Through them, our language can be reconstructed. This is one of the difficulties about reading Greek and Latin, and, for that matter, Hebrew also: it is awfully hard to tell how the ordinary people spoke to one another, since almost all we have is literature, gracefully or powerfully stylized, far above the level of daily conversation; and regional dialects are not common either. But both in American English and in British English, and in several other Western languages, there are many modern books that give marvelously vivid echoes of actual speech: the soft rhythms and slurred syllables of the deep South, the brisk, hard, sharp utterance of New York's business streets, and (in some modern French novels) the crude and bitter, yet lively, slang of the slums. The short stories of O. Henry are a wonderful document for the history of our language.

But, if they are historically minded, our descendants will wonder why we left so many interesting and important things out of our novels. Our amusements, for example. There are very few fictional descriptions of horse racing, or a big fight, or the World Series; and yet millions of people enjoy them year after year. In just the same way, we have no full-length description of a Roman chariot race or the gladiatorial combats: we have to reconstruct these events from sculptures and inscriptions and casual allusions. My favorite satirist Juvenal has one poem in which he invites an old friend to spend the afternoon with him, and have a comfortable dinner. He adds, 'We can take our ease, because all Rome is at the races. Let the young fellows go: they enjoy shouting, and making long-shot bets, and sitting beside smartly dressed girls. We old fellows can relax, and enjoy the sunshine.' Very agreeable. But I wish he had once, just once, at an earlier stage, gone to the races himself and written one of his brilliant satires describing the crowd, their clothes and manners, how they sat or stood, which teams they backed, and the unreasoning excitement that rose to a roar when the heavy chariots rounded the last curve and broke into the straight, with the horses foaming and the drivers lashing and the dust whirling high, and death keeping pace with the leading chariot. But he never did. Once, by the way, he remarks that the winner got a bonus equal to the entire yearly salary of a schoolteacher. That sounds quite familiar.

One other oddity is that modern fiction will not tell our descendants very much about our chief occupations: about our business, our industry, and our science. Sinclair Lewis and Arnold Bennett both wrote novels about the hotel business. Jules Romains has several interesting businessmen and skilled workers in his *Men of Good Will*. Victor White has just completed a big trilogy called *Peter Domanig in America,* about an immigrant to America making his career in heavy industry. There is a good deal of fiction about doctors, lawyers, and teachers; but many important and interesting fields of endeavor—such as shipping, banking, and chemical engineering —are scarcely ever mentioned by our novelists, far less described with full detail, in the tradition of Balzac and Zola.

There is a further omission—which is very hard to account for. It is this. Our fiction does not contain nearly enough vivid descriptions of places. America is full of wonderful and beautiful landscapes, from the Bayous of Louisiana to the Bad Lands of the Dakotas, but very few authors have described them. That was one of the great talents of Fenimore Cooper, whose evocations of the lakes and forests of our northeastern frontier are really magnificent; but it is a talent we don't seem to cultivate today. The only description of Niagara Falls I know in modern fiction comes in H. G. Wells's fantasy, *The War in the Air* (published in 1908). In this respect at least, the movies are well ahead of the novelists: in some of them, the only thing worth admiring is the scenic photography. Then, further, although most fiction-readers are townsfolk, it is strange that so few novels catch the physical appearance, the smells, the sounds, the atmosphere of interesting towns and cities. I don't mean books about crowded city living: no; something more; books that would enable strangers, distant in place or time, to reconstruct in imagination the actual look of a place they had never visited. There is much of this in John Dos Passos, and in Jules Romains; something of it, too, in

Virginia Woolf's *Mrs. Dalloway,* and in an exquisitely written collection of stories by Joseph Hergesheimer called *Quiet Cities*; but that is not enough. Are our novelists too interested in introspection, so that they neglect observation?

In six or eight hundred years, assuming that scientific research continues, our descendants will know much more about psychology than we do. Probably, they will laugh at our ignorance, as we laugh at the medieval doctors with their startling ignorance of pathology and physiology. When they look over our novels, in which psychological description is so frequent and so engrossing, what do you think they will decide about us, and about our authors? They may say—as we say about Shakespeare and the best Greek writers—that our psychological observation of individuals was extremely acute, though sometimes eccentric and always unsystematic. But they will surely add that we knew, or at least wrote in fiction, practically nothing about other important areas of psychical activity. In particular, little or nothing about the psychology of crowds (though we live in a crowd-culture), or about the psychology of organized groups—a team, a regiment, or a church. In fiction, the broad field of criminal psychology still needs much exploration. Our authors have done something with the psychic life of children and of the insane, but we need much more about primitives, and members of other cultures—along the lines of those splendid novels on the southwestern Indians by Oliver La Farge.

From psychology to sex. Some authors seem to think that the two subjects are identical, but the best-informed opinion is that they are not. Still, what will our successors think, in the year 3000? They will find far more detailed and gluttonous descriptions of sexual activity in our novels than in those of any previous period in history. It seems to me that they will look at them with surprise, judging them fanciful or unnecessary. We ourselves, when we read *The Pickwick Papers,* find it hard to maintain an interest in all the elaborate descriptions of eating and drinking and family jollifying; and when we turn to Proust, it takes a tremendous effort to attend to the complex system of aristocratic precedence and etiquette that runs all through his novels. Of course *we* eat and drink and have parties and obey a system of etiquette—but we don't think about these things with so much concentration. Perhaps our descendants will look back on us in the same way; and even find us (as we find the soldiers who decorate their barracks with nothing but pictures of half-naked women) a little immature, a little pathetic.

'Too much sex,' they will say; and they may add, 'Too little intellect.' Not that we are oversexed and underbrained, but that our novelists n̲_____pped. It is possible to look through large numbers of modern novels and get the impression that no human being ever goes to a concert, reads a serious book and remembers it, enjoys pictures, or owns a collection of records. The characters seem to talk and think about nothing except the emotional aspects of personal relationships. And yet, you know, lots of interesting people who are perfectly real and would make good characters in a novel have their minds full of other things as well. Think what goes on in the head of someone like Diaghilev, or Paul Claudel, or Keynes, or Thomas Wolfe. Music, and large fragments of poetry, and remembered scenes and pictures, and complex intellectual explorations all occupy them: sometimes meaning more than all but the most intense personal association. More ordinary people (like you and me) often find their minds actively inhabited by questions raised by a recent book, or memories of an exciting discussion. Such experiences are important. They ought not to be omitted from novels; but they usually are—as though they did not exist, or the author thought they might scare off nervous readers. That was one of the many good things about J. D. Salinger's novel of adolescence, *The Catcher in the Rye*: it actually showed you the boy's mind at work, on books as well as other things; and it is one of the fascinations of Proust, whose hero is haunted by a phrase from a string quartet and by a Vermeer picture— experiences not superficial or decorative, but destined to become essential elements of his life.

Yes, fiction (like art and like philosophy) is only one way of trying to interpret our world; and, like them, it is imperfect. Never think our life is narrow or monotonous. It is infinitely varied, incomprehensibly rich. The greatest authors who ever lived have failed to record more than a fraction of what they saw and knew. The first condition for appreciating any book, or any collection of books, is to realize that it is inadequate; and the best ambition of any writer is to produce a work that contains at least some part of the essential truths without which no book will survive.

## Books of Wisdom

---

OCCASIONALLY, if you are lucky, you meet an exceptionally wise and brilliant man. He does not talk much, but he does not remain morosely taciturn. Even in silence, you can see he is thinking, calmly and fruitfully; and when the right time comes he re-enters the conversation with a wise epigram, an illuminating story, or a trenchant argument. You are bound to envy him. And yet envy is useless, for how could *you* ever be so balanced in judgment, so keen in logic, and so personal and memorable in expression? You can only listen, and admire. Such a man (you think as you go home) is in the realm of thought and speech what Heifetz is in violin-playing or Matisse in drawing. He has trained so long, and set his standards so high, that he cannot without a deliberate and unnatural effort say anything banal or shallow, any more than Heifetz can play a wolf-note or Matisse draw a coarse and obvious curve. Pope says that such skillful thinking and talking come

> from Art, not Chance,
> As those move easiest who have learned to dance.

There are three or four writers like this. Once met, they are never forgotten. They meant not to be forgotten. They wrote to be thought over, and carried next the heart, and even committed to memory. I remember an occasion when the organist of Trinity College, Hartford, was playing for a few visitors to that beautiful chapel: one Bach fugue after another, he played them as soon as we named them. I said to him afterward (naïve amateur): 'It's wonderful to hear you rattling off all these fugues by memory.' He answered, 'I don't see how else one could play them.' I sighed; but I knew he was right; and so it is also with this special type of book. It was well put by the author of one of them, when he said

> Some books are to be tasted, others to be swallowed,
> and some few to be chewed and digested.

They are not religious, these works: no; usually rather worldly, although their authors are thoughtful men who recognize religion as one of the powers of life. They are not scientific, although at least one of them was composed by a scientist. Works of art they are, in a peculiar way: they were written principally to be *true*, but because their authors knew that a truth is not completely viable unless it is perfectly expressed, they worked hard at their style as well as at their thought, until the two, thought and expression, coalesced more completely than in any other form of literature except lyric poetry.

Everyone knows the name of one of these books, and the writers of two or three more. The most famous is surely the Book of Proverbs, in the Old Testament: they say that some of it was composed by the wise King Solomon himself. The best-known modern author of such a work is Francis Bacon, the brilliant philosopher of science and of politics. His book (called simply *Essays*) came out when he was thirty-six and went on to two more editions (each much enlarged) before he died. The meditative Spaniards have another: *The Pocket Oracle*, by Baltasar Gracián; and the witty French prize the *Maxims* of La Rochefoucauld. There are one or two such books in nearly every language.

They are really wise advice on how to live. There is no very good name for them. Essays means either 'experiments' (which is too indecisive to convey their real nature) or 'balancing of opinions,' which is judicial enough but plays down their strongly positive and didactic nature. The name Proverbs is poor, for surely a proverb is something composed and circulated anonymously. The Biblical scholars call them Wisdom Books, which is as useful a title as any: they are books of worldly wisdom, books of lasting value; they are teaching books, on a high level, with a broad application: handbooks of practical living.

For example, what is the best way to negotiate? If you want to reach an agreement with another man and to obtain something from him, what is the best way to go about it? Obviously there cannot be a single universally true answer: human affairs are not like chemistry, where proportions and powers remain fixed. But there ought to be a central principle, with intelligible qualifications and exceptions. So Bacon says:

> It is generally better to deal by speech than by letter; and by the mediation of a third than by a man's self.

But then he qualifies:

> Letters are good when a man would draw an answer back again; or when it may serve for a man's justification

afterwards to produce his own letter; or where it may be danger to be interrupted, or heard by pieces.

And then he goes on with equally shrewd advice about the advantages of negotiating personally and about the correct choice and use of intermediaries. Another of these wise men makes the essential point that every negotiator ought to offer some profit to the other party:

> Enter into another man's plans in order to come out with your own. This is a great trick, because it offers him advantages as a bait to catch his good will, and while it looks as though his purposes were being served, the ground is being prepared for your own.

The very next paragraph in Gracián, though on a different subject, gives such sound advice and shows his style so admirably that it must be quoted:

> Do not show your sore finger for everyone else to strike, and do not complain of it, for malice always pounds where it hurts most. No use to get angry; that will only add to the general amusement. Evil intent goes sneaking around to uncover the infirmity, and prods about to discover where the suffering is greatest, in a thousand different ways, until it hits the spot.

But there are very few of the wisdom books that give advice in such detail. Most of the wise men know that (as Bacon said) 'there is in human nature generally more of the fool than of the wise,' and therefore their advice is usually much shorter. Here is the Book of Proverbs on negotiation:

> As vinegar to the teeth and as smoke to the eyes,
>     so is the sluggard to them that send him.
> The simple believeth every word,
>     but the prudent man looketh well to his going.

So, then, most of the wisdom found in such books is not in the form of plans or systems of behavior, but in simple epigrams, which look sometimes like common sense deepened and sometimes like poetry flattened out: thus—

> The virtue of prosperity is temperance; the virtue of adversity is fortitude.
> Leave something to wish for, so as not to be glutted with happiness.
> The desire of appearing clever often keeps us from becoming clever.
> Youth is continual drunkenness.

Most of the epigrams sound pessimistic, even cynical. Their authors know that men are governed partly by reason and partly by emotion, and that emotion often challenges reason or even wears reason as a mask. They themselves, devoted to thought, are therefore surgically adept at searching out hidden defects. They will say:

> We have all enough strength to bear the misfortunes of others.
> He who rejects praise wants to be praised twice.
> If we had no faults, we should not enjoy finding them in others.

Sometimes you can see these writers thinking. They will weigh two opinions against each other and say:

> Answer not a fool according to his folly, lest thou also be like unto him. Answer a fool according to his folly, lest he be wise in his own conceit.

Montaigne started his essays with this idea; and Bacon, in his *Advancement of Learning,* collected antitheses, pros and cons on various important subjects: evidently since he derived 'essay' from 'assay,' the instrument of the man who tests gold for purity.

The authors of wisdom books often seem to know one another, and weigh each other's thoughts. They quote one another's epigrams with relish and digest them into their own substance. Reading the Book of Proverbs, you see again and again how a good idea has been voiced four or five times, apparently by four or five different people; and Bacon is constantly quoting Solomon's proverbs as well as other apophthegms from classical and modern literature.

Such books are not written down all at once, as we might compose a story. They grow. They grow slowly. They seed one another. Their authors often start by meditating on the wisdom of others; and many a good book of essays has grown out of a collection of 'commonplaces,' pithy generalizations or memorable sayings copied from different authors. (Making such a commonplace book is a most valuable habit, a perpetual self-education, commended to us by the examples of great men such as Jefferson.) After considering such wisdom for a long time, an intelligent man begins to create wisdom of his own, and to put it into durable form. The best such works are shaped by long and careful preparation; whenever I read or think of them, two images of the making of jewels come into my mind: the slow process which layer by layer creates the pearl inside the oyster, and the patient elaboration of the cutter with his lens and his wheel, shaping a diamond; and I recall La Rochefoucauld, an aging and defeated man, meditating in his lonely country castle; Gracián in the silence of his monastery, elaborating his counsels with the endless patience of the Jesuits; and Bacon, putting his essays together as neatly as a watchmaker constructing his delicate machine.

They are literature, these wisdom books. They have transfused more sentences into our daily speech than any other genre, except the great dramas. Think of these fine sayings, only a few out of many:—

From Proverbs and Ecclesiastes:

—Where there is no vision, the people perish.

—A merry heart doeth good like a medicine.

—The fear of the Lord is the beginning of knowledge.

—Whatsoever thy hand findeth to do, do it with thy might.

—Dead flies cause the ointment of the apothecary to send forth a stinking savour; so doth a little folly him that is in reputation for wisdom and honour.

—Cast thy bread upon the waters: for thou shalt find it after many days.

And one gem which always occurs to me at breakfast time. I learned it when I used to commute from New Jersey:

—He that blesseth his friend with a loud voice, rising early in the morning, it shall be counted a curse to him.

From Bacon:

—God Almighty first planted a garden.

—Revenge is a kind of wild justice.

—Suspicions are like bats: they ever fly by twilight.

—All rising to great place is by a winding stair.

—There is no excellent beauty that hath not some strangeness in the proportion.

From Gracián:

—A wise man does at once, what a fool does at last.

—Act always as though you were seen.

—Know your unlucky days.

—To jog the understanding is a greater feat than to jog the memory: for it takes more to make a man think than to make him remember.

—All men worship idols, some of honor, others of greed, and most of pleasure.

—Time and I, against any two.

From La Rochefoucauld:

—In her first passion a woman loves her lover; later, she loves love.

—Quarrels would not last long if all the wrong were on one side.

—The chief secret of cleverness is to know the price of things.

—More people are made cruel by vanity than by natural ferocity.

—We are never so happy, nor so unhappy, as we imagine.

Enlivening, to see all this wisdom displayed so concisely, so powerfully; and yet discouraging. We feel it is almost impossible for us to live so intensely and intelligently, to do everything by the power of reason, to plan constantly and to succeed frequently, to dominate life.

And then we console ourselves by remembering that those who wrote the books were not so wise or so successful as the books they wrote. Bacon advises us to save half of our income to keep level, and two thirds of it in order to grow rich; but he himself was wildly extravagant and died in debt. He preaches caution, and care, and the long view; but he was impeached for corruption which he himself explained as 'frailty' rather than depravity; that is, he wished to seem a fool rather than a scoundrel. La Rochefoucauld did not begin setting down his maxims until he was a beaten man: he took the losing side in a civil war, was defeated, outwitted, and impoverished. As for Gracián, he suffered worst of all. At the age of nearly sixty, when he had been a Jesuit for about forty years and held an important post in a Jesuit college, he was crushed for the two blunders no one would expect from a wise man and a Jesuit: imprudence and disobedience. He had been publishing books under an assumed name, with considerable success (and apparently keeping the money in spite of his vow to possess no private property). He was expressly forbidden to issue another. He disobeyed (it was the third part of *El Criticón*). He was deprived of his professorship, publicly reprimanded, and condemned to penance on bread and water; the General ordered him to keep nothing under lock and key and to be refused the use of pen, ink, and paper. He asked permission to leave the Jesuit order and join another; lingered on a few months; and died in virtual exile and disgrace—he, the man who once wrote, 'Keep in mind the happy ending; he who wins does not have to explain' and 'Think ahead: to the ready there are no accidents, and to the forewarned no dangers.'

The wisest of them all, King Solomon, reached heights of glory such as the others never conceived, with vast wealth, unparalleled power, and the vision of God, and yet 'it came to pass, when Solomon was old, that his wives turned away his heart after other gods . . . And the Lord was angry with Solomon . . . and said "I will surely rend the kingdom from thee, and will give it to thy servant." ' Within a few years after his death, the mighty monarchy which he and his father had built up fell into pieces; before his death, he perhaps foresaw its collapse. And after him there were other thinkers who created profoundly pessimistic maxims, and set them under the name of Solomon.

Perhaps it is not possible both to act wisely and also to write wisely about conduct—because action needs will power, which no book can teach; or else because the wisest men of all are those who never give away their secrets.

---

Francis Bacon, Lord Verulam, *Essays* (ed. C. S. Northup, Houghton Mifflin, 1908).

Baltasar Gracián, *The Art of Worldly Wisdom* (tr. J. Jacobs, Macmillan, 1892).

Baltasar Gracián, *El Criticón* (ed. M. Romera-Navarro, University of Pennsylvania, 1938).

Baltasar Gracián, *The Oracle* (tr. L. B. Walton, Salloch, 1953).

Baltasar Gracián, *A Truthtelling Manual* (tr. M. Fischer, C. C. Thomas, 1945).

F. Guicciardini, *Ricordi* (tr. N. H. Thomson, Vanni, 1949).

François, duc de la Rochefoucauld, *Les Maximes* (ed. by F. C. Green, Cambridge, England, 1945).

*An Eminent Historian*

---

IT is rather over twenty years since one of the darlings of the London intellectual world died. He was a thin bearded man with a squeaky voice and an air of extreme fragility. From his pictures, he must have been rather like Mr. Justice Shallow as Falstaff recalled him in *Henry IV*:

> I do remember him . . . like a man made after supper of a cheese-paring; when a' was naked he was for all the world like a forked radish, with a head fantastically carved upon it with a knife: a' was so forlorn that his dimensions to any thick sight were invincible: a' was the very genius of famine.

Except that Mr. Justice Shallow was tiny, and this fellow was tall and loose-jointed, they were brothers. Acquaintances described him as the very genius of famine, his lugubrious appearance enhanced by a long silky red beard and enormous eyeglasses and pale boneless hands. His full name was Giles Lytton Strachey; dropping the robust and rustic Giles, he preferred to be known as Lytton Strachey.

Lytton Strachey wrote six or eight biographies, and a large number of critical essays on literature. The critical essays did not much impress the general public. The biographies had a tremendous effect: they enriched him, they made him a best-seller, they infuriated many of the most serious historians here and in England, and they enlisted an army of admirers and camp followers. You know them: they are the 'debunkers.' It was Lytton Strachey who made debunking fashionable. Perhaps in the United States it was encouraged by people like Lincoln Steffens and H. L. Mencken, but it was Strachey who really brought it into literature. He was a witty and delightful writer; but as a historian, he was feline and cruel.

Is he read nowadays at all? I never hear anyone talk of him. Of course, this proves nothing. Many a writer, including some of those whom he admired, has failed of admiration until long after his death. Perhaps the time has not come for Strachey to be enjoyed. If our own civilization should move more and more completely into a period of perfect officialdom and supreme organization, with everything arranged by the State, everything authorized and docketed in triplicate and quadruplicate, with a group of unchallengeably powerful officials at the top directing everybody's lives, then the clawed and sharp-toothed critics like Strachey will be prized more and more—not as historians but as satirists—and, if they survive at all, will be read with more and more enthusiasm. At least, until the officials find out . . .

Lytton Strachey was little known outside the Cambridge and Bloomsbury group of aesthetes and wits until 1918, the final year of the First World War. Then he brought out a collection of four long biographical essays called *Eminent Victorians*. This book utterly ignored the war, paid no attention to the twentieth century, and concentrated on four saints, or heroes, of the nineteenth century. These were three men and one woman who had been famous for their self-sacrifice and their suffering in four very different and equally important fields of life: they had been treated as almost superhuman, and statues of them had been erected for succeeding generations to admire. Now came Lytton Strachey, carrying phials of acid. He delicately deformed their features. He burned holes in their robes of state. He added amusing and insulting phrases to the inscriptions on their pedestals. His acids gnawed at their supports, so that they tottered in the gale of laughter which began to rise and blow harder and harder. According to Strachey, Florence Nightingale, the founder of modern nursing and the hospital system, was efficient, yes, terribly efficient, painfully efficient, murderously efficient, and slightly crazy, something of a monomaniac, and sometimes drastically wrong, and finally more than a little mad. Cardinal Manning—the man who was largely responsible for re-establishing the influence of the Roman Catholic Church in England—ah, according to Strachey he was an accomplished intriguer: hence his success, far greater than that of the more saintly Newman; and what did it all lead to? If you descend into his tomb, you will see his only remaining relic, dusty and neglected, the cardinal's Hat. And then, General Gordon, with a long record of amazing gallantry in exploration and something very like genius in the command of native troops—well, according to Strachey he was also a religious faddist and sustained himself on brandy: brave, yes, but shall we say . . . a bit of a barbarian? And as for Dr. Arnold, who reformed the English public-school system by his fourteen years of hard work and noble teaching at Rugby—well, his legs were too short, and he confused his own ideas with those of Almighty God. Silly fellow . . . These are the implications of Lytton Strachey's gracefully written essays, *Eminent Victorians*. The very title is a sneer, for who wants to be Victorian? and 'eminent' implies 'pompous' and 'self-satisfied.' *Eminent Victorians*: really!

The book was an immediate success with the public. Three years later, Strachey followed it with a full-length biography of Queen Victoria, which was even better written and was even more successful. Nearly everyone turned to laughing at the Victorians. Queen Victoria herself, who had been for so many years a sort of grandmother-image, was—well, wasn't she a small, pudgy, dowdy, self-centered old woman with a frown that implied stupidity and a pout that spoke eloquently of vanity and obstinacy? There was a famous occasion on which Queen Victoria utterly annihilated a young member of her Court. He used to do imitations of her, in private. She heard of this. At a State banquet she commanded him to repeat the imitation. Miserably embarrassed, he did so. Of course nobody ventured to laugh. Victoria sat unflinching until the end. Then, in Strachey's words,

> the royal lips sank down at the corners, the royal eyes stared in astonished protrusion, and in fact the royal countenance became inauspicious in the highest degree;

and the Queen crushed the jester with the single sentence, 'We are not amused.' But now, after the publication of Strachey's biography, everybody was amused: and Queen Victoria, with her bourgeois tastes and her emphatic widowhood and her prim moral code, ceased to be formidable and became a figure of fun.

These two books came out in 1918 and 1921. But that was the middle of the reign of King George V. The Victorians were all dead; dead long ago. The Victorian age was separated from Strachey and his public by—not a gulf, but a very considerable gap, filled in with the completely different reign of Edward VII and several important wars and political transformations. Victorianism prevailed no longer in most parts of Britain. Strachey's work succeeded not because it said anything startlingly new but because it expressed a change which had been going on for at least twenty years. He was the heir of Max Beerbohm and Oscar Wilde.

Like some other English writers, he delighted in sly jokes, designed to be appreciated only by those who had equally aristocratic connections or comparably delicate sensibilities. He liked (for instance) to gloat over names that sounded middle class or pedantic. One of his critics * calls this an ingredient in his humor, adding that he quotes unfortunate names 'with such deadly effect that he needs to add no comment. Arthur Clough is recorded as writing to a Rugby schoolfellow:

> I do not think this has made me really forgetful of my personal friends, such as, in particular, Gell and Burbridge and Waldron, and yourself, my dear Simpkinson.

Strachey is never so happy as when he is able to sport with such names, especially when they are attached to divines, scholars, and high officials, as Wegg-Prosser, Monseigneur Dupanloup, Dr. Döllinger, Bosius, Wolfius, Torentius, and Ratgersius, Baron de Stosch, Sir Mount-Stuart Elphinstone Grant-Duff, and the Reverend R. McChyne. To allow such names to fall into the hands of Lytton Strachey was to present an urchin with a water-pistol.' True; yet there is something ridiculous to the sensitive ear about any name which is the tiniest bit pretentious, as for instance that rococo triptych Giles Lytton Strachey. But perhaps he would not think of that.

However, there is a striking anomaly about his historical

* Guy Boas, cited in the bibliography.

books. They are cynical and satiric: so are many historians. But what is much worse, they are not true. From time to time, ever since they appeared, critics have pointed out one misstatement after another; and some of the worst misstatements are apparently deliberate. There is a really shocking alteration of fact—which amounts to a lie—in a passage describing how Manning was converted to Roman Catholicism. Manning visited Rome and had an audience with the Pope while he was still a Protestant. Strachey says that nobody knows what happened at this interview, and later goes on to suggest that the genial and diplomatic Pope Pius IX invited Manning to become a Roman Catholic and promised him some sort of bribe if he would:

> 'Ah, dear Signor Manning, why don't you come over to us? Do you suppose that we should not look after you?'

This absurd and rather vulgar implication is carefully prepared by Strachey's earlier statement that the subject of the interview is unknown, so that we can only wonder . . . But this is false. We know the subject of the interview, for it is in the printed records of Manning's own diary: he states quite clearly what its purpose was. Strachey read this diary; but, trusting that nobody else would, he suppressed the evidence. This is only one of several sinister alterations of the truth in his historical writings.

But the rest of his work is very different, and very much more pleasant. It is a long series of essays on books and authors, written with sensitive appreciation and scarcely a trace of spite. Its emphasis is heavily on the period which he obviously preferred to the energetic, ugly, and moral nineteenth century: the idle, refined, and immoral eighteenth century. On the whole, he prefers France to England. Other countries, other literatures—Italy, the United States, Spain,

Germany, Austria—scarcely exist for Strachey. But within those limits, his taste is delicate, his intellectual penetration is keen, and his style is nearly always worthy of the subject. These essays are grouped under vague names, *Books and Characters, Portraits in Miniature,* and so forth: they are admirable criticism, and I recommend them highly to any student of literature.

Now, these two different sets of books make a singular problem. It is this. Why does Strachey tell the truth about literature, and falsify history? Why is he positive and appreciative about the eighteenth century, and scornful of the nineteenth? Why does he exalt those who read and wrote and talked, and caricature those who did things? If we look into his own life, and visualize him carefully, we can see why the anomaly occurred. Clearly, it sprang from certain discomforts that haunted him all his life. He came of a large and brilliant family, boasting of many centuries of distinguished achievement in public affairs. Strachey's own father was an eminent Victorian: a general; one of the builders of the British Empire in India—quite literally, for he was a famous engineer and helped to construct the Indian railways as well as to set up an adequate forestry service; he was a Fellow of the Royal Society; President of the Royal Geographical Society; a lieutenant-general. He was knighted for his services and became Sir Richard Strachey. In the eyes of most people, he was four times the man his son would ever be. He was sixty-three when Lytton Strachey was born. He lived to be ninety-one. The son of such a man sometimes becomes a complete waster, in despair of equaling his father; sometimes he is inspired to work hard and do well in a totally different kind of career; and sometimes he spends much of his life being refined, and idle, and poetic, and sneering at his father, or the people who represent his father. (Think of Samuel Butler, that horrible little worm.) Lytton Strachey chose to defend himself by sneering.

One important symbolic gesture was Strachey's beard. He grew it at the age of thirty-one, three or four years after the death of his father. We hear also that when he was at Cambridge he read an essay, a humorous essay but perhaps serious in intention, to a society of his intimates, called *Ought the Father To Grow a Beard?* One might almost say that in his personal appearance he tried to look both eminent and Victorian.

There was another motive in his writing. Strachey was always delicate, and his mummy brought him up very carefully. When he was thirty-four the war broke out. At once he declared himself a conscientious objector. In his statement to the examining board, he said that for some time he had been 'strongly critical of the entire social structure,' and that the war had intensified his convictions. It is not that he was a fascist or communist; no; he was by conviction an aristocrat: he would have preferred to live in an era when work was not expected of a man of taste; and he hated the whole notion of Duty, seeing it as another of the hideous mechanical inventions of the nineteenth century. (Ogden Nash might put it, 'When Duty whispers low, "Thou must," Strachey replied, "I just can't." ') Therefore, when he chose to write history, he selected the Victorian age, in which moral obligations were felt strongly and social responsibilities developed rapidly. The persons he chose to satirize were all reformers: they actually tried to do what they thought was right, and to encourage others to do the same. Duty! Responsibility! Morality! Work! Oh (said Lytton Strachey), fudge! Even his splendid account of the death of General Gordon under Sudanese spears, coupled with his savage mockery of the British diplomatic representative in Egypt, Evelyn Baring, meant that Strachey disliked and distrusted peaceful negotiators (like his father) and admired violent and tragic and picturesque heroes who lived mainly on their emotions.

That is part of the answer to the problem of Strachey. If your emotions are narrowly personal, if you have little experience of the world, if you know nothing about command and responsibility and the necessity of decision, you should write aesthetic criticism, not history. Criticism must be sensitive. History must be true.

------

G. L. Strachey, *Landmarks in French Literature* (Oxford, 1912).
    *Eminent Victorians* (Putnam, 1918).
    *Queen Victoria* (Harcourt, Brace, 1921).
    *Books and Characters* (Harcourt, Brace, 1922).
    *Elizabeth and Essex* (Harcourt, Brace, 1928).
    *Portraits in Miniature* (Harcourt, Brace, 1931).
    *Characters and Commentaries* (Harcourt, Brace, 1933).

Max Beerbohm, *Lytton Strachey* (Knopf, 1943).
Guy Boas, *Lytton Strachey* (Oxford, 1935).
C. R. Sanders, *The Strachey Family* (Duke University, 1953).

## Arms and the Woman

---

THERE is a boom in historical romances. They have always been popular, I suppose, but in the last decade or so more of them have been coming out every year. And just recently one special fashion in them has been getting much stronger. This is *History for the Ladies*.

First, consider a hard and brutal truth. Men make history. Except in a few very special periods, men have always made history; and they still make it. History is masculine.

Now, look at a soft and charming fact. Women like romance; and nowadays women read most of the historical romances. Romance is chiefly feminine.

Men make history. Women like to read historical romance. And, on the whole, women would rather read about women than about men. A contradiction arises. But it can be solved, with the help of the imagination. An author who wishes to write a historical romance for the ladies simply takes a large, exciting piece of historical fact; then he humanizes the men in it and polishes them up a bit, making them handsome, susceptible, and gallant; and then he either discovers a real woman somewhere inside it and rearranges the story around her, or else invents a woman, puts her into the middle of it all, and imagines what would happen if she had really existed.

For example . . . Recently an Austrian lady, Annemarie Selinko, published a long, pleasant, chatty story about the era of Napoleon. It centers on a French girl, not pretty but very attractive in spite of her turned-up nose. The heroine has the admirably romantic name of Désirée, and lives up to it; for she is proposed to by Napoleon himself, then by several of his officers; she is finally married to a big, strong general, Jean-Paul Bernadotte, who is elected crown prince of Sweden. In time, she becomes the Queen of Sweden, and lives happily ever after.

It is rather charming. It is rather Austrian: you know, optimistic and frivolous and a little irresponsible, let us not take things too seriously, *glücklich ist wer vergisst,* can this really be I?, these changes are bewildering but terribly gay, like a fast waltz, time out to change partners or costumes once again, the waltz keeps playing and one need never stop, or think. Yes, it is charming. But it is something considerably different from history: from reality. Those were terrible times, when Napoleon was threatening the entire world. He was not cruel and murderous like Hitler; but he was power-mad; and for a long time many people in Europe felt as though their lives were being dominated by a very strong, intensely clever, utterly ruthless maniac. That feeling does *not* appear in Fräulein Selinko's book: why, her heroine knew Napoleon when he could not even afford a proper uniform; she sent him sandwiches when he was imprisoned; she used to race down the garden with him; how could she take him seriously? He was only a man after all, no doubt very clever and ambitious, but still . . . That is history as a feminine romancer sees it.

It is strange to turn away from *Désirée*, and to read the sober chapters of a masculine history of those times—for instance, J. M. Thompson's biography of Napoleon. At once the whole thing becomes more difficult, more gloomy; individuals are seen in their proper proportion against the vast multitudes whom their actions affected; problems appear; implications reaching back and forward for centuries have to be considered; the waltz music dies away, to be succeeded by the whispers of diplomats, the scratch of busy pens, the relentless march of troops, the thunder of guns.

For instance, take one important episode in the struggle of Europe against Napoleon. *What was to happen to him after Waterloo?* He was still Emperor; he had to be persuaded or compelled to abdicate; and then to be got out of Paris, if possible out of France. If you can imagine a game of chess in which one of the chief pieces is filled with high explosives, and has to be moved *very delicately,* you will understand the movements of Napoleon and the other leaders of Europe during the summer of 1815.

This is how Thompson tells the story, from the abdication of the Emperor onward.

A Provisional Government with Fouché at its head sent a message to [the German general] Blücher, who was advancing at full speed on Paris, telling him of the abdication, and asking for an armistice. This he refused, unless Napoleon surrendered in person. On June 25th Fouché asked Napoleon to leave Paris, and he obeyed, going for the last time to [the country palace of] Malmaison and the sad ghost of Joséphine. On the 29th Blücher was

near enough to make an attempt to kidnap his enemy—
he was in a mood to have him shot: but Fouché again
baulked him, by ordering Napoleon away to [the sea-
port of] Rochefort. On the day he arrived there,
Blücher granted an armistice.

(From other sources—such as the memoirs of Bourrienne—
we even know who it was who carried the message to Napoleon ordering him to leave Malmaison; and of course we know
that St. Helena was not mentioned until all these negotiations
were over.)

These are the facts. But how about romance? For romance,
a woman must be introduced, to play some important part.
So Miss Selinko makes her heroine Désirée carry the message
to Napoleon, accept his surrender, and tell him he has to go to
St. Helena, all in the same short, touching interview. This is
how Désirée herself describes it. She drove from Paris to Malmaison, with a message from the French government . . .

'Joseph,' I gulped, 'I must—please, I must speak to
your brother immediately.'

'His Majesty,' he said, 'is on the bench in the maze.
You remember the maze and his bench, Désirée?'

I knew the intricacies of the maze, so charmingly devised by Josephine. I knew how one turns so as not to run
into the hedge, but comes suddenly and surprisingly to
the little white bench on which only two can sit very
close together.

On this little bench sat Napoleon.

No one heard him call me Eugénie. No one saw him
move over to one side of the little bench for two, who
had to sit very close together. When I sat close beside
him, he turned to me and smiled. 'It's been many long
years since you and I looked at a flowering hedge
together.'

Then I said, 'The French Government has asked me

to inform you that the Allies will consider the surrender of Paris only after you have left France.'

'Madame.' He was so close to me I had to lean back my head to see his face. 'You say, the French Government wishes me to leave. And—the Allies?' His face was contorted; in the corners of his mouth were tiny bubbles.

'The Allies insist on taking you prisoner, General.'

He breathed very heavily.

'When I saw you awhile ago, and recognized your face, Madame, I felt for a moment that my youth had come back. I was wrong.'

'Why? I remember perfectly the evenings we faced each other. You were already a general, a very young and handsome general.' I spoke as in a dream, the words came of themselves. 'Once—it was late in the evening, and the meadow beyond our garden was all dark—you told me that you knew your destiny. Your face was so white in the moonlight.'

'That was the first time I kissed you, Eugénie.'

Shortly after this tender moment, Napoleon hands over his sword to the enchanting lady and thus surrenders both to Désirée and to the Allies; and a few moments later she breaks the news to him that he will be interned in St. Helena—thus anticipating history by at least a month.

There is the difference between masculine history and feminine romance. One is all logic and the struggle for power. The other is chiefly personal relationships and emotion. One is anxious and difficult; the other is exciting but easy. One is prose, the other is part way toward poetry.

Couldn't we work out a pattern for the heroine of a historical romance? Surely. Let us try.

(1) She is energetic, constantly facing crises which men cannot master.

(2) But she never has a consistent plan; instead, she has a series of adventures, and waltzes from climax to climax.

(3) She is beautiful; or at least very attractive.

(4) She has a flair for dress, and her costumes must be described with considerable details.

(5) She is amorous, inspiring love in others and enjoying it herself. Sometimes she can be what other people call wicked— but for a very good motive. The great example here is, of course, Miss Kathleen Winsor's Amber, whose motto was, apparently, 'Love Conquers All.' Another instance is a rather painful romance about the founding of Christianity, called *The Galileans*. The heroine is Mary Magdalene. At one point she does a strip tease in a large public theater—but for the best possible motive, to save her friends from a massacre. Immediately after it is over, 'the flame of her hair envelops her like a protecting cloak,' and she buries her face in her hands. It was the only solution. In a romance, however naughty the heroine may *seem,* she is good at heart, and thus has it both ways.

(6) She is very clever. Some girls are not; but in a historical romance the heroine solves the most complex problems.

You see how such a heroine differs from normal women. It it not a normal nature and normal experiences which are described; it is rather the dream-experience of her creator and of the readers. She is a pattern of wish-fulfillment; she is the achievement of the improbable, the combination of opposites. (The heroine of *The Galileans* is a really outrageous example of this. Mary Magdalene has been known for many centuries as a very wicked woman, who was miraculously redeemed by the intervention of Jesus. Now, a good novel could be written about such a woman, although it would need careful psychological analysis, especially of the sense of sin and the process of conversion. But the author airily brushes aside the motivation of the Bible story. He sets out to show us that Mary Magdalene was really very nice all along. This means, you see, that the power of Jesus to convert her was scarcely needed, and it makes nonsense of the original tradition; but it contains the romantic pleasure of allowing Mary to be the heroine, and to have it both ways.)

Thinking over all this, I began to reflect that there must be a gold mine in history, for dozens of romantic writers. Almost any incident, almost any period can be livened up by putting a woman into it. Suppose we take a typical romantic heroine, green-eyed and red-haired, sexy but pure in heart, a tasty dresser, clever and energetic, with a touch of the gamine, the gay, and the irresponsible; suppose we call her Molly Madcap: why, we might spend thirty profitable years writing one historical adventure after another with the same heroine.

Just imagine the titles. *Molly Madcap and the Civil War*—no, that's been done, hasn't it? Well, then, *Molly Madcap and the Missouri Compromise*. Or *Molly Madcap and the Fourth Crusade*—we could make her a Byzantine princess who almost outwits the Crusaders, and sets them all to fighting for her sake. Or take Rome. *Molly Madcap and Julius Caesar*—no, Bernard Shaw wrote that one and Vivien Leigh acted it. Well, then, *Molly Madcap and the Other Borgias*. Or this, the best of all—*Molly Madcap and Her Little Ship the Niña*. We could bring in Columbus as a subordinate character, but we should make it clear that it was really the irresistible charm and energy of our heroine which convinced the crew to sail on and on. Columbus may have thought he was working out a new route to India, but Molly knew very well that she was discovering America. Never underestimate the power of a Madcap.

---

Annemarie Selinko, *Désirée* (tr. Joy Gary, Morrow, 1952).
F. G. Slaughter, *The Galileans* (Doubleday, 1953).
J. M. Thompson, *Napoleon Bonaparte* (Oxford, 1952).

## The Outsider

———————————

HE had no real home. He had not many friends. He did not even like or trust himself very much. His best friend was humanity; he liked the people.

Most of us know his name—at least the name under which he published his books. He called himself 'George Orwell.' That sounds rather maladjusted, because his real name was much stronger. It was Eric Blair, which somehow suited his long, thin, strong, bony face; while 'George Orwell' sounds like one of those dainty young men with wavy hair and brocade waistcoats whom one met in Bloomsbury during the 1930's. Still, let us call him George Orwell, for that is the name he chose.

Nearly all of us know his powerful novel about the inverted utopia of the future totalitarian state, *1984*; and his satire on

Stalinism, *Animal Farm*. But almost everything he wrote is worth reading—and, for young writers, worth studying. Recently I enjoyed what is, I am afraid, the last book of George Orwell's which we shall ever see: a collection of his essays, called by the ironic title, *Such, Such Were the Joys*. It is full of amusing remarks mixed with sadness, wit mingled with gloom, clear-eyed perception tempered by soft-hearted sympathy. For instance, take this simple description of Orwell feeding a gazelle in the park at Marrakech, in Morocco:

> Gazelles are almost the only animals that look good to eat when they are still alive, in fact, one can hardly look at their hindquarters without thinking of mint sauce.*
> The gazelle I was feeding seemed to know that this thought was in my mind, for though it took the piece of bread I was holding out it obviously did not like me. It nibbled rapidly at the bread, then lowered its head and tried to butt me, then took another nibble and then butted again. Probably its idea was that if it could drive me away the bread would somehow remain hanging in mid-air.
>
> An Arab navvy working on the path nearby lowered his heavy hoe and sidled slowly towards us. He looked from the gazelle to the bread and from the bread to the gazelle, with a sort of quiet amazement, as though he had never seen anything quite like this before. Finally he said shyly in French:
>
> '*I* could eat some of that bread.'
>
> I tore off a piece and he stowed it gratefully in some secret place under his rags.

At this time, Orwell was a poor man himself; yet he had the kindness to share his small possessions with a stranger and an

---

* Orwell can never have contemplated a duck on a Sunday morning, waddling plumply toward its pond with an almost visible halo of green peas floating above it; or a trout, still, fresh, and glistening in the river. Perhaps he meant quadrupeds only, or perhaps he had finer feelings.

animal, and also to sympathize with the humility and hostility imposed on them by their hunger. He had a warm heart.

He is dead now. He died in 1950, at the age of forty-seven, of tuberculosis: perhaps also of anguish for humanity, since he loved mankind and yet found that so much of it was not lovable. You see, he could be both a philanthropist and a critic. It seems to me that the secret of George Orwell was that he was an outsider: almost a displaced person. Throughout much of his life he was on the outside looking in, and during the rest he was a prisoner yearning to escape.

His family was Scottish by origin; but he went to English schools and tried to make himself into an Englishman. His pseudonym Orwell comes from a tiny river in southern England, near a place which his family owned; and as for George, that is the name of the English patron saint.

He was born in Bengal, a land in the far eastern part of India, the richest and most confusingly mixed province of the subcontinent. By his very birth in this crowded and difficult region, he was an outsider—just like Rudyard Kipling: both British and Indian, neither British nor Indian. And, like Kipling, he was sent back to England at a very early age, to feel himself even more of an exile than before. (Kipling, you remember, was put in the charge of a horrible old woman who ran a kind of home where he and his sister were the only inmates: the woman and her son tortured him with all the more gusto because he was lonely and eccentric and half-blind.) The next five or six years were spent in a small hell, none the less tormenting because it was miniature in size, a hell of loneliness and persecution and paranoia. The school did not even want him. Its headmaster thought he was too poor, a sort of charity-boy, kept only because he was clever and might bring credit on the place by winning a big scholarship. And the dirt and squalor! Long afterward, long, long afterward, Orwell remembered being so hungry that he tiptoed downstairs to steal stale bread from the pantry at two in the morning; and he recalled the filthy metal bowls out of which the boys ate porridge, the rims flaked and scabbed by leavings from yesterday and the day before and the day before that . . .

In one way, the school did do its job. Orwell won a scholarship to the most famous and the proudest school in the world, Eton College. At Eton, a scholarship-boy is an outsider, because he lives apart from the other boys, who are richer and usually less clever; and yet he is an outsider compared with boys in all other schools, too; he is above them because Eton is so splendid in its reputation and so brilliant in the education that it does give. There are reminiscences of Orwell in the autobiographies of several contemporaries: Cyril Connolly remembers him as someone who was too contemptuous and self-possessed to be an open rebel, but was certainly not a typical Etonian.

Normally, the next stage of his career would have been for him to win another scholarship—to Oxford or Cambridge— and then to aim at the Foreign Office or some other government department. Either he failed, or he rebelled, or his people made him change the routine. Aged eighteen, he entered the Indian Imperial Police, serving in Burma—where he felt even more of an outsider: surrounded by people who feared, hated, or despised him. (This part of his life is reflected in two books, *Burmese Days* and *Shooting an Elephant*.) Finally, at the age of twenty-four, he cast loose, returned to Europe, and became a bum. He felt that all organized society was a racket: he became a down-and-out, a hobo, living and sleeping in filth, homeless and hopeless. He has left some unforgettably hideous descriptions of this period: the filthy kitchens of fine restaurants in Paris, full of roaches and dirty cloths, with sweat falling into the gravy; and the even filthier kitchens of mean lodging houses in Britain. Try his *Down and Out in Paris and London* and something not yet published in the United States, *The Road to Wigan Pier*.

By the age of thirty-two or thirty-three (always a climacteric period) he was beginning to remake his life, and was setting out to be a writer, while keeping himself alive by running a small country store. He had been absorbing a good deal of Marxist theory (you remember, the 1930's were a time of keen Communist penetration and conversion); so, when the Spanish revolution broke out, he went to Spain and joined the left-wing forces. But even in his fighting there he was nonconformist, for he joined a unit that was not sympathetic to the Communists (it was the POUM, which was later denounced and sabotaged by Stalin's agents): so he was now an outsider of outsiders among outsiders.

He was wounded in Spain. He wintered in Morocco—already feeling the pull of the disease that was to kill him. He wrote a book about the Spanish war which was received with hostility by the pinkos in Britain and ignored by the others; it was not even published in this country until last year, when some of the scales had fallen from our eyes. It is called *Homage to Catalonia.*

Returning to Britain, Orwell settled down to become a professional writer. He had many enemies. The Stalin clique and their allies did their best to wreck his work; still, he wrote so well that he got into print oftener than they would have liked. His masterpiece is a story already famous: a description of the grim, state-worshiping, police-ridden, torture-dominated socialist future, without permanent truths or permanent values, when the dictatorship of one class has become the dictatorship of one gang, the new Dark Ages, called *1984.* It is a splendid book, worthy to be classed with Voltaire's *Candide* and Swift's *Gulliver.*

In the remainder of his work, what will last is his extremely sharp social and literary criticism. His writing is delightfully clear and convincing, without rhetoric or evasiveness. Oh heavens, how hard it is to acquire a good clear style, as honest as decent stitching in a shoe, as clean as a well-laundered shirt, as economical as an efficient surgical operation, as tireless as a fine machine, as graceful as a fast runner! It is particularly hard when one writes about politics, for then one tends to become shrill and excitable, or else to fall into clichés about democratic values and class conflicts and the heritage of history and the mission of the people and so forth, stereotypes which usually conceal an absence of thought. Also, when a man is lonely, as Orwell was, it is hard for him not to be savagely bitter, to strike back at personal enemies, to put in poisoned parentheses, to produce a negative effect. But Orwell did manage to maintain his balance, to keep thinking, to continue his kindness to most of his fellow men, to hammer out and to polish into brilliance a sharp, honest style.

Then again he was able to do something which few modern writers can do: he could compose equally well in three or four different types of writing, and sometimes blend them: fiction; personal reminiscences; literary criticism; and social commentary. There are many literary critics who write as though prose and poetry were somehow detached from the world in which they were written and from the individuals who wrote them; there are innumerable novelists who write as though none of their characters ever read a single book, in fact, as though literature were something to be ashamed of; there are many autobiographers who know little about society and think aesthetic experience is not worth recalling; and there are social writers who seem to believe that art is not essential to life. These people are usually wrong; and Orwell was right to blend all these ways of thinking and of writing, although it made his task more difficult.

But the best of his qualities was his vision. He looked at everything with detachment, even at himself; and he saw things clearly. Right up to the end, you can see him conquering his own earlier illusions, such as the absurd Marxist doctrine that there are only two classes and that they hate each other; you can see him in his latest essays ruthlessly exposing the intellectual, emotional, and moral weaknesses of the very people who were most likely to read him, the intelligentsia; you can watch him working out a difficult and penetrating analysis of nationalism as a drug-habit of the mind—and under nationalism he includes not only jingoism but communism and Zionism and color feeling (both black and white) and class feeling (both types) and pacifism and anti-Semitism and Trotskyism, in fact most of the obsessive group-beliefs which are now held, above and beyond the call of reason, by the majority of the world's population. (This essay alone, 'Notes on Nationalism,' is worth the price of admission.) It is delightful also to watch Orwell sympathizing with outsiders, such as Henry Miller, and the artists who draw comic postcards, and children (for children are certainly outsiders—which is why they see us so clearly). Most of us can agree with him in these sympathies, and these analyses. Few of us would have been able to think them out for ourselves; or, if we did, to express them so neatly. He was an unhappy, dissatisfied man, poor Orwell, like the man in the Schubert song, *ein Fremdling überall*, 'a perpetual outsider'; but, like some others, like Thoreau and Pascal, he was able to see most clearly because he was lonely and stood apart from the crowd, yet without hating either the large stupid mass or the poor crushed individuals.

G. Orwell, *Animal Farm* (Harcourt, Brace, 1946).

    *Dickens, Dali, and Others* (Reynal and Hitchcock, 1946).

    *1984* (Harcourt, Brace, 1949).

    *Burmese Days* (Harcourt, Brace, 1950).

    *Coming Up for Air* (Harcourt, Brace, 1950).

    *Down and Out in Paris and London* (Harcourt, Brace, 1950).

    *Shooting an Elephant* (Harcourt, Brace, 1950).

    *Homage to Catalonia* (Harcourt, Brace, 1952).

    *Such, Such Were the Joys* (Harcourt, Brace, 1953).

## Words and Meanings

---

A CYNICAL diplomat once said that language was given to us in order to conceal our thoughts. Like most epigrams, this is more witty than true; but it points the way to a truth which we sometimes miss. The truth is that language sometimes serves to confuse our thoughts, and never manages to convey them completely.

The more difficult our thoughts are, the less able is language to express them. This is not simply a matter of style, or eloquence. Of course some people are tongue-tied. Even when they love a woman dearly, or feel they have been bitterly wronged, or experience tremendous happiness, they cannot say more than a few silly clichés, which they themselves feel to be embarrassingly inadequate. And still, the finest speaker and writer who ever lived, using the most sensitive language yet devised by man, would be incapable of putting certain of his own thoughts into words—words which he himself and others would recognize as carrying more than a fraction of the intended meaning. That is one of the reasons why people write poetry instead of prose: poetry conveys more meanings than prose. That is one of the reasons why we love music: music conveys meanings which we know to be powerful, but which cannot be put into words.

And yet most of us somehow believe that language and thought are usually identical. We have a false equation in our minds:

$$1 \text{ word} = 1 \text{ thought.}$$

But in fact, very often

$$1 \text{ word} = 2 \text{ or } 3 \text{ different thoughts;}$$

and sometimes

$$10 \text{ words} = \text{no thought whatever.}$$

Language can be used to conceal the absence of thought.

There is one easy example of this which we all know: double-talk. This is the art of uttering sentences which sound coherent, but which contain absolutely meaningless words and are therefore absolutely meaningless. An expert double-talker can slip sentences like this into a clear and reasonable speech, and can utterly bemuse his listeners, who guess wildly at his meaning, his nonexistent meaning. Early in 1952 a radio reporter who went out and interviewed people with a concealed recording machine took along a famous double-talker, who asked unintelligible questions about the coming elections and got detailed answers. For instance, he talked to one lady about Truman, saying,

> When Truman went into office, he made many promises: one thing the presstrill and taxes with the

nextren of intramat, to make payment for the fraysted
or less than other Presidents, didn't he?

The lady replied:

Well, at the time he got into office, he thought he could
do all the things he said he could. Then he found out
he couldn't. It wasn't all up to him, either.

The interviewer pursued this point, objecting:

But he did make the definite statement that when he
traysnod the vaus, and snapid for the boys taking out
the taxes, and more taxes, didn't he?

This worried the lady, but at last she replied:

He said that in good faith, and couldn't follow through.

Brutal, isn't it? But extremely funny. Here is the finest piece of
such mystification I know. A professor who was studying
James Joyce with a class of graduate students thought they
needed a little more humor, and a little more sense of the
irrational. So he introduced a 'distinguished visiting scholar'
to lecture to them. The man stood up very solemnly, and
began:

The style of James Joyce presents many difficulties
peculiar to itself. Among these surely the most complex
and vilpurt is the sentence-rhythm. A slow and careful
worker like Joyce, who always entwendered to promin
the sound of ordinary speech, and nevertheless hennepe
mousa with other significances (both turp and stal),
was bound to create a mixed, and sometimes (although
I say this with reservations) a perkinstic effect.

Fiendish. They say he went on like that for twenty minutes,
while the professor stood at the back of the classroom and
watched his students struggling to take notes.

There is almost every kind of humor in the work of François

Rabelais; and so we should expect to find double-talk there, too. And there it is, three chapters of it in the Second Book. It seems that there was a famous lawsuit, which had been discussed for nearly a year, but could not be settled, or even understood, by the greatest lawyers in France. They consulted Pantagruel. He heard the case. Each party made a speech; Pantagruel gave his decision; they went away satisfied. And the beauty of it is that both the speeches and the decision are absolutely unintelligible, for that is what Rabelais thought about lawyers and the law. For example, the defendant ends his speech by citing a precedent: he says,

> Such another sentence after the homeliest manner was pronounced in the 17th year, because of the bad government of Louzefougarouse, whereunto it may please the Court to have regard. I desire to be rightly understood: for truly I say not but that in all equity, and with an upright conscience, those people may very well be dispossessed who drink holy water as one would do a weaver's shuttle, whereof suppositories are made to those that will not resign except on the terms of ell and tell and giving one thing for another. *Tunc*, my lords, *quid juris pro minoribus?*

Exactly!

I remember once when I was teaching Rabelais one of my students, a freshman, came to me much distressed. He said that his father was a lawyer and that he himself was hoping to become one; he had often heard difficult cases discussed at home; but this in Rabelais—he had read the speeches three times and the decision four times, and he still could not make head or tail of it. What should he do? I tried to be very helpful. I advised him to go off and make a *précis* of the speeches, and then everything would be clear to him. He found out . . .

That kind of deliberate mystification reminds us that there

is another interesting use of language: as a code, a method of conveying secrets between members of a group. Back-slang is the best known and the easiest to detect: the words are partly or wholly inverted, so that BACK becomes KAB or else ACKBAY. Criminals' talk is usually covered with slang as a disguise; and the tight little groups of hot musicians develop their own language, to conceal the poverty of their ideas. As for rhyming slang (which is found in several parts of the British Empire), it is hard to determine whether it started as a secret language or merely as a set of inventive and humorous variations on ordinary words, a sort of vulgar poetry. The essence of this is that for an ordinary word you substitute a more or less meaningless phrase that rhymes with it. Then, to be even cleverer, you use the first, the non-rhyming part of the phrase alone. In regular rhyming slang, instead of your wife, you speak of the old trouble-and-strife; and the kids are the Gawd-forbids. But a more sophisticated slangster will put his titfer on his loaf and go round to the rubbedy: that is, he puts his tit-for-tat (his hat) on his loaf-of-bread (his head), and goes to the rubbedy-dub (the pub), just round the Johnny Horner.

A vulgar poetry. But there is a loftier poetry, built upon alterations and confusions of language. This is the poetry which makes new words to show meanings not yet fully expressed. I am not thinking of Dadaist poetry, which is usually either straight imagist verse or else sound without logic; but of poetry as a creator of language. Do you recall the fine heroic ballad that Alice read in the Looking-Glass book? The plot is simple— the same as St. George and the Dragon, or *Beowulf*: a hero slays a mighty monster. But the language is complicated. It begins:

> 'Twas brillig, and the slithy toves
>   Did gyre and gimble in the wabe;
> All mimsy were the borogoves,
>   And the mome raths outgrabe.

This atmospheric stanza puzzles Alice, until that plump and pleasing person, Humpty Dumpty, explains it. *Brillig* is neither morning nor evening, but about 4 p.m., when you start broiling and grilling things for dinner; *toves, raths,* and *borogoves* are obviously strange animals (their names are not queerer than coypu or chinchilla); *slithy* means lithe and slimy; to *gyre* is to whirl like a gyroscope, and to *gimble* is to make holes in the ground like a gimlet, perhaps gamboling a little from time to time. *Mimsy* is like ZaSu Pitts, flimsy and miserable; *mome* is like Kafka, feeling lost and far from home; and *wabe* is the grass round a sundial, like the perspective in a Chirico painting, going a long way beyond it on every side.

This reminds us of James Joyce. 'Jabberwocky' was only a short poem, but Joyce wrote a book that went a long way beyond it in every direction. Out of every thousand of us, thirty or forty have heard of it; about four own a copy; and perhaps only one has ever read it. It is *Finnegans Wake*. It appeared just fifteen years ago. I have tried fifteen times to read it all through, and fifteen times I have failed. Edmund Wilson has read it; Thornton Wilder has read it several times, and is said to have annotated it in detail; but it really is a thing for specialists to study rather than for readers to read—and I feel there are other more important things for me to study. And yet . . . and yet . . . I can feel its fascination. *Finnegans Wake* is the story of a long night of sleep and dreams, told in dream language. Events and persons of the present are confused with recent history and distant myths; and the language mixes up words of one meaning with words of another meaning but similar sound, words of English origin with words of German and Greek and Gaelic and a score of other tongues— because, in dreaming, we sink below the level of articulate, precise thought and a single logical language. The result is a blend of poetry nonsense obscurity obscenity humor and grotesque fancy. Here is a sentence from Joyce's fable of the Ondt and the Gracehoper:

Now whim the sillybilly of a Gracehoper had jingled through a jungle of love and debts and jangled through a jumble of life in doubts afterworse, wetting with the bimblebeaks, drikking with nautonects . . . he fell joust as sieck as a sexton and tantoo pooveroo quant a churchprince, and wheer the midges to wend hemsylph . . . alick, he wist gnit!

We can see at once what it means: that the grasshopper (called gracehoper because he did not *earn* his salvation) spent a summer singing and reveling, and then fell into poverty, not knowing where to turn. And we can hear some of the double meanings: midges are gnats; it is not far from gnat to gnit; a sylph, too, is a little airy creature; the whole sentence is a dancing maze of tiny-insect names. There is a lot more which we cannot possibly get without careful study and a dozen rereadings and hours spent with that useful guide book, Campbell and Robinson's *Skeleton Key to Finnegans Wake*. Some of us will wonder (in the words of Sam Weller) 'vether it's vorth goin' through so much to learn so little, as the charity-boy said ven he got to the end of the alphabet.'

And yet, even if I shall never read *Finnegans Wake* all through in detail, I still like to keep it and to wander about in its maze: it is a land of fancy, described in fantasy-speech. So much language is taken up with a dull and unsuccessful attempt to be precise, so much poetry is blunt and realistic even when it deals with difficult images, that a little imaginative double-talk now and then is a relief. Sometimes I can cure insomnia by repeating to myself the end of the dialogue between the two old women, washing clothes on the river bank and gradually changing into a tree and a rock:

Can't hear with the waters of. The chittering waters of. Flittering bats, fieldmice bawk talk. Ho! Are you not gone ahome? What Thom Malone? Can't hear with bawk of bats, all thim liffeying waters of. Ho, talk save us! My foos won't moos. I feel as old as yonder elm. A tale told of Shaun or Shem? All Livia's daughtersons. Dark hawks hear us. Night! Night! My ho head halls. I feel as heavy as yonder stone. Tell me of John or Shaun? Who were Shem and Shaun the living sons or daughters of? Night now! Tell me, tell me, tell me, elm! Night night! Telmetale of stem or stone. Beside the rivering waters of, hitherandthithering waters of. Night!

---

J. Campbell and H. M. Robinson, *A Skeleton Key to Finnegans Wake* (Harcourt, Brace, 1944).

James Joyce, *Finnegans Wake* (Viking Press, gallant fellows, 1939).

'The Jaskpurt of Naustrent,' *Time*, 7 April 1952.

# The Christians and the Lions

ONE of the greatest subjects in the world is still waiting for a gifted writer—someone with really special talent and knowledge and understanding—to make it into a book. It could hardly be converted into a play, unless by a stupendous genius. It would make the theme of a magnificent novel, on the lines of *War and Peace*. A historian could devote his life to it. There have been some operas dealing with it; some spectacular but superficial films; and not enough poetry—although it could also become the basis of a dramatic poem like Thomas Hardy's *The Dynasts*. It is a superb subject, one of the most important which has ever emerged: it combines horror and beauty, hard fact and the loftiest mysticism, violent physical action and complex political intrigue and difficult philosophical discussion; it merges the past with the present, and both with eternity. The subject is the conversion of the ancient world, the Greek and Roman world, to the religion of Christianity.

Because I am a classical scholar and was brought up as a practicing Christian, the subject has always interested me deeply: I have been reading and thinking about it for nearly thirty years. But we are all interested in it, for we live in an age which is seeing powerful and widespread spiritual changes, adaptations of belief, dislocations of tradition, conversions and reconversions and apostasies and martyrdoms; and perhaps we shall all understand ourselves and our times better if we understand the rise of Christianity a little more clearly and vividly.

The one thing I am sure of is a principle I have found to be valuable in all historical and philosophical discussion. It is this:

*Complex events have complex causes.*

It sounds simple, doesn't it? But how many people have racked their brains and wasted their time trying to find one single explanation to which everything else can be reduced? It is like trying to find one single essential root in the life-system of an enormous tree. No isolated fact, no one-sided approach, will solve the problem and answer the complicated question: how and why was the ancient world converted to Christianity?

Some of the explanations given in modern fiction and history are not only limited but downright wrong. I remember a book by Naomi Mitchison called *Blood of the Martyrs*, which was built on the idea that Christianity succeeded as a social revolution, promising economic relief to the poor and freedom to the slaves. This sounds nice, but it is untrue. St. Paul explicitly told slaves that they ought to go on being slaves; and the early Christians in general paid little attention to things like that. Their problems were different. In fact, it was the first Christian Emperor, Constantine, who set up something like serfdom for the poor peasants. Slavery, and serfdom, and bondage—all these make an important subject, but they are not closely connected with the rise of Christianity.

In the motion pictures, and in some of the more naïve novels about the subject, the usual explanation is stamped out, on the black-and-white pattern of so many Western films: that all the pagans were vicious, bloodthirsty monsters who persecuted the Christians with fire and torture and brutal execution; that the world had never before seen men and women sacrificing themselves for their convictions; and that the spectacle of their martyrdom converted the better spirits to overthrow paganism and embrace Christianity. The movie version of the Polish novel *Quo Vadis?* falsified history by making us believe that one of the Emperor Nero's officers turned upon him after watching the Christians suffering, and that Nero was then overthrown by a demonstration of popular feeling. This is nonsense. Nero was much beloved by the common people, and his overthrow, which came later than the persecution, was due to quite different causes. A later persecution authorized by Diocletian is the subject of Cardinal Wiseman's once famous novel, *Fabiola*, which has been filmed several times; but it is equally crude and equally unsatisfactory. In fact, Christianity was not persecuted systematically and unremittingly, like the Jews under Hitler or the opponents of communism in a communist state; there were long periods when nothing whatever was done to hinder its growth; and at last the organization of the Empire and the organization of the Church merged into one another almost painlessly, within less than a generation after the final persecution.

We can never understand such a process, unless we realize how complicated it was. Any novel which treated it adequately would be a huge social and intellectual panorama, and would show many different types of people turning toward Christianity or away from it, for many different reasons. It would have to show the conflict between Christianity and the lofty philosophical systems to which so many of the intellectuals belonged. Not many novelists are competent to write about that struggle nowadays, because few people have the training to assimilate an advanced philosophical doctrine such as Stoicism, together with the imagination to understand how it could grip both the mind and the emotions of a mature man; and still fewer have the power to make the process clear in a novel. There is one nineteenth-century novel which conveys something of the violence of the conflict, Charles Kingsley's *Hypatia*—named after the beautiful young woman who taught Platonism and was hacked to pieces by a Christian mob; and there is one which tries to show the relations of the philosophical creeds to Christianity, Pater's *Marius the Epicurean*; but neither of them is subtle enough to show us the depths and the heights of these philosophies and their opponent.

Then again, the true depicter of early Christianity would have to show how it competed with other mystical religions. Kipling was interested in this, and wrote several good short stories in which he described Mithraism, that picturesque Persian cult which contained a blood sacrifice, a communion meal, and a hierarchy of initiation rather like that of his own favored creed Masonry; but I do not know of any novel that does justice to it, or to the other mystery-religions and their links with Christianity. Do you know that the very date of Christmas was taken over from one or more of them? The Bible does not say in what month Jesus was born. The Church took over the festival of the winter solstice, which was celebrated as the birthday of the Unconquerable Sun—and traces of that cult remain in our celebrations, when we hang out evergreen wreaths and set up evergreen trees, which show nature conquering winter but have nothing directly to do with Christian doctrine.

A still more ticklish point is that some of the strongest opposition to Christianity in its early phases came from the Jews. I notice that this subject is almost entirely neglected in most modern stories and films about the first three centuries of our era: yet one of the most interesting things about the Christian religion is that it carried some Jewish beliefs into the Greco-Roman world and left others outside. The Greeks and Romans had no seven-day week, and no regular day of rest; the week, with the Sabbath, came in from Judaism. But circumcision and dietary laws were not imported. And, on a far higher level, a new conception of the relation between God and man was worked out during the transition. Anyone who wrote about this would have to think long and hard about St. Paul, who was 'three times flogged' by the Jews, and also about the fascinating relation between Jewish thought and Greek philosophy.

Some of the pagans who opposed the new religion were well intentioned. They were not devils incarnate. And they insisted that the Greco-Roman world was sustained by certain long-standing traditions. In contrast with these traditions, Christianity appeared to them to be simple anarchism, the cult of a naïve group of mystics who expected the world to come to an end at any moment, and who therefore cared nothing about the duties and responsibilities involved in administering a civilized community—public health, and education, and taxation, and commerce, and national defense, and day-to-day social progress. They pointed to the fact that Rome, as it came closer and closer to accepting Christianity, had been growing weaker and weaker under the attacks of the barbarians: some of them said that Christianity meant the abandonment of the will to live. They were wrong; and they were right; but certainly any novelist or historian who approaches the subject should make their fears and their courage intelligible.

And then there are the barbarians, infiltrating over the

frontiers, cutting the roads, looting the towns, besieging the cities. In the Western empire, their activities coincided with some of the enterprises of Christianity. Mr. Toynbee has worked out a connection between the two: he calls them an external and an internal proletariat. But one of the things that surprises us when we look at the barbarians is that many of them were not heathen, but simple Christians: too simple: they were called heretics, because they believed that God was supreme and Jesus merely a created being. In time this belief passed away (except in so far as it is now represented by Unitarianism), but it certainly could not be called paganism.

If I were attempting a book on this subject, the problem which would concern me most would be this. Christianity depends on a sense of sin. The Christian believes that we are all guilty: every man and woman is guilty; not even the sincerest repentance is enough, alone, to cure us. Now, most of the pagan Greeks and Romans had a sense of duty; but they did not have a sense of pervading and overwhelming sin. Provided they did their duty, they saw nothing wrong in enjoying the rest of their lives. But how was that feeling replaced by the Christian sense of inadequacy and guilt? For example, the Greeks and Romans loved going to the theater. How did the Christians convince them that it was immoral, and abolish the theater for a thousand years? And so with many other fields of the ethical life: how did the Christians create a new sense, or enlarge an existing sense, of guilt? It is easy enough to understand conversion in our own time, when the convert turns from what he knows (through education or inclination or example) to be wicked toward what he knows to be good; but what did conversion mean in a pagan world? A. D. Nock of Harvard, in an erudite little book called *Conversion*, has told us something of that: but not quite enough.

There have been many novels recently on the rise of Christianity, and more of them are appearing every month. Some of them are awful nonsense. Mr. Costain's *Silver Chalice* deals with an early period soon after the Crucifixion; and although it is vivid, it is pretty superficial and pretty improbable. Others are much worse, with the most ridiculous mistakes in language and historical fact. Gladys Schmitt's *Confessors of the Name* is the only recent novel which seems to me to cover the ground with anything like completeness. It is not really possible to write about the rise of Christianity without long and careful meditation on the works of the early Church Fathers, without a sympathetic study of that fascinating subject, Christian art (did you know that some of the early representations of Jesus showed him as Orpheus and Hermes?), without knowing much Jewish lore, and without understanding the rival Greco-Roman philosophies which Christianity was in part to destroy, in part to transcend, and in part to assimilate. As long as we think of the Christianization of the Western world as a simple story of persecution followed by victory, we shall misunderstand it. Forget the lions; remember the men and women. It was the Greeks and the Romans who, slowly, gradually, and after many generations of thought and experiment, became the Christians; and so, at a distance of fifty generations, they are ourselves.

———

Thomas Costain, *The Silver Chalice* (Doubleday, 1952).
Naomi Mitchison, *Blood of the Martyrs* (Whittlesey House, 1948).
A. D. Nock, *Conversion* (Oxford, 1933).
Gladys Schmitt, *Confessors of the Name* (Dial, 1952).

# The Gettysburg Address

---

F*OURSCORE and seven years ago* . . .

These five words stand at the entrance to the best-known monument of American prose, one of the finest utterances in the entire language, and surely one of the greatest speeches in all history. Greatness is like granite: it is molded in fire, and it lasts for many centuries.

Fourscore and seven years ago . . . It is strange to think that President Lincoln was looking back to the 4th of July 1776, and that he and his speech are now further removed from us than he himself was from George Washington and the Declaration of Independence. Fourscore and seven years before the Gettysburg Address, a small group of patriots signed the Declaration. Fourscore and seven years after the Gettysburg Address, it was the year 1950,* and that date is already

* In November 1950 the Chinese had just entered the war in Korea.

receding rapidly into our troubled, adventurous, and valiant past.

Inadequately prepared and at first scarcely realized in its full importance, the dedication of the graveyard at Gettysburg was one of the supreme moments of American history. The battle itself had been a turning point of the war. On the 4th of July 1863, General Meade repelled Lee's invasion of Pennsylvania. Although he did not follow up his victory, he had broken one of the most formidable aggressive enterprises of the Confederate armies. Losses were heavy on both sides. Thousands of dead were left on the field, and thousands of wounded died in the hot days following the battle. At first, their burial was more or less haphazard; but thoughtful men gradually came to feel that an adequate burying place and memorial were required. These were established by an interstate commission that autumn, and the finest speaker in the North was invited to dedicate them. This was the scholar and statesman Edward Everett of Harvard. He made a good speech—which is still extant: not at all academic, it is full of close strategic analysis and deep historical understanding.

Lincoln was not invited to speak, at first. Although people knew him as an effective debater, they were not sure whether he was capable of making a serious speech on such a solemn occasion. But one of the impressive things about Lincoln's career is that he constantly strove to *grow*. He was anxious to appear on that occasion and to say something worthy of it. (Also, it has been suggested, he was anxious to remove the impression that he did not know how to behave properly—an impression which had been strengthened by a shocking story about his clowning on the battlefield of Antietam the previous year.) Therefore when he was invited he took considerable care with his speech. He drafted rather more than half of it in the White House before leaving, finished it in the hotel at Gettysburg the night before the ceremony (not in the train, as sometimes reported), and wrote out a fair copy next morning.

There are many accounts of the day itself, 19 November 1863. There are many descriptions of Lincoln, all showing the same curious blend of grandeur and awkwardness, or lack of dignity, or—it would be best to call it humility. In the procession he rode horseback: a tall lean man in a high plug hat, straddling a short horse, with his feet too near the ground. He arrived before the chief speaker, and had to wait patiently for half an hour or more. His own speech came right at the end of a long and exhausting ceremony, lasted less than three minutes, and made little impression on the audience. In part this was because they were tired, in part because (as eyewitnesses said) he ended almost before they knew he had begun, and in part because he did not speak the Address, but read it, very slowly, in a thin high voice, with a marked Kentucky accent, pronouncing 'to' as 'toe' and dropping his final R's.

Some people of course were alert enough to be impressed. Everett congratulated him at once. But most of the newspapers paid little attention to the speech, and some sneered at it. The *Patriot and Union* of Harrisburg wrote, 'We pass over the silly remarks of the President; for the credit of the nation we are willing . . . that they shall no more be repeated or thought of'; and the London *Times* said, 'The ceremony was rendered ludicrous by some of the sallies of that poor President Lincoln,' calling his remarks 'dull and commonplace.' The first commendation of the Address came in a single sentence of the Chicago *Tribune*, and the first discriminating and detailed praise of it appeared in the Springfield *Republican*, the Providence *Journal*, and the Philadelphia *Bulletin*. However, three weeks after the ceremony and then again the following spring, the editor of *Harper's Weekly* published a sincere and thorough eulogy of the Address, and soon it was attaining recognition as a masterpiece.

At the time, Lincoln could not care much about the reception of his words. He was exhausted and ill. In the train back to Washington, he lay down with a wet towel on his head. He had caught smallpox. At that moment he was incubating it, and he was stricken down soon after he re-entered the White House. Fortunately it was a mild attack, and it evoked one of his best jokes: he told his visitors, 'At last I have something I can give to everybody.'

He had more than that to give to everybody. He was a unique person, far greater than most people realize until they read his life with care. The wisdom of his policy, the sources of his statesmanship—these were things too complex to be discussed in a brief essay. But we can say something about the Gettysburg Address as a work of art.

A work of art. Yes: for Lincoln was a literary artist, trained both by others and by himself. The textbooks he used as a boy were full of difficult exercises and skillful devices in formal rhetoric, stressing the qualities he practiced in his own speaking: antithesis, parallelism, and verbal harmony. Then he read and reread many admirable models of thought and expression: the King James Bible, the essays of Bacon, the best plays of Shakespeare. His favorites were *Hamlet, Lear, Macbeth, Richard III,* and *Henry VIII,* which he had read dozens of times. He loved reading aloud, too, and spent hours reading poetry to his friends. (He told his partner Herndon that he preferred getting the sense of any document by reading it aloud.) Therefore his serious speeches are important parts of the long and noble classical tradition of oratory which begins in Greece, runs through Rome to the modern world, and is still capable (if we do not neglect it) of producing masterpieces.

The first proof of this is that the Gettysburg Address is full of quotations—or rather of adaptations—which give it strength. It is partly religious, partly (in the highest sense) political: therefore it is interwoven with memories of the Bible and memories of American history. The first and the last words are Biblical cadences. Normally Lincoln did not say 'fourscore' when he meant eighty; but on this solemn occasion he recalled the important dates in the Bible—such as the age of Abram when his first son was born to him, and he was 'fourscore and six years old.' * Similarly he did not say there was a chance that democracy might die out: he recalled the somber phrasing of the Book of Job—where Bildad speaks of the destruction of one who shall vanish without a trace, and says that 'his branch shall be cut off; his remembrance shall perish from the earth.' † Then again, the famous description of our State as 'government of the people, by the people, for the people' was adumbrated by Daniel Webster in 1830 (he spoke of 'the people's government, made for the people, made by the people, and answerable to the people') and then elaborated in 1854 by the abolitionist Theodore Parker (as 'government of all the people, by all the people, for all the people'). There is good reason to think that Lincoln took the important phrase 'under God' (which he interpolated at the last moment) from Weems, the biographer of Washington; and we know that it had been used at least once by Washington himself.

Analyzing the Address further, we find that it is based on a highly imaginative theme, or group of themes. The subject is—how can we put it so as not to disfigure it?—the subject is the kinship of life and death, that mysterious linkage which we see sometimes as the physical succession of birth and death in our world, sometimes as the contrast, which is perhaps a unity, between death and immortality. The first sentence is concerned with birth:

* Gen. 16.16; cf. Exod. 7.7.
† Job 18.16–17; cf. Jer. 10.11, Micah 7.2.

> Our *fathers brought forth* a *new* nation, *conceived* in liberty.

The final phrase but one expresses the hope that

> this nation, under God, shall have a *new birth* of freedom.

And the last phrase of all speaks of continuing life as the triumph over death. Again and again throughout the speech, this mystical contrast and kinship reappear: 'those who *gave their lives* that that nation might *live*,' 'the brave men *living* and *dead*,' and so in the central assertion that the dead have already consecrated their own burial place, while 'it is for us, the *living*, rather to be dedicated . . . to the great task remaining.' The Gettysburg Address is a prose poem; it belongs to the same world as the great elegies, and the adagios of Beethoven.

Its structure, however, is that of a skillfully contrived speech. The oratorical pattern is perfectly clear. Lincoln describes the occasion, dedicates the ground, and then draws a larger conclusion by calling on his hearers to dedicate themselves to the preservation of the Union. But within that, we can trace his constant use of at least two important rhetorical devices.

The first of these is *antithesis*: opposition, contrast. The speech is full of it. Listen:

> The world will little *note*
> nor long *remember*     what *we say* here
> but     it can never *forget*     what *they did* here.

And so in nearly every sentence: 'brave men, *living* and *dead*'; 'to *add* or *detract*.' There is the antithesis of the Founding Fathers and the men of Lincoln's own time:

> Our *fathers brought forth* a new nation . . .
> now *we* are testing whether that nation . . . can *long endure*.

And there is the more terrible antithesis of those who have already died and those who still live to do their duty. Now, antithesis is the figure of contrast and conflict. Lincoln was speaking in the midst of a great civil war.

The other important pattern is different. It is technically called *tricolon*—the division of an idea into three harmonious parts, usually of increasing power. The most famous phrase of the Address is a tricolon:

> government of the people
>          by the people
>   and  for the people.

The most solemn sentence is a tricolon:

> we cannot dedicate
> we cannot consecrate
> we cannot hallow      this ground.

And above all, the last sentence (which has sometimes been criticized as too complex) is essentially two parallel phrases, with a tricolon growing out of the second and then producing another tricolon: a trunk, three branches, and a cluster of flowers. Lincoln says that it is for his hearers to be dedicated to the great task remaining before them. Then he goes on,

> that from these honored dead

—apparently he means 'in such a way that from these honored dead'—

> we take increased devotion to that cause.

Next, he restates this more briefly:

> that we here highly resolve . . .

And now the actual resolution follows, in three parts of growing intensity:

```
        that these dead shall not have died in vain
        that this nation, under God, shall have a new birth
                of freedom
and  that
                (one more tricolon)

                    government of the people
                            by the people
                    and   for the people.
                shall not perish from the earth.
```

Now, the tricolon is the figure which, through division, emphasizes basic harmony and unity. Lincoln used antithesis because he was speaking to a people at war. He used the tricolon because he was hoping, planning, praying for peace.

No one thinks that when he was drafting the Gettysburg Address, Lincoln deliberately looked up these quotations and consciously chose these particular patterns of thought. No, he chose the theme. From its development and from the emotional tone of the entire occasion, all the rest followed, or grew —by that marvelous process of choice and rejection which is essential to artistic creation. It does not spoil such a work of art to analyze it as closely as we have done; it is altogether fitting and proper that we should do this: for it helps us to penetrate more deeply into the rich meaning of the Gettysburg Address, and it allows us the very rare privilege of watching the workings of a great man's mind.

W. E. Barton, *Lincoln at Gettysburg* (Bobbs-Merrill, 1930).

R. P. Basler, 'Abraham Lincoln's Rhetoric,' *American Literature* 11 (1939–40), 167–82.

L. E. Robinson, *Abraham Lincoln as a Man of Letters* (Chicago, 1918).

# Poetry and Poets

# What Use Is Poetry?

CHILDREN ask lots and lots of questions, about religion, about sex, about the stars. But there are some questions which they never ask: they leave grown-ups to ask them and to answer them. Often this means that the questions are silly: that they are questions about nonexistent problems, or questions to which the answer is obvious. Sometimes it means that the questions *should* be asked, but that the answer is difficult or multiplex.

So, children never ask what is the good of music. They just like singing and dancing, and even drumming on a low note of the piano. In the same way, they never ask what is the use of poetry. They all enjoy poems and songs, and very often come to like them before they can even talk properly; but it never occurs to them that they ought to find reasons for their enjoyment. But grown-ups do inquire about the justification of poetry: they ask what is the point of putting words in a special order and extracting special sound effects from them, instead of speaking plainly and directly. And often—because they get no adequate answer, either from the poets or from the professors—they conclude that poetry is only a set of tricks like conjuring, or a complicated game like chess; and they turn away from it in discouragement . . . until, perhaps, a poetic film like *Henry V* shocks them into realizing something of its power; or, as they grow older, they find that a poem learned in childhood sticks in their mind and becomes clearer and more beautiful with age.

What is the use of poetry?

There must be a number of different answers to the question. Just as a picture can be meant to give pleasure, or to carry a puzzle, or to convey information, so poems are meant for many different things. We can begin to get some of the answers if we look at the poetry that children themselves naturally enjoy, and then see how it is connected with the most famous grown-up poems.

The first pleasure of poetry is the simplest. It is the same pleasure that we have in music—the pleasure of following a pattern of sound. Everyone loves talking, and most people like what might be called doodling in sound. So, if you look through the *Oxford Dictionary of Nursery Rhymes*, you will find several tongue-twisters, like this:

> Peter Piper picked a peck of pickled pepper;
> A peck of pickled pepper Peter Piper picked;
> If Peter Piper picked a peck of pickled pepper,
> Where's the peck of pickled pepper Peter Piper picked?

On a grown-up level, many a famous poem is little more than a pattern of sound: for instance, Shakespeare's love song:

It was a lover and his lass,
  With a hey and a ho and a hey nonino,
That o'er the green cornfield did pass,
  In the spring time, the only pretty ring time,
    When birds do sing, hey ding a ding ding;
    Sweet lovers love the spring.

Much of the best poetry of Swinburne is pattern-making in sound, with a very light core of meaning. Here are four exquisite lines which really mean very little more than the sound of spring showers:

When the hounds of spring are on winter's traces,
  The mother of months in meadow or plain
Fills the shadows and windy places
  With lisp of leaves and ripple of rain.

Small meaning, but lovely rhythm and melody.

Now, there is a second pleasure in poetry. This is that it is sometimes better than prose for telling a story. It even gives authority to a story which is illogical or incredible, or even gruesome. That is one reason children love the poem that tells of the tragic fate of Jack and Jill. There is an interesting variant of it: the cumulative story, in which one detail is piled up on another until the whole story has been set forth with the simple exactitude of a primitive painting: for instance, 'The House That Jack Built,' and the funeral elegy, 'Who Killed Cock Robin?' and the famous old Jewish rhyme, 'Had Gadyo,' about the kid bought for two pieces of money—which is said to symbolize a vast stretch of the history of the Jewish people. Another variant is the limerick, which is simply a funny story in verse. Many a man who would protest that he knew no poetry, and cared nothing for it, could still recite eight or ten limericks in the right company.

In serious adult poetry there are many superb stories, including the two oldest books in Western literature, the *Iliad* and the *Odyssey*. Every good collection of poems will include some of the most dramatic tales ever told, the English and Scottish ballads, which are still occasionally sung in our own southern states. One of the strangest things about the stories told as ballads is their terrible abruptness and directness. They leave out a great deal. They give only a few details, a name or two; they draw the outlines, harsh and black or blood-red, and they concentrate on the actions and the passions. Such is the ballad about an ambush in which a knight was killed by his own wife's brother. It is called 'The Dowie Houms of Yarrow' (that means the sad fields beside the river Yarrow, in the Scottish borders), and it opens immediately with the quarrel, almost with the clash of swords:

> Late at een, drinkin' the wine,
>   And ere they paid the lawin',
> They set a combat them between,
>   To fight it in the dawin'.

Within only a few verses, the knight has been surrounded, and treacherously murdered, fighting against heavy odds; and when his widow goes out to find his body, her anguish is described in one of the most terrible stanzas in all poetry:

> She kissed his cheek, she kamed his hair,
>   As oft she did before, O;
> She drank the red blood frae him ran,
>   On the dowie houms o' Yarrow.

That story in poetry and a few others like 'Edward, Edward' —in which a mother persuades her son to kill his own father, and drives him mad—are absolutely unforgettable.

But besides storytelling, poetry has another use, known all over the world. This is mnemonic. Put words into a pattern, and they are easier to remember. I should never have known the lengths of the months if I had not learned:

> Thirty days hath September,
> April, June, and November;
> All the rest have thirty-one,
> Excepting February alone,
> And that has twenty-eight days clear
> And twenty-nine in each leap year.

This is certainly four hundred years old, for it occurs in an English manuscript dated about 1555, and there is a French poem, with the same rhyme scheme, written three hundred years earlier. (It might be easier to change the calendar, but mankind is by nature conservative.) On a simpler level there are many nursery rhymes in every language which are designed to teach children the very simplest things; for instance, counting and performing easy actions:

> One, two,
> Buckle my shoe,
> Three, four,
> Shut the door.

And even earlier, before the child can speak, he is lucky if his mother can recite the poem that goes over his five toes or fingers, one after another:

> This little pig went to market,
> This little pig stayed at home,

up to the comical climax when the child is meant to squeak too, and to enjoy staying at home.

Adults also remember facts better if they are put into verse. Nearly every morning I repeat to myself:

> Early to bed and early to rise
> Makes a man healthy and wealthy and wise.

And nearly every evening I change it to Thurber's parody:

> Early to rise and early to bed
> Makes a male healthy and wealthy and dead;

or occasionally to George Ade's variant:

Early to bed and early to rise
Will make you miss all the regular guys.

This is the source of what they call didactic poetry, poetry meant to teach. The best-known example of it is the Book of Proverbs in the Bible, which ought to be translated into rhythmical prose, or even verse. The third oldest book in Greek literature, not much younger than Homer, is a farmer's handbook all set out in poetry, so that it could be learned off by heart and remembered: it is the *Works and Days* by Hesiod. To teach has long been one of the highest functions of the poet: great poetry can be written in order to carry a message of philosophical or practical truth—or sometimes an ironical counsel, as in this strange poem by Sir Walter Scott:

Look not thou on beauty's charming;
Sit thou still when kings are arming;
Taste not when the winecup glistens;
Speak not when the people listens;
Stop thine ear against the singer;
From the red gold keep thy finger;
Vacant heart and hand and eye,
Easy live and quiet die.

There is one peculiar variation on the poem that conveys information. This is the riddle poem, which tells you something—but only if you are smart enough to see through its disguise. There are some such riddles in the Bible: Samson created a good one, about the dead lion with a hive of wild bees inside it. Legend has it that Homer died of chagrin because he could not solve a rather sordid poetic puzzle. The nursery rhyme 'Humpty Dumpty' was really a riddle to begin with (before Lewis Carroll and his illustrator gave it away). We are supposed to guess what was the mysterious person or thing which fell down, and then could not possibly be put together again, not even by all the king's horses and all the king's men, and nowadays by all the republic's scientific experts: the answer is an egg. There is a beautiful folk song made up of three such riddles: the cherry without a stone, the chicken without a bone, and the baby that does not cry. It is at least five hundred years old, and yet for four hundred years it was passed on from one singer to another, without ever being printed.

Again, there are some famous and splendid poems that deal with mystical experience in riddling terms, phrases which have two meanings, or three, or one concealed: these are also didactic, informative, and yet riddles. One such poem, by an American poet, deals with the paradox of God—the complete God, who includes all the appearances of the universe, both the appearance of good and the appearance of evil. This is Emerson's 'Brahma.'

> If the red slayer think he slays,
>   Or if the slain think he is slain,
> They know not well the subtle ways
>   I keep, and pass, and turn again.
>
> Far or forgot to me is near;
>   Shadow and sunlight are the same;
> The vanished gods to me appear;
>   And one to me are shame and fame.
>
> They reckon ill who leave me out;
>   When me they fly, I am the wings;
> I am the doubter and the doubt,
>   And I the hymn the Brahmin sings.
>
> The strong gods pine for my abode,
>   And pine in vain the sacred Seven;
> But thou, meek lover of the good!
>   Find me, and turn thy back on heaven.

This is a riddle which is meant not for children but for adults. There are similar riddles in the Bible, sometimes equally beautiful. Such is the meditation on old age at the end of that mysterious and rather unorthodox book called *Koheleth*, or *Ecclesiastes*:

> Remember now thy Creator in the days of thy youth,
>> while the evil days come not,
>>> nor the years draw nigh, when thou shalt say, I have
>>>> no pleasure in them;
>
> while the sun or the light or the moon or the stars be
>> not darkened, nor the clouds return after the rain;
>
> in the day when the keepers of the house shall tremble,
>> and the strong men shall bow themselves,
>> and the grinders cease because they are few,
>> and those that look out of the windows be darkened,
> and the doors shall be shut in the streets,
>> when the sound of the grinding is low,
>> and he shall rise up at the voice of the bird,
>> and all the daughters of music shall be brought low,
> also when they shall be afraid of that which is high,
>> and fears shall be in the way,
>> and the almond tree shall flourish,
>> and the grasshopper shall be a burden,
> and desire shall fail:
>> because man goeth to his long home
>> and the mourners go about the streets;
>
> or ever the silver cord be loosed,
>> or the golden bowl be broken,
>> or the pitcher be broken at the fountain
>> or the wheel broken at the cistern.
>
> Then shall the dust return to the earth as it was;
>> and the spirit shall return unto God who gave it.

All these enigmatic and memorable phrases are descriptions of the symptoms of the last and almost the bitterest fact in life, old age. They show that it is pathetic, and yet they make it beautiful.

Such poetry is unusual. Or rather, its manner is unusual and its subject is a fact of common experience. It is possible for poets to speak plainly and frankly about everyday life; and that is one more of the uses of poetry—one of the best known. Poetry can express general experience: can say what many men and women have thought and felt. The benefit of this is that it actually helps ordinary people, by giving them words. Most of us are not eloquent. Most of us—especially in times of intense emotion—cannot say what we feel; often we hardly know what we feel. There, in our heart, there is the turmoil, be it love or protest or exultation or despair: it stirs us, but all our gestures and words are inadequate. As the emotion departs, we know that an opportunity was somehow missed, an opportunity of realizing a great moment to the full. It is in this field that poetry comes close to religion. Religion is one of the experiences which the ordinary man finds most difficult to compass in words. Therefore he nearly always falls back on phrases which have been composed for him by someone more gifted. Many, many thousands of times, in battles and concentration camps and hospitals, beside death beds, and even on death beds, men and women have repeated a very ancient poem only six verses long, and have found comfort in it, such as no words of their own would have brought them. It begins, 'The Lord is my shepherd; I shall not want.'

If we look at poetry or any of the arts from this point of view, we shall gain a much greater respect for them. They are not amusements or decorations; they are aids to life. Ordinary men and women find living rather difficult. One of their chief difficulties is to apprehend their own thoughts and feelings, and to respond to them by doing the right things and saying the right sentences. It is the poets who supply the words and sentences. They too have felt as we do, but they have been able to speak, while we are dumb.

Not only that. By expressing common emotions clearly and eloquently, the poets help us to understand them in other people. It is difficult to understand—for any grown-up it is difficult to understand—what goes on in the mind of a boy or girl. Parents are often so anxious and serious that they have forgotten what it was like to be young, and vague, and romantic. It is a huge effort, rather an unpleasantly arduous effort, to think oneself back into boyhood. Yet there are several poems which will allow us to understand it, and even to enjoy the experience. One of them is a fine lyric by Longfellow, called 'My Lost Youth':

> I remember the gleams and glooms that dart
>    Across the schoolboy's brain;
> The song and the silence in the heart,
> That in part are prophecies, and in part
>    Are longings wild and vain.
>       And the voice of that fitful song
>       Sings on, and is never still:
>       'A boy's will is the wind's will,
> And the thoughts of youth are long, long thoughts.'
>
> There are things of which I may not speak;
>    There are dreams that cannot die;
> There are thoughts that make the strong heart weak,
> And bring a pallor into the cheek,
>    And a mist before the eye.
>       And the words of that fatal song
>       Come over me like a chill:
>       'A boy's will is the wind's will,
> And the thoughts of youth are long, long thoughts.'

If you have a young son who seems to be woolgathering half the time, and who sometimes does not even answer when he is spoken to, you should read and reflect on that poem of Long-fellow.

This function of poetry is not the only one, but it is one of the most vital: to give adequate expression to important general experiences. In 1897, when Queen Victoria celebrated her Diamond Jubilee, the Poet Laureate was that completely inadequate little fellow, Alfred Austin; but the man who wrote the poem summing up the emotions most deeply felt during the Jubilee was Rudyard Kipling. It is called 'Recessional.' It is a splendid poem, almost a hymn—Biblical in its phrasing and deeply prophetic in its thought:

> The tumult and the shouting dies—
>     The captains and the kings depart—
> Still stands Thine ancient sacrifice,
>     An humble and a contrite heart.
> Lord God of Hosts, be with us yet,
> Lest we forget, lest we forget!

However, as you think over the poems you know, you will realize that many of them seem to be quite different from this. They are not even trying to do the same thing. They do not express important general experiences in universally acceptable words. On the contrary, they express strange and individual experiences in abstruse and sometimes unintelligible words. We enjoy them not because they say what we have often thought but because they say what we should never have dreamed of thinking. If a poem like Kipling's 'Recessional' or Longfellow's 'Lost Youth' is close to religion, then this other kind of poetry is close to magic: its words sound like spells; its subjects are often dreams, visions, and myths.

Such are the two most famous poems by Coleridge: 'The Ancient Mariner' and 'Kubla Khan.' They are scarcely understandable. They are unbelievable. Beautiful, yes, and haunting, yes, but utterly illogical; crazy. Coleridge himself

scarcely knew their sources, deep in his memory and his subconscious—sources on which a modern scholar has written a
superb book. Both of them end with a mystical experience
that none of us has ever had: 'The Ancient Mariner' telling
how, like the Wandering Jew, he must travel forever from
country to country, telling his story with 'strange power of
speech'; and 'Kubla Khan' with the poet himself creating a
magical palace:

> I would build that dome in air,
> That sunny dome! those caves of ice!
> And all who heard should see them there,
> And all should cry, Beware! Beware!
> His flashing eyes, his floating hair!
> Weave a circle round him thrice,
>> And close your eyes with holy dread,
>> For he on honey-dew hath fed,
> And drunk the milk of Paradise.

Not long after those fantastic verses were written, young
Keats was composing a lyric, almost equally weird, which is
now considered one of the finest odes in the English language.
It ends with the famous words which we all know, and which
few of us believe:

> Beauty is truth, truth beauty,—that is all
> Ye know on earth, and all ye need to know.

It is the 'Ode on a Grecian Urn'; but how many of us have
ever stood, like Keats, meditating on the paintings that surround a Greek vase? and, even if we have, how many of us
have thought that

> Heard melodies are sweet, but those unheard
> Are sweeter?

It is a paradox. The entire ode is a paradox: not an expression of ordinary life, but an extreme extension of it, almost a
direct contradiction of usual experience.

Most modern poetry is like this. It tells of things almost unknown to ordinary men and women, even to children. If it has power over them at all, it is because it enchants them by its strangeness. Such is the poetry of Verlaine, and Mallarmé, and Rimbaud; of the difficult and sensitive Austrian poet Rilke; in our own language, such is most of Auden's poetry, and Ezra Pound's; and what could be more unusual than most of T. S. Eliot—although he is the most famous poet writing today? Suppose we test this. Let us take something simple. Spring. What have the poets said about the first month of spring, about April? Most of them say it is charming and frail:

> April, April,
> Laugh thy girlish laughter;
> Then, the moment after,
> Weep thy girlish tears!

That is Sir William Watson: turn back, and see Shakespeare talking of

> The uncertain glory of an April day;

turn forward, and hear Browning cry

> O to be in England
> Now that April's there!

and then hundreds of years earlier, see Chaucer beginning his *Canterbury Tales* with a handshake of welcome to 'Aprille, with his shoures soote.' Indeed, that is what most of us feel about April: it is sweet and delicate and youthful and hopeful. But T. S. Eliot begins *The Waste Land* with a grim statement which is far outside ordinary feelings:

> April is the cruellest month, breeding
> Lilacs out of the dead land, mixing
> Memory and desire, stirring
> Dull roots with spring rain.

And the entire poem, the best known of our generation, is a description of several agonizing experiences which most of us not only have never had but have not even conceived as possible. Yet there is no doubt that it is good poetry, and that it has taken a permanent place in our literature, together with other eccentric and individual visions.

But some of us do not admit it to be poetry—or rather claim that, if it is so extreme and unusual, poetry is useless. This is a mistake. The universe is so vast, the universe is so various, that we owe it to ourselves to try to understand every kind of experience—both the usual and the remote, both the intelligible and the mystical. Logic is not enough. Not all the truth about the world, or about our own lives, can be set down in straightforward prose, or even in straightforward poetry. Some important truths are too subtle even to be uttered in words. A Japanese, by arranging a few flowers in a vase, or Rembrandt, by drawing a dark room with an old man sitting in it, can convey meanings which no one could ever utter in speech. So also, however extravagant a romantic poem may seem, it can tell us something about our world which we ought to know.

It is easier for us to appreciate this nowadays than it would have been for our grandfathers in the nineteenth century, or for their great-grandfathers in the eighteenth century. Our lives are far less predictable; and it is far less possible to use logic alone in organizing and understanding them. Therefore there are justifications, and good ones, for reading and memorizing not only what we might call universal poetry but also strange and visionary poetry. We ourselves, at some time within the mysterious future, may well have to endure and to try to understand some experience absolutely outside our present scope: suffering of some unforeseen kind, a magnificent and somber duty, a splendid triumph, the development of some new power within us. We shall be better able to do so if we know what the poets (yes, and the musicians) have said

about such enhancements and extensions of life. Many a man
has lived happily until something came upon him which made
him, for the first time, think of committing suicide. Such a man
will be better able to understand himself and to rise above
the thought if he knows the music that Rachmaninoff wrote
when he, too, had such thoughts and conquered them, or if
he reads the play of *Hamlet*, or if he travels through Dante's
*Comedy*, which begins in utter despair and ends in the vision
of

> love, that moves the sun and the other stars.

And even if we ourselves are not called upon to endure such
extremes, there may be those around us, perhaps very close to
us, who are faced with situations the ordinary mind cannot
assimilate: sudden wealth, the temptations of great beauty,
the gift of creation, profound sorrow, unmerited guilt. The
knowledge of what the poets have said about experiences
beyond the frontiers of logic will help us at least to sympathize
with them in these experiences. Such understanding is one of
the most difficult and necessary efforts of the soul. Shelley
compared the skylark, lost in the radiance of the sun, to

> a Poet hidden
> In the light of thought
> Singing hymns unbidden,
> Till the world is wrought
> To sympathy with hopes and fears it heeded not.

To create such sympathy is one of the deepest functions of
poetry, and one of the most bitterly needed.

*Seventeen Syllables*

---

IN SOME ways, the Japanese are an exquisitely civilized people. In some ways . . .

A splendid exhibition of their art was displayed in the chief cities of the United States in 1953. It was impossible to look at the best of the Japanese pictures in it without feeling a deep sympathy, almost an affection, for the artists who produced them. They loved nature. They loved nature dearly. Portraying human beings, they were usually conventional and trivial; in most of their religious pictures, they were remote and even surrealist; but they could paint a pine branch covered with thick, fluffy snow, or a tall, lonely heron in a pool, or a group of bright-eyed ducks among the reeds, with a tender grace and certainty which came only from love.

Their technique was masterly. Within their limitations (particularly those of perspective) they could depict practically anything they wanted. And they had the rare art of omission. Sometimes, in a large composition containing trees and crags and weather, they would leave one quarter of the area blank —except for a faint cloud or a few snowflakes. But far above their technique was their deep understanding and passionless love of nature. As Auden says in *The Age of Anxiety,*

> one knows from them what
> A leaf must feel.

We think of most Oriental art as detailed, and intricate, and rather too closely finished; in fact, some of the pieces in that exhibition were clearly the work of laborious years. Yet there were others which, although finished pictures, seemed to be scarcely more than sketches. A trunk of a tree would be rendered with three or four rapid strokes of the brush dwindling away into thin streaks of ink or color, making no effort to sustain the illusion that the tree was real. The Japanese like that. They enjoy it as we enjoy our Impressionist painters. They admire the quality of play, almost of magic, in it: the little miracle by which an artist, with a few blobs of color or a few dashes of black, conjures up a pool of water or a clump of bamboos, and then—simply by not *trying* to be complete and literal—reminds us that art is not reproduction but vision, and induces us to complete the picture by our own imagination.

There is one kind of Japanese poetry in which the same principles seem to be applied: incompleteness, feathery delicacy of touch, sympathetic love of nature mingled with humor and tenderness, noble subjects indirectly approached, tact, suppleness, an apparent absence of effort.

Have you ever looked out over the roofs of a large city, in the early morning or the evening after rain, when the light is falling aslant, making some windows bright and others dark? At such a time, gazing into the cloudy sky, you sometimes see a sudden curving glint in mid-air, a silver-gray flash which is really reflected but which seems, for a second or so, to shine by its own light. It vanishes again; but if you keep watching, a little lower down you will see a flock of pigeons in flight. A few moments before they were startled by something; they rose above the housetops, invisible because they were gray against gray clouds; then all in one movement they swooped round, to fly over and settle elsewhere; and, as they turned, the light caught their wings.

A particular type of Japanese poetry is like that sudden glint on the wings of flying birds. Other writers would make a complete poem out of the incident: sudden noise, fluttering birds, beating hearts, soaring flight, gradual reassurance, and the returning calm as the flock comes to rest in some safer spot. But *this* kind of poetry mentions only the rapid curving glitter in the sky; the reader must do all the rest.

The Japanese call it a *haiku*, or *hokku*, which means something like 'a beginning,' and so carries the meaning of deliberate incompleteness, or a creative activity shared between poet and reader. Surely it is one of the shortest poetic forms ever invented. It has seventeen syllables: no more, no less. They are arranged in three lines, of five, seven, and five syllables each. (Here we might see a parallel to the Japanese system of flower arrangement, where the standard pattern is a triad, with a strong central unit flanked by two weaker units in a harmonious but asymmetrical balance.) There is no rhyme, and no fixed meter: merely the brief outline, three groups of syllables, seventeen in all. The subjects of these poems are unlimited, but usually they contain some reference to the seasons or the time of day. Practically every Japanese knows some of the famous *haiku* off by heart, and thousands of new ones are composed every year.

Let us look at a few of these little things—to see how an effective poem can possibly be written within the compass of seventeen syllables. Like the originals, our translations will be brief, ending almost as soon as they begin; but they will not keep the triadic Japanese form, and their grammar will be a little clearer than the abrupt, almost telegraphic language of the Japanese poets.

First is a single sentence by Hyakuchi:

> I enjoyed the evening coolness
> with one who does not say all he thinks.

That is all. But you see how much is in it, and how much more is implied. There are: the season of the year (it is summer, hot summer, because the poet has been longing for the evening); the sounds of the world (after the noisy day, it is becoming quiet, so that even speech would be an intrusion); the light (growing dimmer into the restful darkness); the situation (two men sitting together, far from noisy parties); the mood (rest and meditation); and the thought behind the whole (that there is greater understanding, of nature and of friends, in almost silent companionship—not in complete silence, but in those brief words which are more eloquent than long speeches or busy conversation). Chopin might have translated that into music, as one of the Preludes.

Here is another *haiku*, by the most famous of all Japanese writers in this style: Basho, who was born just over three hundred years ago, gave up the life of a nobleman and courtier, and became an ascetic, a nature-loving pilgrim, a student of Zen Buddhism (most imaginative of all Buddhist sects), and a superb poet, teacher of poets: he says—

> The cry of the grasshoppers
> does not show how soon they are to die.

All life is brief—the life of the man as well as the life of the insect. But the vivid energy of the grasshoppers' perpetual shrill chorus makes them the masters of the summertime; they are wise; they live their lives without worrying about death, and enjoy life so intensely that they drown out the very thought of death with their song. Or do they know, and therefore sing all the more eagerly?

Next, a delightful springtime poem by a modern poet, Sho-u:

> The birds, singing among the flowers,
> laugh at men who have no leisure.

Observe how every one of these poems at once suggests a picture: usually a picture containing some *contrast*. In this, the contrast of bird song and glum human activity, of carefree creatures enjoying the beauty of the spring and harried men worrying about their work and their families and their property, is clear enough. But it would not surprise me to learn that the poet also had in his mind a painting in which the sparkling eyes of a bird on a flower-laden branch and the delicate lines of his head and his feathers were contrasted with the stodgy, thick face and heavy, drooping clothes of a man passing beneath, with his head bent by his anxieties, his short-sighted anxieties, which are making him as ugly as he is unhappy.

Here is a very early *haiku*, which within three lines contains as much as an entire short story, or one chapter of a novel. It is by Kigin, and is called 'Love Unconfessed':

> 'Oh, my thinness is caused by summer heat,'
> I answered, and burst into tears.

It is a little drama. The speaker is evidently a girl: she is in love, so much in love that she is growing thin and pale, letting concealment, like a worm i' the bud, feed on her damask cheek. And it is the young man she loves who, knowing nothing of her sufferings, asks her why she is so thin (and by implication, ugly); and then—unkindest cut of all—suggests that she must be in love with someone and pining away. If he is as blind as that, he could never love her: so she has just enough strength left to lie once again:

> 'Oh, my thinness is caused by summer heat,'
>     I answered, and burst into tears.

A sad little poem. Two cheerful *haiku* to take the bitter taste away: one by Kikaku:

> Blessed is the beggar,
>     wearing heaven and earth for summer clothes.

And another word painting by Soseki:

> In this crystal-clear spring
>     the stones at the bottom seem to move.

And one more, a sublime and rapid thought by the eighteenth-century poet Ryota:

> Moonlight. May I be reborn
>     as a pine tree on a mountain peak!

It is a great deal to get into seventeen syllables, isn't it?

Yet the oddest thing about these exquisite poems and the equally exquisite paintings is that they should have been produced by a nation which is also capable of such beastly treachery, violence, and cruelty. Invasion, corruption, torture, cold-blooded medieval savagery of the vilest kind—how can they even exist in the same world as such works of art? The delicate sensibilities of *The Tale of Genji*, the tea ceremony, and the flower arrangers—how can they possibly belong to people who would blindfold a captured soldier, make him kneel, and behead him over his own grave, and photograph this filthy crime while it was being committed?

I believe the answer is to be found in another of these poems. Some time before the outbreak of the Second World War, when the Japanese were pressing forward into China and were about to threaten the whole Pacific and Asian world, the emperor announced that the subject for the annual *haiku* competition would be Peace; and he himself wrote a model poem:

> Peaceful is morning in the shrine garden:
> if the whole world were filled with such peace!

At the time, some Western observers interpreted this as absurd hypocrisy; but they misunderstood the Japanese, and did not know the art of the *haiku*, which depends on suggestion and implication. By choosing that subject and expressing that wish in his own poem, the emperor stated his own policy, and indicated that he had been unwillingly overruled by the army. He was lining up the artists, the thinkers, the sensitive people on his side. He was in fact declaring that Japan was—like many civilized peoples—not one nation but two. Japan has two souls: one, that of the soldier and the businessman; the other, that of the poet and the sage. Occasionally they coincide; sometimes they conflict; sometimes they have little or nothing to do with one another. To understand any nation fully is to understand *both* aspects of its character. But although we may admit the courage of the *samurai* and the energy of the Japanese industrialist, they are scarcely likable, and often repulsive. As human beings we can admire only those others, the men who transferred to paper the rustle of rain-lashed reeds, who could build a snow-loaded mountain with a few lines and dots of an agile brush, and who could put into seventeen syllables the whole beauty of a valley lying white under the harvest moon.

---

A. Miyamori, *An Anthology of Haiku Ancient and Modern* (Maruzen Co., Tokyo, 1932).

C. H. Page, *Japanese Poetry* (Houghton Mifflin, Boston, 1923).

*The Poet and His Vulture*

---

WE KNOW the faces of most poets only as stereotypes: the frail, earnest features of John Keats, Tennyson's dark beard and brooding eyes, the suave, enigmatic mask of Shakespeare. But there is one dramatic figure which, as we think of it, lives and moves. It stamped its appearance on the memory of a whole generation, and even set the style for young men's faces and young men's clothes and young men's manners. It still lives. It is Lord Byron.

Mention the name: at once the man appears. Slender; handsome, nobly, arrogantly handsome even in an age of fine-looking men; bold and unconventional, with collar open on a strong white neck; dark curling hair; intense gray eyes with dark lashes. And then the figure moves, and we see that it is lame. Byron could ride a spirited horse, he could swim for hours in rough seas, he could even box if he did not have to move about much, but he could not walk normally, because one or both of his feet were deformed. This (he said) was due to his mother's behavior while he was being born; he could never forgive her; it worried him all his life, and he overcompensated for it. His lameness adds a touch of penetrating grief to our picture of him. Melancholy seems to surround Byron. No; something deeper: a gloom almost Satanic. Men and women were actually afraid of him. He created new characters, who lived in darker worlds: Manfred, the wizard of the high Alps, knowing more of spirits than of mankind and oppressed with a nameless guilt; savage Turkish pashas; daring rebels; lonely pirates whose names are

> linked with one virtue, and a thousand crimes.

Byron wrote one splendid poem in which he addressed the Titan Prometheus—crucified on a remote mountain by an unjust god—as a fellow sufferer. And his life ended in bitter frustration. He died not as he would have chosen, on the battlefield, but of fever in a small Greek town, foreseeing no success for the struggling of liberation which he was endeavoring to keep alive, and leaving his finest, most ambitious poem forever incomplete. A somber destiny. Before he had worn his laurels long, their leaves were blackened.

When you first read Byron's poems, you are struck by their unrelenting pessimism. It is not hysterical, or revolutionary, nor is it the pessimism of the isolated intellectual. It sounds like the considered verdict of an educated, experienced, reflective man who has the gift of poetry. Here is a brief meditation on the heaped ruins of Rome, in a vision that evokes the pessimistic historian of a later century, Oswald Spengler.

> Cypress and ivy, weed and wallflower grown
> Matted and massed together—hillocks heaped

On what were chambers—arch crushed, column strown
In fragments—choked up vaults, and frescos steeped
In subterranean damps, where the owl peeped,
Deeming it midnight:—Temples—Baths—or Halls?
Pronounce who can: for all that Learning reaped
From her research hath been, that these are walls—
Behold the Imperial Mount! 'tis thus the Mighty falls.

There is the moral of all human tales;
'Tis but the same rehearsal of the past,
First Freedom, and then Glory—when that fails,
Wealth—Vice—Corruption,—Barbarism at last;
And History, with all her volumes vast,
Hath but *one* page.

That is the tone of most of Byron's poems. That is the tone
which caught the ear of so many other young poets, and
molded the minds of Heine, Lamartine, De Musset, Leopardi,
Pushkin; yes, and Berlioz: lonely pessimism; heroic disillusion-
ment; Promethean endurance; Titanic scorn. That is the
dark vision that appears when we hear the name of Byron:
proud face, lame foot, tragic gaze, tormented heart.

But look through his poems again; or, better still, open
his letters and his diaries. At once a new Byron appears. Roars
of laughter strike th' astonished ear. A constant flow of epigrams, personal jokes, and nonsense rhymes gushes out. Byron
turns out to be extremely good company, a loyal and cheerful
friend, and a young man full of animal spirits, who would
write a funny letter as readily as he would box five rounds
with a visitor. That was the age of wits and eccentrics, when
a reputation could be made by a brilliant talker. It was the
age of Sydney Smith—who said that Daniel Webster was
like a steam engine in trousers, and declared it required a
surgical operation to get a joke into a Scotchman's head.
Byron was brought up in Aberdeenshire, far in the northeast

of Scotland, and that is where his strong character and his love of solitude were formed; but when he went to school at Harrow and then on to Cambridge, he was thrown into a rough but cheerful society, in which a man needed both wits and guts to make his mark. Byron made his mark.

Occasionally he hated it: society, and success, and his mother, and his wife, and the whole thing. But quite often he enjoyed it. When he did, out poured his gaiety and his fun. His letters are full of jollity. It must have been a cheerful fellow who described a stag party as 'all hiccup and happiness.' In his letters he kept improvising satirical poems like this:

> The world is a bundle of hay,
>   Mankind are the asses who pull,
> Each tugs it a different way,—
>   And the greatest of all is John Bull!

And in conversation he was equally amusing. Lady Blessington wrote down some of the epigrams he threw out to her:

After a season in London, one doubts one's own identity.
I have not quite made up my mind that women have souls.
No man dislikes being lectured by a woman, provided she be not his wife, sister, mother, or mistress.

Really, Byron seldom became bitter unless when he spoke of the British climate, his own reputation, or his female relatives. It was a little naughty of him to describe his honeymoon as the treacle-moon (or we should say the 'molasses-moon'). There is a very funny letter, too, in which he talks about the poem that brought him fame, *Childe Harold*:

I was half mad during the time of its composition, between metaphysics, mountains, lakes, love unextinguishable, thoughts unutterable, and the nightmare of my own delinquencies. I should, many a good day, have blown my brains out, but for the recollection that it would have given pleasure to my mother-in-law; and, even *then*, if I could have been certain to haunt her . . .

Yet Byron's humor goes deeper than that; it runs all through his work. His first poems were lyrical, and sentimental. When they were badly reviewed, he published a sharp, vigorous, and very funny satire called *English Bards and Scotch Reviewers*. (He still thought of himself, at that time, as an Englishman; he was cured later.) Thenceforward, although he was best known for his gloomy works, he kept producing poems of laughter also. Probably he is the last of the great satiric poets writing in English. The favorite of most readers who know Byron's satires is his *Vision of Judgment*, which pokes irresistible fun at the Poet Laureate's conception of George III's arrival at the pearly gates and his triumphal entry into heaven. And his final work, *Don Juan*, was a cross between epic, romance, and satire, in the manner of the gayest and most irreverent of Italian poets, Ariosto. It is full of good things. It specializes in one difficult but amusing art, which could be practiced only by a genuine humorist: comic multiple rhymes. Here is Byron's epitaph on Keats, whose death was partly brought on by bitter reviews of his poetry:

John Keats, who was killed off by one critique
    Just as he really promised something great,
If not intelligible, without Greek
    Contrived to talk about the gods of late.
Much as they might have been supposed to speak.
    Poor fellow! His was an untoward fate;
        'Tis strange the mind, that very fiery particle,
        Should let itself be snuffed out by an article.

From the same poem, here is a magnificent description of London, huge, fogbound as so often, and crowned by St.

Paul's Cathedral. This is worth putting beside Wordsworth's sonnet on London:

> A mighty mass of brick and smoke, and shipping,
>   Dirty and dusky, but as wide as eye
> Could reach, with here and there a sail just skipping
>   In sight, then lost amidst the forestry
> Of masts; a wilderness of steeples peeping
>   On tiptoe through their sea-coal canopy;
>     A huge, dun Cupola, like a foolscap crown
>     On a fool's head—and there is London Town!

In fact, the whole of *Don Juan* gives us a better impression of Byron's real character than any other of his poems. The tragedies and romances are pervasively somber. The satires are uproariously scornful. This poem contains love affairs, battles, shipwrecks, splendid descriptions of scenery, scornful vignettes of society, the love of travel, and fits of hearty laughter: all these, we know, were parts of Byron's life. Small but important details of his personality come out of it, usually illuminated by flashes of wit. There is recurrent anxiety about money, once pointed by an allusion to Machiavelli:

> Alas! how deeply painful is all payment!
>   Take lives—take wives—take aught except
>     men's purses:
> As Machiavel shows those in purple raiment,
>   Such is the shortest way to general curses.
> They hate a murderer much less than a claimant
>   On that sweet ore which everybody nurses.
>     Kill a man's family, and he may brook it,
>     But keep your hands out of his breeches pocket.

There is some very acute observation of the psychology of women: for instance, this description of the Englishwoman, with a cold manner and a hot heart. Byron looks for a suitable image, and then cries:

What say you to a bottle of champagne?
Frozen into a very vinous ice,
    Which leaves few drops of that immortal rain,
Yet in the very centre, past all price,
    About a liquid glassful will remain;
        And this is stronger than the strongest grape
        Could e'er express in its expanded shape:

'Tis the whole spirit brought to a quintessence;
    And thus the chilliest aspects may concentre
A hidden nectar under a cold presence . . .
        And your cold people are beyond all price,
        When once you've broken their confounded ice.

Besides this, there are several hangovers, and quite a lot of
liver trouble; listen:

I think, with Alexander, that the act
    Of eating, with another act or two,
Makes us feel our mortality in fact
    Redoubled; when a roast, and a ragout,
And fish, and soup, by some side dishes backed,
    Can give us either pain or pleasure, who
        Would pride himself on intellects, whose use
        Depends so much upon the gastric juice?

Now, reading Byron's life and letters, and thinking over
that last stanza, I believe I can suggest one reason for the
extraordinary variations in his outlook and his personality. It
is this. He was not naturally a slender, elegant, athletic, grave
young man at all. Naturally, he was a plump, pleasant, pot-
bellied person, and he spent tremendous, almost unremitting
efforts on keeping down his natural fat. He was about five
feet eight. When he was nineteen years old, he weighed 202
pounds. Because of his lameness and his difficulty in taking
normal exercise, this corpulence would soon have become
quite irremovable. Byron had a strong will. He resolved to get
it off, and keep it off. He did so by painful exercises and the

most Spartan regime of dieting, which may well have wrecked his liver. He took exercise wearing seven waistcoats and a heavy topcoat; then he took hot baths; he ate hardly anything. By the time he was twenty, he had got down to 147 pounds. Only once or twice throughout the rest of his life did he rise above that. But it meant that he was constantly hungry. He would sometimes fast for forty-eight hours. In 1816 he lived on a diet of one slice of thin bread for breakfast, a dinner of vegetables, and green tea and soda water in between. To keep down his hunger, he chewed tobacco and mastic gum; sometimes he took laudanum. He was starving.

The Anglo-Irish critic Cyril Connolly says that inside every fat man there is a thin man, screaming to be let out. The reverse is sometimes true, I think, and it was true for Byron. He was a thin man, and inside him there was a fat man roaring to be set free. Or, to put it in scientific terms, Byron was by nature what Sheldon calls a viscerotonic, plump and jovial. He converted himself, by a terrible effort, into a muscular, balanced somatotonic with strong touches of the nervous, gloomy cerebrotonic. All three Byrons played their parts in his life and his poetry. The thin cerebrotonic conceived the grim otherworldly tragedy of *Manfred*; the tough athlete swam the Dardanelles, and wrote of pirates and duels and the storming of cities; the invisible fat man poured out the jokes and satires at which we still laugh. We can see now why Byron chose to compare himself to Prometheus, for that unhappy giant not only was crucified, but had a vulture tearing eternally at his flesh. Byron had several vultures with their beaks buried deep in his vitals; but the one which he felt most constantly, if not most painfully, was that haggard-eyed, sharp-clawed, tireless monster, a starvation diet.

---

Byron, *Letters and Journals* (ed. R. A. Prothero, Scribner, N. Y., 1898—).

*Rhythm in Poetry*

---

W HEN the poet Goethe first went to Italy, he found
new experiences in love and new impulses in poetry and art.
He also found that the two were closely connected. He wrote
a fine book of poems about his visit, called *Roman Elegies*.
In one of these he says that he found himself making love and
making poetry at the same time. He would have his arms
around his sweetheart, and be playing a little tune with his
fingers on her back. She thought he was caressing her. He
*was* caressing her; yes; but he was also working out the rhythm
of a new poem. It is an amusing little picture; but it is very
revealing to people interested in the work of creation: for it
shows that one of the things Goethe felt to be essential in
poetry was rhythm.

Most of the good poetry in English and other Western

languages is strongly rhythmical. There are some fields in which poetry links up with logic, and religion, and metaphysics, and rhetoric; but in this particular field, it is close to music, and the rhythms of poetry give us the same sort of psychical excitement and satisfaction as the swing and the percussion of an orchestra.

The reasons for this are clear. Our love for rhythm is part of our subconscious and emotional endowment. It springs from one of those mysterious regions in which the mind and the body are interlinked: it is possible to read a poem in silence to oneself, and, by sympathy with its pulsations, to feel one's heart beating more rapidly and strongly.

The importance of rhythm in poetry is understood; but the methods poets use in producing and employing it are not obvious. They are worth discussing, for one of the ways in which good poetry differs from trash is in its rhythmical subtlety.

Let us take a simple case—the best-known meter in English, the heroic line. It is the verse of Shakespeare's dramas, of Milton's epics, of most of Tennyson and Browning and Keats and Shelley and Byron, of Dryden and Pope and scores of lesser men. Sometimes it rhymes, sometimes it is blank. But the basis of it is always the same.

It is built on one simple fact. English is a stressed language, in which nearly every word and every group of words have one or more stresses, and in which we use stress for emphasis. Normally we say

        Énglish is a stréssed lánguage

with three stresses; and for emphasis we can also say

        Énglish ís a stréssed lánguage

with four. Every sentence we utter in English contains stresses;

when these stresses form a regular pattern, we are speaking verse.

Now, the heroic line contains five more or less regularly spaced stresses, separated by five weak syllables which are not stressed. The two alternate, like this:

And óne, and twó, and threé, and foúr, and fíve.

And here are two typical lines from Tennyson, both quite regular:

Come dówn, O Maíd, from yónder moúntain heíght:

What pleásure líves in heíght? the shépherd sáng.

The basis is clear and simple:

And óne, and twó, and threé, and foúr, and fíve.

That is the iambic pentameter, sometimes called the heroic line because it is used for heroic subjects.

But if a poet wrote every line in a long poem on that same rhythmical pattern, it would become intolerably monotonous. Therefore he exerts himself to vary it: delicately, for if he varies too widely, he will get away from the feeling of regularity altogether, and his readers will lose the sense of controlled and sustained excitement; but still, within a wide range of rhythmical values, so as to express more sensitively the varying emotions and ideas with which he is dealing.

The first way of doing this is to take the five beats, the five equal stresses, and make one of them a little weaker than the others. This gives our inner ear a short rest, and also imposes a slightly stronger emphasis on the two neighboring beats. You remember the beautiful prologue to the fourth act of Shakespeare's *Henry V*, where the Chorus describes the night

watch before the decisive battle, with the young king walking
among his soldiers to encourage them. It is a splendid piece.
Now, some of the lines in it are perfectly regular:

> The húm of eíther ármy stílly soúnds . . .

> The coúntry cócks do crów, the clócks do tóll . . .

But in one inimitable line Shakespeare says that all shall see

> A little touch of Harry in the night.

Now, this cannot be spoken in five exactly equal beats:

> A líttle toúch of Hárry ín the níght.

Instead, it must be this:

> A líttle toúch of Hárry . . . in the níght.

And so, from the weakness of the word 'in,' the poet gets a
little extra strength for the affectionate and gallant name,
'Harry,' and for its dark romantic contrast, 'night.'

Another variation on the regular pattern of rhythm is
equally simple and equally valuable. It is to add one weak syllable at the end of the line. Instead of

> And óne, and twó, and threé, and foúr, and fíve,

this gives us

> And óne and twó, and threé, and foúr, and fíve, and . . .

Obviously, this is a change and a rest for the ear; but it can
also convey doubt or hesitation or wonder, for it makes the
line end not with a definite final stress but with a weak syllable trailing away into silence. So in the most famous monologue in English poetry, Hamlet's meditation on suicide,
there are many lines which close on the strong stress, like
these:

> To sleep; perchance to dream: ay, there's the rúb
> For in that sleep of death what dreams may cóme
> When we have shuffled off this mortal cóil
> Must give us pause.

But the opening lines of the same speech all have an extra syllable, hanging in hesitation, drifting away into doubt, not this:

> To be or not to be, that is the chóice—

but this:

> To be or not to be, that is the question:
> Whether 'tis nobler in the mind to suffer
> The slings and arrows of outrageous fortune,
> Or to take arms against a sea of troubles,
> And by opposing end them?

English is particularly lucky in this: our poets can end either with a strong stressed syllable or with an extra weak syllable, as they wish. In Italian it is almost mandatory to end with the weak one:

> Nel mezzo del cammin di nostra vita
> Mi ritrovai per una selva oscura . . .

And in French dramatic poetry written in couplets, it has become compulsory to end one couplet with strong syllables, and the next with weak syllables, like this:

> Non: vous avez beau faire et beau me raisonner,
> Rien de ce que je dis ne me peut détourner:
> Trop de perversité règne au siècle où nous sommes,
> Et je veux me tirer du commerce des hommes.

But to make a variation so rigidly regular as that really destroys the beauty of variation: the emotional range of poetic drama in French is therefore a good deal smaller than that of English drama.

Now, take a third type of variation. The basic flow of rhythm in this kind of verse is an alternation of weakly and strongly stressed syllables, evenly balanced. Now, good poets often invert the succession in one pair of syllables, so as to bring two weak syllables together and two strong syllables together. This produces surprise and extra emphasis. Consider the opening of Milton's *Paradise Lost*. Milton is announcing his subject, which is the Fall of Man; and he is praying for the help of the Holy Spirit in writing on this great theme. He begins:

> Of Man's first disobedience, and the fruit
> Of that forbidden tree, whose mortal taste
> Brought death into the world, and all our woe,
> With loss of Eden, till one greater Man
> Restore us, and regain the blissful seat,
> Sing, Heavenly Muse!

You hear the steady pulsation of the alternating weak and strong syllables. But you also hear telling variations on the regular succession of weak and strong. In the very first line there is an eloquent change of emphasis: for we cannot say

> Of Mán's first disobédience, and the frúit . . .

Instead, we must say

> Of Mán's fírst disobédience, and the frúit . . .

Then in the fourth line, with its reference to Jesus as the Redeemer, we are not intended to say

> With loss of Éden, till one greáter Mán
> Restore us,

but rather

> With loss of Éden, till one greáter Mán
> Restore us . . .

Milton is particularly good at this kind of thing, almost as good as his master Vergil. A hundred lines later in the same book, we hear the fallen archangel Lucifer speaking. He recalls how he fought against God

> In dubious battle on the plains of Heaven
> And shook his throne. What though the field be lost?
> All is not lost . . .

Here it would be impossible for us to say:

> And shook his throne. What thóugh the fíeld be lóst?
> All ís not lóst.

Instead, we are compelled to echo the bold self-confidence of Lucifer, as he shouts

> And shóok his thróne. Whát though the fíeld be lóst?
> Áll is not lóst.

You can hear the same use of variation throughout Shakespeare. So Hamlet's soliloquy does not begin:

> To be or not to be, that ís the quéstion.

No, it begins

> To be or not to be, thát is the quéstion.

And in Macbeth's wonderful speech of remorse, made just after he has murdered a sleeping man, he begins with a regular rhythm:

> Methought I heard a voice cry 'Sleep no more!
> Macbeth does murder sleep, the innocent sleep . . .'

And then twice, for emphasis, he inverts the stresses of the opening: first this:

> Sléep, that knits up the ravelled sleave of care,

then a regular line

The deáth of each day's life, sore labour's bath,

and then another emphatic inversion:

Bálm of hurt minds, great nature's second course . . .

so that we can hear his mounting excitement in the urgency
of the rhythm.

We have been talking only of inverting the stresses in one
single foot of the line. But good poets can carry this much
further, and invert several different stresses, so that we—as
it were—feel the regular pulse working backward, and get
additional excitement from the strangeness of the rhythm.
*Hamlet* is full of such effects. When the young prince is in his
mother's room reproaching her, and his father's ghost appears,
you remember she cannot see it. In wild excitement and irregular rhythm, he cries

Why, loók you thére! Loók, how it steáls awáy!

Next, a slow regular line, in which two weak words are stressed
in order to make them powerfully emphatic:

My fáther ín his hábit ás he líved,

And then a passionate double inversion:

Loók where he góes, even nów, oút at the pórtal!

As soon as an actor reads out a scene of Shakespeare, even a
page, we can tell whether he understands its meaning or not.

Finally, let us look at a really remarkable effect from Milton's *Paradise Lost*. It comes from the climax of the primal
war in heaven, describing the fall of the rebel angels. In
battle they have defeated the loyal angels, but now the Son
of God himself goes forth to war against them, and drives
them in rout to the frightful gulf at the edge of heaven. Now

see how the violence of their overthrow is imaged in three inversions:

The monstrous sight

Stro´ok them with horror backward; but far worse
Urg´ed them behind; headlong themselves they threw
Do´wn from the verge of heaven: eternal wrath . . .

And then, to describe their catastrophic fall down through space into hell, a wonderful line which is all distorted and chaotic:

eternal wrath

Burnt after them to the bottomless pit.

Impossible, utterly impossible, to read this as

Burnt a´fter the´m to the´ botto´mless pi´t.

Instead, the line crashes down like the dizzy plunge of the outcast spirits, its rhythms altered and unnatural like the angels changing into devils, and its terrible pace ending only in the last, lowest, terrible syllable:

Bu´rnt a´fter the´m to the botto´mless pi´t.

Only good poets can venture on such tremendously daring effects. That is why we not only read the best poetry but reread it and study it. It never suffers from being better understood. The first time we hear one of Shakespeare's great speeches, we are moved. The fiftieth time we hear or read it, we understand it better, and are far more deeply moved. Even such a simple thing as the rhythm of ten syllables can make us hear the thudding of a tormented heart, or open up the utmost gulfs of space.

*Melody in Poetry*

———————————

A GOOD poem has many different approaches, many different methods of exerting power over its readers. Or should we say—over its readers, speakers, and hearers? We lose a great deal nowadays because we seldom read poems aloud, even to ourselves. Yet most poems in the enormous treasury of the world were meant to be spoken, or chanted in chorus, or sung to music. Much of their meaning is in their sound.

The rhythm of poetry is only one of its powers. Equally important is its melody. Rhythm is the pulse which, through its regularity, enhances our interest and sustains our excitement, and through its variations, emphasizes the meaning. Melody is the music of syllables and words, which delights the hearer and emphasizes the meaning in a different way. Much of the best poetry in our own language and in others has a powerful rhythm. Some of the best poetry also has a subtle and delightful melody. This is another of its ties with music. Poets know that there are many words which sound ugly but have interesting meanings, and many beautiful noises which have little or no meaning, at best a vague significance. One of the problems of the poet's art is therefore to use such sounds in order to help the total effect of a poem.

The most obvious of the poetic devices based on sound is the regular echo which we call rhyme. Here the chime of repeated sounds gives us pleasure just as we enjoy a piano and a violin playing in concord and echoing one another. But beyond the pleasure of the ear, there is in rhyme a pleasure which is connected with the mind. Two lines that rhyme seem to have a secret kinship: their meanings are somehow closely allied, and support one another, either by contrast or by similarity. For instance, here is Pope describing one of his many enemies, Lord Hervey, the effeminate courtier. Notice how the rhymes sometimes stress a contrast, and sometimes play on a resemblance, since the man himself was a conglomeration of opposites.

> Yet let me flap this bug with gilded wings,
> This painted child of dirt, that stinks and stings . . .
> Eternal smiles his emptiness betray,
> As shallow streams run dimpling all the way . . .
> His wit all seesaw, between that and this,
> Now high, now low, now master up, now miss,
> And he himself one vile antithesis.
> Amphibious thing! that acting either part,
> The trifling head, or the corrupted heart,
> Fop at the toilet, flatterer at the board,
> Now trips a lady, and now struts a lord.
> Eve's tempter thus the Rabbins have expressed,
> A cherub's face, a reptile all the rest:

> Beauty that shocks you, parts that none will trust,
> Wit that can creep, and pride that licks the dust.

Without the sound effects that splendid description would have lost much of its energy and its clarity. The brisk clear rhymes, following in relentless pairs, sound like the double knock of a hammer driving nails into a coffin.

Sometimes again rhyme helps the sense, by being odd. If the poet is describing something absurd, he will amuse his hearers by adding ridiculous noises: by putting in unimaginable and almost impossible rhymes. W. S. Gilbert was good at this: you recall the Major-General's song in *The Pirates of Penzance*, which rhymes *gunnery* to *nunnery* and *strategy* to *sat a gee*. In English, the most successful such rhymester was probably Samuel Butler, the seventeenth-century satirist. Here is his description of the power of imagination stimulated by terror—with suitably ridiculous rhymes:

> Fear does things so like a witch,
> 'Tis hard to unriddle which is which;
> Sets up communities of senses
> To chop and change intelligences;
> As Rosicrucian virtuosi's
> Can see with ears and hear with noses;
> And when they neither see nor hear,
> Have more than both supplied by fear,
> That makes them in the dark see visions,
> And hag themselves with apparitions.

Since nearly every rhyme here is unexpected, the subject sounds unnatural and absurd.

But beyond rhyme there is a much older device, both to make the sound echo and to improve the sense. This is alliteration: the echo of a single sound (vowel or consonant) from one word to another within a line or two. This can be used either for emotional emphasis or for the actual imitation of natural sounds. If you study how our best poets use it, you soon find that the various letters have quite different emotional connotations—s shows hatred, т disgust, ʟ and ᴠ soft affection, and so forth. In this, we are getting very close to the mysterious and still unknown origins of language.

Let us look at some examples.

First, a short and striking one from W. H. Auden, using s to show horror. In a description of a nightmare, he says,

> Behind you swiftly the figure comes softly,
> The spot on your skin is a shocking disease.

The same letter s, the letter of disgust and sinister cunning, the letter which begins the words *snake* and *serpent* and *Satan*, occupied one of the great scenes in Milton's *Paradise Lost*. Here the devil has returned from his successful mission: he has partly ruined God's newly created world, corrupted mankind, and established a bridgehead into the otherwise happy and virtuous universe, a bridgehead on this earth. Satan announces this to his comrades in hell; and then

> A while he stood, expecting
> Their universal shout and high applause
> To fill his ear; when, contrary, he hears
> On all sides, from innumerable tongues,
> A dismal universal hiss . . .

He and his accomplices have all been transfigured into snakes; and in a few moments the poetry itself begins to hiss:

> Now were all transformed
> Alike, to serpents all, as accessories
> To his bold riot; dreadful was the din
> Of hissing through the hall, thick-swarming now
> With complicated monsters, head and tail,
> Scorpion, and Asp, and Amphisbaena dire,
> Cerastes horned, Hydrus, and Ellops drear,
> And Dipsas . . .

A little later in the same scene, s spits with the very sound of disgust, as the defeated fiends fill their mouths with the apples of Sodom, and then

> instead of fruit
> Chewed bitter ashes, which the offended taste
> With spattering noise rejected . . .

Now let us take a gentler sound. The letter F is quiet, almost mute, like a tiny breeze blowing: so it can echo the soft activities of nature in springtime. Here is a stanza by Swinburne almost entirely based on F: notice how the repetition of the sound makes you think of the rustle of zephyrs and the almost audible movement of growth:

> The full streams feed on flower of rushes,
>   Ripe grasses trammel a travelling foot,
> The faint fresh flame of the young year flushes
>   From leaf to flower and flower to fruit.

There are some s sounds in this stanza too; but they are nearly all softened down into SH: rushes, flushes; that sound is less bitter and makes us think rather of the gush of rain-filled brooks. The T's in the second line somehow reflect the complicated growth of fresh vegetation, crossing and interlocking:

> Ripe grasses trammel a travelling foot.

And finally, notice the skillful and delightful broadening of the vowels in the last line, to show the passage of spring into summer:

> From leaf to flower and flower to fruit.

There is a good natural effect of this kind in Tennyson. In two lines he contrives to describe a stormy sky overcast by thunderclouds, some of them already breaking. To do this, he uses the rolling letter R, two soft s sounds, broad open

vowels for the thunder, and narrow vowels for the rain: and
here is the result:

> The ragged rims of thunder brooding low,
> With shadow-streaks of rain.

Without doubt, Tennyson was the master of this kind of thing
in English. His teacher was the Latin poet Vergil, who is
simply superb, probably the greatest poet of sound effects in
all Western literature. Listen: here are two lines from an
early poem about country life in which Vergil imitates not
only the sound but actually the rhythm of cooing doves and
pigeons:

> Nec tamen interea raucae, tua cura, palumbes,
> Nec gemere aëria cessabit turtur ab ulmo.

That is only one of a thousand such brilliant effects in Vergil.
Tennyson tried very hard to rival them, often adding his own
sense of quaintness and fun. For instance, here is his half-
humorous imitation of the music of a little brook: first two
lines full of T and R, to show the grinding of gravel:

> I chatter over stony ways
> In little sharps and trebles . . .

And then two lines full of B, P, and D, to sound like bursting
foam:

> I bubble into eddying bays
> I babble on the pebbles.

Here is an even more amusing effect, also by Tennyson, describing an explosion; you can actually hear the separate
stages: first the detonation, then the harsh rip of the torn
air, then the waves of sound expanding and growing duller:

> High above, I heard them blast
> The steep slate-quarry, and the great echo flap
> And buffet round the hills from bluff to bluff.

Different consonants have different powers. w sometimes sounds like the wind; hard c and g clatter like ice. Shelley describes a bitter frost mainly through these three letters:

> For Winter came: the wind was his whip:
> One choppy finger was on his lip:
> He had torn the cataracts from the hills
> And they clanked at his girdle like manacles.

The explosive initials, T, D, and P, can be used to suggest disgust and derision. This is splendidly conveyed in Macbeth's famous speech:

> Tomorrow, and tomorrow, and tomorrow
> Creeps in this petty pace from day to day
> To the last syllable of recorded time;
> And all our yesterdays have lighted fools
> The way to dusty death.

We have been talking about consonants, because the effects they produce are clearer at a first hearing. But the best poets also work with vowel effects, although English is less well endowed with resonant vowels than Latin or Greek or Italian or French. One of the most exquisite lines in French poetry is a little masterpiece by Verlaine, describing a children's choir, with its music echoing round the hollow of a dome:

> Et ô, ces voix d'enfants chantant dans la coupole!

Finally, here are two astonishing descriptions of nature, based on musical vowels and eloquent consonants. The first is an evocation of a thunderstorm in only seven lines. Of course it is by Shakespeare. It is made of four sentences, each with a different tempo and different types of sound. The first evokes brief and violent gusts of *wind*. The second (built on R and S, with plunging and splashing rhythm) makes us hear a deluge of savage *rain*. The third, filled with immensely varied vowels and clashing consonants, shows us multiple flashes of *lightning*; and the fourth booms like *thunder*.

> Blow, winds, and crack your cheeks! rage! blow!
> You cataracts and hurricanoes, spout
> Till you have drenched our steeples, drowned the cocks!
> You sulphurous and thought-executing fires,
> Vaunt-couriers to oak-cleaving thunderbolts,
> Singe my white head! And thou, all-shaking thunder,
> Strike flat the thick rotundity of the world!

Tremendous; magnificent. Now, finally, three lines from Tennyson which image the exact reverse: the peaceful sound of water, the cooing of doves, and bees humming somewhere out of sight:

> Myriads of rivulets hurrying thro' the lawn,
> The moan of doves in immemorial elms,
> And murmur of innumerable bees.

*The Madness of Hamlet*

---

TOGETHER with his best friend, his only friend, Prince Hamlet enters a churchyard. He watches a man digging a grave, and tossing skulls out of it, and singing. After a time he speaks to the fellow, asking how long he has been a gravedigger. Without recognizing him, the man replies:

> Of all days in the year I came to it . . . the very day that young Hamlet was born; he that is mad. (5.1.154f.)

The scene, one of the most wonderful in all drama, goes on with grim jokes and puns and obscenities, until the skull of the jester Yorick is thrown up. Hamlet talks to it, gloomily and meditatively; but not madly. Yet a few minutes later he is in the grave himself, wrestling with Laertes; and then standing beside it raving and shouting like a lunatic; finally, after a horrible display of feverish violence, he rushes wildly off, babbling nonsense (5.1.313–14). It is a fearfully difficult scene to act—because the player must, within a very few minutes, pass from a tone of courtly wit (remember, Hamlet was a poet and a humorist as well as many other things) into elegiac melancholy and ironic bitterness; and then, after a long pause of almost complete silence while he sees his sweetheart's body carried in for burial, into masterful princely energy (5.1.281–5), and thence into shocking yells and rants and imprecations, ending at last in a few vague sentences, half pathetic and half crazy. Difficult as it is to act and harrowing as it is to watch, this scene contains some of the essential problems of the play, and it epitomizes the most absorbing of them. The gravedigger says Hamlet is mad. Hamlet behaves very strangely and furiously toward the end of the scene. Is he mad, or not?

It is a subtle and enthralling problem. It haunts nearly everyone in the drama: they keep worrying about it and talking of it, each in his own way. It fascinates nearly everyone who sees the play or acts in it—although Sir Laurence Olivier apparently never thought about it one way or the other, and introduced his handsome but stupid version of it by calling it 'the story of a man who could not make up his mind.' The connection of madness and sanity concerned Shakespeare himself very deeply: nearly every one of his plays has either an extreme eccentric, or a halfwit, or a melancholic in it somewhere; and, in his other great tragedies, Lady Macbeth goes slowly mad and Macbeth is threatened with madness, Timon of Athens is a hopeless psychotic, while *King Lear* is a play filled with lunacy feigned and real, cruel and innocent. But in these dramas there is no doubt, although there is grief and horror. We know who is mad, and who is sane. In *Hamlet*, we do not know. The plot and the character of the hero are a mystery. They fascinate us both with puzzlement and with a strange mixture of terror and delight. Dozens and dozens of critics have written brilliantly about the mystery, and still it remains a darkness, shot with flashes of light that blind us.

Of course we shall not expect to find a complete solution for it. One of the essences of character drawing like Shakespeare's, and one of the foundations of tragic poetry, is insolubility. Life is not logical, and logic neither controls nor explains life. Much of the finest art is built on an unanswerable *Why?*

Yet surely we can solve some of the mystery if we read the play carefully. It was one of Shakespeare's most deeply felt works, revised much more extensively and written with far more detailed attention than most of his others. (His only son, who died in childhood, was called Hamnet.) Since he thought about it so intensely, he intended us to think about it. Hamlet himself, in those incomparable dying words, asks his friend to live on so as to explain him to the world.

Was he mad, then? I have heard it said that if Hamlet had been mad there would have been no play. That is not quite true. The spectacle of a powerful man—prince or giant or genius—transformed into a dangerous maniac does make an exciting drama; but it is a play of a different type from *Hamlet*, and of a different pattern. The essence of this play is doubt. If we knew all along that the hero was hopelessly mad, there would still be tension, but of a more obvious, an external kind.

Contrariwise, Hamlet is not sane. He is intelligent, but he is not 100 per cent sane, a wily man merely pretending to be a lunatic in order to plot in safety against a usurping king. That was the original story of Hamlet the Dane, the viking's son—a bloody and primitive saga from the Dark Ages. But although Shakespeare's Hamlet often speaks of pretense and carries out several cunning stratagems, his main adventure is not one of disguise, conspiracy, and successful revenge. His most elaborate plots are fruitless or needless, and the killing of his enemies —Polonius, Laertes, Claudius—is accomplished almost by chance: Horatio calls it 'accidental judgments, casual slaughters' (5.2.396).

Let us look inside the play. What do the people there think of Hamlet?

The simpler souls all believe he is mad through and through. (Simple people generally believe that complicated people are mad.) The gravedigger says so; poor Ophelia is convinced of it; so (with a few misgivings) is her father, Polonius, and so is Hamlet's own mother, Gertrude. They think that his insanity comes and goes by spasms of violence; they find it hard to suggest any real origin for it, except love, in which they do not wholly believe; but on the whole they are sure Hamlet is not responsible for his actions.

His friend Horatio always treats him as perfectly sane— although very excitable. He restrains him now and then (1.4.69–78, 1.5.133–5, 5.1.226), but he never doubts him, he is dedicated to him, and he even attempts to die with him.

The king? Ah, the king. One of the best things in the play is that duel between the king and Hamlet, between the Machiavellian usurper and the brilliant amateur. Claudius is a noble villain, every inch an autocrat, and with any other opponent he would have won the contest and survived victorious. He speaks to Hamlet with imperturbable courtesy, with wise firmness when necessary, and even with what looks like affection; while Hamlet consistently ignores or insults him, adding ironic provocations which would make a lesser man lose his control. The king swallows every insult with perfect composure, except the actual re-enactment of his crime. But he watches Hamlet constantly. He sees him first of all as a disturbing element, a silent protest; later as a man incalculable but dangerous, and therefore sane, in the strategic essentials of purpose and planning.

And Hamlet himself? Does he think he is mad? Surely that is one of the major keys to the play. We are so well accustomed to seeing sane and harmonious characters, full of conviction, that we somehow assume a hero must be sure of his own sanity. But when we watch Hamlet alone and listen to his thoughts, seeing him twice contemplating suicide (1.2.129f., 3.1.56f.) and twice reproaching himself bitterly for the un-natural, incomprehensible faults of his mind and will (2.2.-584f., 4.4.32f.), hearing him talk (2.2.638) of his own 'weak-ness and melancholy,' or warn himself against murdering his own mother; or when we see him in a more level mood, speak-ing to others of his 'bad dreams' and his 'madness' we recog-nize a special and a rare tragedy—that of the brilliant man who fears he is losing his mind, and who, nevertheless, subtly enjoys it. He cannot do what he ought to do. He cannot act when he should act. He cannot feel what he ought to feel. His life is divided into two main periods, one of profound gloom, which he knows as melancholy, and the other of wild excite-ment in which he acts almost without thinking; and these two phases of his life are almost wholly separate from each other.

Yet, there are between-times, when he is calm, balanced, energetic, extremely intelligent. No trace of madness then. He is a good (though severe) critic of the drama, a brilliant social satirist, a thoughtful moralist, a wit in the best Renaissance fashion. Alone on ship, he spies on the agents who are com-missioned to have him executed, alters their Top Secret orders so that they will die instead of him, then leads a counter-attack on a pirate cruiser, is captured, talks his way out of captivity and ransom, and thus survives both a merciless con-spiracy and a sinister chance.

Hamlet suffers, then, from intermittent madness. As we

would say nowadays, he is 'mentally disturbed'; and his disturbances occur only in certain limited situations. When we first see him, his life has been dislocated by the sudden smooth maneuver through which his uncle has slipped onto the throne of Denmark and made him, once the rightful heir, now a pretender or a hanger-on, almost a displaced person. He is sullen. He is trying to get away, back to the university where he met his friend Horatio. Later, he learns that his father did not die naturally but was murdered, and that his mother committed adultery and incest with Claudius before the murder—so that all those closest to him are victim, criminal, and accomplice. In particular, his mother, after giving birth to him, has now unmade him by abolishing his father and his own existence as heir to the throne. Henceforward, whenever he is brought face to face with this central set of facts, his father's murder, his uncle's treachery, and his mother's guilty folly, he alternates between profound gloom and raving excitement. At those times he distrusts and insults almost everyone who crosses his path, even his own sweetheart. He is sane only when he is away from the court, when he is not faced with that problem which he finds too brutal even to contemplate, far less to solve. Within that prison, he is like a trapped bird, now fluttering wildly, now (as his mother says, 5.1.308–10) passive and drooping.

This is a pattern which *we* know too: we call it manic-depressive. Shakespeare knew it both from life and from books. In particular, the young Earl of Essex behaved in a manner very close to manic depression, alternating crazy excitement and illogical daring with periods of timeless silence and lethargy. (Essex was executed in 1601, and *Hamlet* was produced about 1602.) But there are literary prototypes, too, for the moody madness of heroes faced with insoluble problems. Shakespeare certainly knew the tragedy of the mad Hercules (by Seneca); he may well have heard of Orestes, who killed his mother for planning the murder of his father, and then went mad; he thought also of the criminal and crazy life of Nero, who killed both his mother and his adoptive father.

Hamlet's tragedy has many roots. His mother's vice and his uncle's crime are two of the central roots, but there are others, deeply buried. The English psychologist Ernest Jones has suggested that Hamlet is also in part Oedipus, that he has long contemplated the crimes of parricide and incest and is maddened and paralyzed by the fact that they were committed *for him*. But the main truth is clear. It is this. Hamlet is not a weakling; he is not a neurotic; he is not a sensitive plant too tender for this world, as Goethe imagined him, or a cynical eccentric, as Laforgue portrayed him. Nor is he a solid, thoughtful type surrounded by uncomprehending eccentrics and sinister plotters, as Olivier apparently imagined him. Like Lear and Macbeth and Othello, he is *both* strong *and* weak— or weakened, or wounded. (That is why the perfect actor would have to be both Maurice Evans and John Gielgud, with touches from other disparate characters also; and perhaps Barrymore was most like him of all.) He is *both* mad *and* sane. His suffering, like that of Macbeth and the others, is that his wound betrays him, it takes him out of himself, so that he sees his once excellent mind partly overthrown. A really weak man would have surrendered at once, or degenerated rapidly, like Bonnie Prince Charlie after his defeat. But one of the highest and deepest forms of tragedy is the losing struggle of the light self against the incalculable self which is dark. There are some magnificent dramas on that theme: but none has ever surpassed the play in which a prince sits beside the grave dug for his own sweetheart, and talks with love and horror to the jester's skull.

## The Poet and the Musician

W E are often told that it is dangerous to compare different arts. I am not sure why. It seems to me to be a legitimate type of criticism. It has its dangers, but it is often very helpful. To understand Debussy's Preludes, it is almost necessary to look at the best French impressionist paintings; if you find it difficult to appreciate baroque architecture, it will become easier if you think of it as parallel to the choral works of Bach.

Sometimes these parallels force themselves upon you, and then it is extremely interesting to follow them out. Recently a new one suggested itself to me, and brought me a new range of understanding. This is the parallel of two men who did not know each other, but who had surprisingly similar characters, lived partly similar lives, and did similar work in different fields—one a poet, the other a musician.

The musician is Johannes Brahms. Last summer I was trying to play his shorter piano pieces: the lovely things he wrote rather late in life—called by unassuming names, like Intermezzi. They are exquisitely beautiful, every note placed with delicate craftsmanship. Only, remembering the portraits of Brahms, I found it hard to understand how this small, fat, cigar-puffing fellow could have produced work of such grace, and almost feminine sensibility. Yet they are characteristic of him: for he wrote well over three hundred songs, and many of those too are ethereally light; and then think of his clarinet quintet, so melodious but so unassuming and tender. The face of Brahms, with his heavy beard and his thoughtful eyes, came up in my mind; and then suddenly it changed to another face, just as thoughtful, less serene and more somber, and also heavily bearded. The new face was that of the poet Alfred Tennyson; and at once I began to recall some of his lyrics:

> Where Claribel low-lieth
> The breezes pause and die . . .

> There is sweet music here that softer falls
> Than petals from blown roses on the grass . . .

> Heavily hangs the hollyhock,
> Heavily hangs the tiger-lily . . .

and many others, so light that when he was young, the critics sneered at him for being niminy-piminy, and when he was older the poems looked quite unsuited to his booming voice and his strong masculine personality.

My mind turned from that to another resemblance between the two men, as creators. The symphonies of Brahms are very powerfully energetic: think of the opening of the first, with the repeated beat beat beat of the big drum, or the tremendous set of variations which closes the fourth; one of the dominant emotions is the sense of struggle, flowing from another side of the man's nature. Now, Tennyson too has his heroic side. It comes out best in his poems on the legends of King Arthur, the *Idylls of the King*, where he writes of powerful men with brutal appetites, warring with other men or with themselves, and makes his verse clang like armor or whistle like arrows.

Now, this might be merely a coincidence between two people working in different spheres; or it might show a real kinship. The next thing to do was to read the biographies of Brahms and Tennyson, and see how deep the similarity went.

The lives of the two men started differently, but their careers followed surprisingly similar lines. Brahms was a slum boy, brought up in one of the poorest quarters of Hamburg and forced at an early age to work hard for a living—playing the piano in cheap dance halls. Tennyson's family was comfortably off, and indeed one of *his* troubles was that he never had to work, and found it a tremendous effort to escape from dreams and idleness. But both Tennyson and Brahms began composing very early indeed, and their first publications were greeted with almost too much enthusiasm. Schumann welcomed Brahms by describing him as the new genius of music; Tennyson's friend Hallam plugged his 1830 volume (*Poems, Chiefly Lyrical*) with a long article 'On the Genius of Alfred Tennyson.' And the result was the same. Wiser critics arose to say it was much too early to tell; sourer reviewers looked for any faults that they could find, to correct the overemphasis; and both Brahms and Tennyson were deeply wounded. To the end of their lives, neither of them could endure hostile criticism; and unfortunately they both got a great deal of it. There is an entire volume full of parodies of Tennyson—some of them very funny indeed, but Tennyson could not see the humor. (One pun simply infuriated him. You know his beautiful line about the early morning, when we hear

The earliest pipe of half-awakened birds.

Once when he went out for a smoke in the garden before

breakfast, a man met him, and said, 'Ah, I see, the earliest pipe of half-awakened bards.' It didn't go down at all well.) Similarily, Brahms got involved in the argument about the merits of Richard Wagner. Wagner's admirers attacked Brahms as stuffy and conventional, Wagner called him a 'Jewish czardas player,' Brahms's supporters returned these attacks; and therefore the real merits of Brahms were obscured to quite a large section of the public, for many years.

Still, by the end of their lives, both Brahms and Tennyson had attained fame. Tennyson was a peer, and Poet Laureate; Brahms was decorated by monarchs, and was the favorite composer of that kindly city Vienna. (Even the post of conductor of the Hamburg Philharmonic, which he had long coveted, was finally offered to him.) Others were known as brilliant experimentalists; these two, each in his own way, were the classics of the later nineteenth century.

Apart from their careers, the two men were like each other in character. They were basically soft-hearted. Early pictures show them as handsome, clean-shaven youngsters with delicate features and a clear candid look, almost too noble for this rough world. Then later, they both grew gruff, and sometimes positively rude. Brahms was so forbidding that extravagant stories were told of his harsh temper: they say that once he paused when he was leaving a party and said, 'If there is anyone here whom I have omitted to insult, I apologize to him,' and certainly he was apt to have diabolical rows with his closest friends. Tennyson, too, always found it a tremendous effort to be even civil to strangers. Yet both of them were sincerely kind and gracious to young shy girls. The beard which both Tennyson and Brahms grew in middle life was both a claim to greater maturity and a mask for the soft-heartedness shown by the lips and mouth.

Brahms never married; Tennyson did. But both men had a

strong and deep attachment in youth, which was broken. Brahms was in love with Clara Schumann, the widow of the composer—although she was fourteen years older, she understood him, admired his work, and liked him at least well enough to be a little jealous. His decision to break away from her meant a good deal of suffering for them both; and though he was in love after that, he died a lonely man. Tennyson's life was altered by the sudden death of his dearest friend Hallam: a charming young man and a good writer, he had been engaged to marry Tennyson's sister, and his brutally unexpected death broke up two families. Seventeen years later Tennyson was still suffering from that shock, but, like a good artist, he channeled his feelings into his work, where they produced that noble elegy, *In Memoriam.*

Even in their working methods the two men were remarkably similar. They both wrote very easily; and they both threw a great amount of their work away. Tennyson would polish and polish a poem long after most others would have published it and moved on; and many of his best-known pieces grew slowly out of sketches conceived many years earlier. (For instance, *Maud* was essentially an expansion of a single lyric, 'O that 'twere possible,' a youthful poem which took root and spread into an entire lyric drama.) Brahms tinkered with his work incessantly: one famous piece began as a string quintet, then became a sonata for two pianos, and finished up as the piano quintet, Opus 34. He said himself that he burned twenty string quartets before he allowed one to be published, and long after he was famous he was still destroying music which he thought not quite good enough.

Finally, there are close resemblances in the actual work of the two men. Differences, yes; Brahms had little taste for drama and could never attempt an opera, while Tennyson did write some verse-plays. But striking similarities. We have already compared Brahms's symphonies to Tennyson's heroic poems, and the songs and lyrical piano works to Tennyson's songs. Then in middle life each men wrote a long elegiac work centering on the death of someone very near his heart: Tennyson's *In Memoriam* surely corresponds to Brahms' *German Requiem*, whose purpose is (as Geiringer says) 'to reconcile the living with the idea of suffering and death.' At the other extreme you will no doubt think of Brahms' fiery Hungarian dances and graceful Viennese waltzes: in the work of Tennyson there are similar pieces, in broad dialect with touches of rough comedy and unbuttoned jollity, in particular 'The Northern Farmer.' Between those extremes, in the work of each man, lies a single masterpiece, strange but characteristic. Tennyson's *Maud* is what he calls a monodrama, a set of lyrics spoken by one man, telling the story of a tragic love. In 1869 Brahms lost the beautiful young Julie Schumann: the result was his famous *Alto Rhapsody*, an extended lyric, in fact a monodrama on the agonies of loneliness in a heart thirsty for love.

The nineteenth century was a nationalistic era, so both Brahms and Tennyson wrote pieces we should now call jingoistic: they are seldom played or read today, but they are part of the total picture. For Brahms the best known was his *Triumph Song* written after the German conquest of France. For Tennyson, it was 'The Charge of the Light Brigade,' and other galloping and shouting lyrics.

Further, their most intellectual pieces seem to have a natural affinity. Tennyson's calm thoughtful monologues, such as 'Tithonus,' 'Ulysses,' and 'Oenone,' each contain enough material for an entire novel, compressed into a few pages of melodious verse. Whenever I read them nowadays, I hear the rich harmonies and the exquisite organization of the Brahms chamber works. And finally, Tennyson's life was closed with the solemn lyric, 'Crossing the Bar'; and Brahms's last considerable work was the wonderful collection of *Four Serious Songs*.

They were inspired by the thought of Clara Schumann's death; he himself (although perhaps he did not know it) had only a few more months to live; and he would never willingly hear them performed because they moved him too profoundly.

Those who love Tennyson and also love Brahms will surely see other resemblances between the work of these fine artists. Those who love one without knowing the other will learn more from tracing the likenesses between the two. Brahms, as far as I know, said nothing explicit about poetry, though he paid superb tribute to it in his songs; but Tennyson wrote two lines on the sister art which are unequaled in their expressiveness: he praised

> Music, that gentlier on the spirit lies
> Than tired eyelids upon tired eyes.

---

H. l'A. Fausset, *Tennyson, a Modern Portrait* (Appleton, 1923).

K. Geiringer, *Brahms, His Life and Work* (second edition, Oxford, 1947).

H. Nicolson, *Tennyson* (Houghton Mifflin, 1925).

Jelle Postma, *Tennyson as Seen by His Parodists* (Amsterdam, 1926).

*A Drinking Song*

———————————

A GOOD idea, in poetry, or prose fiction, or art or philosophy, lasts for centuries. It can be used by many different creators, and will inspire each of them differently. It is one of the greatest pleasures of literature, to recognize a cadence from one good writer in the work of another—not a theft, but an echo, or a tribute.

There is one beautiful little echo which has traveled over sixteen centuries, first sounding in Greek and then coming down through French to English. It is a drinking song, which turns at last into a love song.

Nobody knows who wrote it originally, and nobody can do much more than guess when. It is in a cheerful little dancing meter:

Ἡ γῆ μέλαινα πίνει,
πίνει δὲ δένδρε' αὖ γῆν,
πίνει θάλασσα δ' αὔρας,
ὁ δ' ἥλιος θάλασσαν,
τὸν δ' ἥλιον σελήνη.
τί μοι μάχεσθ', ἑταῖροι,
καὐτῷ θέλοντι πίνειν;

(*Anacreontea* 21)

Now here it is translated into English:

The black earth drinks and drinks again,
The trees in turn drink in the earth,
The sea drinks up the breezy air,
The sun in heaven drinks the sea,
The moon drinks up the glowing sun.
Tell me, friends, why do you think
That I myself ought not to drink?

It is a simple little poem, based on a good idea. For a long time, people used to believe it was written by the famous Greek poet Anacreon, who loved parties, and pretty girls, and drinking, and wrote fine poems about them all. It is in the meter which was one of his favorites. But the experts now believe it was not by him but by one of his many imitators. This particular poem can scarcely be placed more accurately than by saying it must have been written fairly late in Greek history; for it is based on a rather advanced philosophical idea—the idea that the whole universe is a unity, which is kept going by a constant process of interaction . . . the sun causing evaporation from the sea, the moon getting reflected light from the sun, and so forth. When the poet says

The sea drinks up the breezy air

he is thinking of the rain clouds that feed the sea; we should think of rivers, but there are very few big rivers in Greece, and they do not flow steadily and voluminously like ours. A

German scholar proposed that the poem was actually written by a fairly distinguished Jewish author called Aristobulus, who lived in the second century before Christ and was one of the first men to apply Greek philosophical ideas to the Old Testament; there are thoughts rather like this, although less frivolous, in his authentic writings; but then some other German scholar blew the idea up, and put the poem among the works of the versatile and copious author Anon.

During the Dark Ages after the fall of the western Roman empire, Greek was forgotten in western Europe. For centuries Anacreon was only a name. Generations passed. In the late Middle Ages Greek began to come slowly back to the West, and scholars and poets began to enjoy for themselves the Greek poetry which they had for so long known only indirectly, through imitations and allusions in the Roman writers. Connoisseurs, like the Medici, began to send agents to the Near East to buy up manuscripts of Greek books; and, one by one, the great writers of Greek literature emerged from the long darkness. It was an age of delighted discovery. Men greeted the appearance of a new classic with the same rapture as that with which they admired a famous piece of sculpture disinterred after a thousand years of burial in the earth, with the same excitement as that felt a few years ago, in our own lifetime, by the Greek fishermen who found something in their nets, and drew up a magnificent statue of Zeus, made for and revered by their distant ancestors.

The poems of Anacreon were first printed in Paris by Henri Estienne in 1554. This little drinking song was among them, for it was believed to be by Anacreon himself. The young French poets were delighted with the new discovery; for after all what could be more sympathetic to the French than poems about good wine and poems about *Amour*? A graceful French translation of them was published very soon, by Remi Belleau;

and even before that the leading poet of all France, Pierre de Ronsard, inserted an imitation of this very poem in his monumental collection of Odes. He added one line, to make two neat four-line stanzas:

> La terre les eaux va boiuant,
>   L'arbre la boit par sa racine,
>   La mer salée boit le vent,
>   Et le Soleil boit la marine,
>
> Le Soleil est beu par la Lune:
>   Tout boit, soit en haut ou en bas:
>   Suiuant ceste reigle commune
>   Pourquoy donc ne boirons-nous pas?
>           (*Quatrième Livre des Odes,* xxxi)

Here is a translation of Ronsard's echo of Anacreon:

> Earth drinks the waters as they run,
>   The earth is drunk up by the trees,
>   The briny ocean drinks the breeze,
> The sea is drunk, too, by the sun;
>
> The moon drinks down the sunbeams' light;
>   The whole world drinks, above, below;
>   It is a general rule, and so
> Why should we not drink tonight?

This is pretty straightforward: just a little fancier in vocabulary than the original Greek; arranged in rhyming stanzas, not in blank verse; but it has one addition. Ronsard is rather careful to explain that, as he puts it,

> The whole world drinks, above, below;
>   It is a general rule . . .

Yet that is just a little less subtle. The Greek poet, whoever he was, gave five lines to describing the interlinked phenomena, and then let his listeners draw their own conclusion;

a great deal of the best Greek literature is built on implication; but Ronsard was a little more obvious, and just a little more prosy.

Another hundred years passed, and the idea was imported into England. This time it was taken up by a brilliant poet, who had been a child prodigy, publishing a remarkable book of poems while he was still at school. He was Abraham Cowley, born in 1618. He is not much read now; we think of his age as the age of Milton and Dryden; but he was immensely ambitious. One of his ambitions was to rival the great lyric poets of Greece and Rome, and so in 1656 he published his own adaptation of some of the poems attributed to Anacreon. Here is what he made of the drinking song:

> The thirsty Earth soaks up the Rain,
> And drinks, and gapes for drink again.
> The Plants suck in the earth, and are
> With constant drinking fresh and faire.
> The Sea itself, which one would think
> Should have but little need of Drink,
> Drinks ten thousand Rivers up,
> So fill'd that they oreflow the Cup.
> The busy Sun (and one would guess
> By 's drunken firy face no less)
> Drinks up the Sea, and when he has don
> The Moon and Stars drink up the Sun.
> They drink and dance by their own light,
> They drink and revel all the night.
> Nothing in Nature's sober found,
> But an eternal health goes round.
> Fill up the bowl, then, fill it high,
> Fill all the glasses there, for why
> Should every Creature drink but I,
> Why, Man of Morals, tell me why?

It is delightful, isn't it? But see what remarkable changes

Cowley has brought in. The original in Greek was seven lines long—just long enough for a toast, as it were. Cowley's version is twenty lines long. The original had Greek economy. This has baroque amplitude. You imagine the Greek singer with a head of short curly hair and a little wreath of flowers on it; but Cowley appears with a long periwig covering both his shoulders, and a huge lace collar.

Then Cowley has made the whole thing much funnier than the original. As Dr. Johnson said (in that well-known clumpy style of his), 'His power seems to have been greatest in the familiar and the festive,' and this proves it. It is quite a good joke to say that the sun must be something of a drunkard because of his jolly red face; and it is rather fine humorous imaginative poetry to make the moon and the stars dance by their own light. The Greek would never have said, 'Nothing in Nature's sober found,' for that would have seemed impossible, perhaps blasphemous, to him. Nature is what is; and the word cosmos means 'order.' But, having said, 'Nothing in Nature's sober found,' Cowley redeems it by a handsome and original metaphor, 'An eternal health goes round.'

There is one small mistranslation, or deliberate change. The Greek spoke of the sea drinking the air, that is, the clouds and mists; Cowley makes it, with true baroque richness, 'ten thousand rivers.'

And there is a great deal of detail, which reminds us of the description of Creation in the poem which came out eleven years later, Milton's *Paradise Lost*. The Greek said only, 'The trees in turn drink in the earth.' Cowley puts in a more vivid word, and adds a little joke:

> The Plants *suck* in the earth, and are
> With constant drinking fresh and faire.

And finally, perhaps we can trace the difference between paganism and Christianity, or at least Puritanism, in the different endings of the two poems. The Greek had friends who were telling him to take it easy; but Cowley in the seventeenth century had a censor, to whom he cried, 'Why, Man of Morals, tell me why?'

About a hundred and fifty years passed. The Greek poem was read by a young English poet of twenty-seven, living in Italy—an eccentric and passionate young man who, although he is often called a romantic, was a devoted student of the classics. This was Shelley, who, if he had not been murdered before he was thirty years old, would have given our literature something to be put on the same bookshelf as the plays of Shakespeare. He knew Greek very well, and he knew this poem as an Anacreontic, a poem about drink. Only he did not care for drinking: he was always intoxicated, simply with pure water and his own wild, whirling imagination. He was like the poet whom Coleridge described in 'Kubla Khan': 'he on honey-dew had fed, and drunk the milk of Paradise.' On the other hand, he was very susceptible to beautiful girls; he had had two wives and several fancies. Beauty was a stimulus to Shelley. So he changed the old drinking song into a love song, and called it 'Love's Philosophy.'

> The fountains mingle with the river,
>   And the rivers with the Ocean,
> The winds of Heaven mix for ever
>   With a sweet emotion;
> Nothing in the world is single;
>   All things by a law divine
> In one spirit meet and mingle.
>   Why not I with thine?—
>
> See, the mountains kiss high Heaven
>   And the waves clasp one another;
> No sister-flower would be forgiven
>   If it disdained its brother;

> And the sunlight clasps the earth
>  And the moonbeams kiss the sea:
> What is all this sweet work worth
>  If thou kiss not me?

Now, for the first time, the little poem became something like a masterpiece. Shelley was a far better writer than the Greek follower of Anacreon; than the French Ronsard, despite all his talents; than the baroque decorator Cowley. And he was more passionate: so he took an idea of the second grade of intensity, and made it strong, and individual, and urgent. We should hardly believe it was based on the Greek original, if he himself had not underlined the connection by calling it 'An Anacreontic.'

It is a splendid little poem, 'Love's Philosophy.' Of course we cannot tell exactly who inspired it; but we know that Shelley wrote a copy of it in his own hand and presented it to Miss Sophia Stacey; and there is another poem, written in the same year, called 'To Sophia,' which speaks of soft limbs and beautiful deep eyes: that particular poem was not published by Shelley's wife, as so many of his others were; and so, perhaps . . .

Anyhow, it is a masterpiece. Again the poet has altered the original theme and treatment. The follower of Anacreon simply said, 'All things drink, why shouldn't I?' Shelley changed it into love; and then he analyzed love into two different aspects, putting each in a single stanza. Love is the delight of two spirits in one another, and so Shelley says,

> Nothing in the world is single;
>  All things by a law divine
> In one *spirit* meet and mingle.
>  Why not I with thine?

But love is also the delight of two people in each other's bodies, the strength of the man, the beauty of the woman: so Shelley finishes his poem with the image of an embrace:

> The sunlight *clasps* the earth
> And the moonbeams *kiss* the sea:
> What is all this sweet work worth
> If thou kiss not me?

He has drawn two images out of one, the old original image of the interlocking unity of all nature.

Being Shelley, he has abolished the slight monotony of the original poem, which spoke rather naïvely of drink, drink, drink; instead, he gives us (or gives his sweetheart) mingle, mix, meet, kiss, and clasp. And he has done the same kind of thing seriously which Cowley carried out humorously: he has brought in pantheism. In Cowley's version, Nature is drunk, and an eternal health goes round. In Shelley's version, Nature is ruled by God, and is happy:

> The winds of Heaven mix for ever
> With a sweet emotion

(exquisite phrase, containing both movement and passion)

> Nothing in the world is single;
> All things by a law divine
> In one spirit meet and mingle . . .

It is astonishing to see a little seven-line poem written by an unknown Greek in imitation of a famous Greek, surviving for something like two thousand years, changing first into a Renaissance ode, then into a lavish baroque witticism, and finally into a romantic love poem aimed at converting one girl to admiring the beauties of nature. As the morality becomes more difficult and limited, the poetry positively improves; or is it we think drinking far less important than making love? And *were* the Greeks better balanced?

## *The Old Wizard*

———————————

A WIZARD; a seer; a mystic; an explorer of the unknown. All these descriptions would suit one of our greatest
modern poets.

I saw him once, and spoke with him, when he was nearly
seventy years old. I recall him as tall, and proud, and grim;
he was wearing a baggy gray suit and a woolly tie, and high
boots, up to his knees. They looked adventurous, as though he
were about to set off on a dangerous voyage, and they made it
clear that he did not relish being shut up within four peaceful
walls and a quiet roof. Our host told me that the wizard had
some malady which the boots were meant to alleviate; but
they looked characteristic of him as a ruffian, a buccaneer,
what he himself called 'a wild old wicked man.' He was harsh
to me when we talked, and he was brusque to our host. At the

time I put this down to my own youth and inadequacy; but now I know the wild old wicked man was terribly unhappy, and found it difficult to be kind, even to himself. He was the poet William Butler Yeats: he hated old age, and his old body, and most of the life that surrounded him.

He said so himself, in a pathetic poem written in the last few years of his tormented life.

> Some think it a matter of course that chance
> Should starve good men and bad advance,
> That if their neighbours figured plain,
> As though upon a lighted screen,
> No single story would they find
> Of an unbroken happy mind,
> A finish worthy of the start.
> Young men know nothing of this sort,
> Observant old men know it well;
> And when they know what old books tell,
> And that no better can be had,
> Know why an old man should be mad.

He himself, in those years, was very nearly mad. The madness of youth is painful but endurable. The madness of old age is unbearable: for it is a struggle between the principle of life and the principle of death, the vigorous spirit and the decaying body, public reputation and private passion, duty and personality, decorum and spontaneity, the finite necessity and the hope of infinity. That was the madness which Yeats was grappling with toward the end. Violent echoes of the struggle come out in his final poems: there is a good study of them by Vivienne Koch, called *The Tragic Phase*; but the poems themselves outrun any analysis.

Yeats was born nearly a century ago, in 1865, and died in 1939. His parents were Protestants; and apparently his ancestry was, like that of Swift and Shaw and other Anglo-Irish authors, a painful and difficult mixture of English and Celtic, poverty and riches and learning and ignorance and orthodoxy and eccentricity and duty and rebellion. Yeats himself said his immediate kinsmen bore the Cornish name of Pollexfen and the English name of Middleton. He recollected hearing stories about some of his ancestors who had fought for the British crown—one of his uncles was killed in the Battle of New Orleans—and about others who had been the friends of Irish patriots; his nurses and playmates in childhood were Celtic Irish, but his father and mother felt their cultural home was London, where Yeats was brought up and lived for some of his most active years. He wrote in English; I doubt if he ever managed to learn Irish Gaelic. And he spent much of his energy trying to bridge the gulf between the English and the Irish—most notably, by trying to create an English-speaking Irish theater. The Irish have always been wonderful story-tellers, but they had never had wholly native plays and play-wrights until Yeats and his friends got to work. Yeats and a few others determined to add something new to Irish literature: a collection of plays on heroic and fantastic subjects from Irish myth and history, written in the English language. Such a thing was bound to have only a limited success. To begin with, most of the themes Yeats chose were shaped not for spoken drama but for storytelling. How can anyone stage a play whose climax is a battle between a warrior prince and the waves of the wild sea? Such things are essentially epic, and undramatic: they must happen off stage and merely be de-scribed: this means that the drama must change back into the story from which it was drawn. And Yeats's poetic plays were not clearly understood by the English-speaking world; not only people living in England but audiences in Toronto and Edinburgh and New York were bound to be puzzled and even estranged by those wild stories that stemmed from the remote pre-Christian world of the Celtic Iron Age. On the other hand the Irish nationalists could not wholly admire them either, since they were written in English and recognizably belonged to the English poetic tradition. Yeats says himself that the first poems to move him were a group of Orangemen's rhymes and Macaulay's *Lays of Ancient Rome*; from these he went on to Scott and Shakespeare, then to Byron, Shelley, Tennyson, Browning, and Spenser; much of his mature work echoes the cadences of Swinburne. His dramatic work was bound to create, or rather to express, a conflict that proved to be insoluble.

Yeats was a man of conflicts; and no one is quite clear to this day what he was trying to do, what he hoped to make of his own active life and unusual talents. He did not know himself. Sometimes he thought it was his duty to write only for a small community of spiritual aristocrats, without caring for the opinion of the mob; and yet, when his work was unsympathetically received by the general public, he was bitterly offended. Later, when he was given the Nobel Prize and almost universally acclaimed, he was often astonished and often ill at ease. As he himself wrote,

> Much did I rage when young,
> Being by the world oppressed,
> But now with flattering tongue
> It speeds the parting guest.

Once the Irish Republic had been established, he worked hard to strengthen its culture; and yet he despised the whole business of states and republics and governments: he thought it was all bosh compared with the life of the individual and the experience of the spirit. Among his later poems there is a strange little lyric which expresses some of that dissatisfaction and reveals something of his trouble. It is called *Politics*; and it is headed by a rather pompous and shallow remark from the pen of Thomas Mann:

> In our time the destiny of man presents its meaning in political terms.

Now, Yeats hated abstract statements like that, and broad universal conclusions; he despised political activity as such; and he was a sensual man with a roving eye; so here is what he thought of a political discussion:

How can I, that girl standing there,
My attention fix
On Roman or on Russian
Or on Spanish politics?
Yet here's a travelled man that knows
What he talks about,
And there's a politician
That has read and thought,
And maybe what they say is true
Of war and war's alarms,
But O that I were young again
And held her in my arms!

Poor Yeats. In such a mood he sounds like the aging Tolstoy. Of course the two men differed in many vital ways. Yeats became a nationalist. Tolstoy ended by ignoring nationalism. Tolstoy was deeply concerned about Christianity, and tried to become like the saints, while most of Yeats's religious thinking was centered on the pagan cults of prehistoric Ireland and the esoteric philosophies of Asia. Tolstoy worried about the peasants, and endeavored to imitate their simplicity; Yeats did not care how the ordinary farm laborers lived, and retreated into a tower to avoid them: can you imagine his working all day in the fields and coming in for dinner, like Tolstoy, sweaty and barefooted? Yeats had a miserably unsatisfactory love affair with a proud, beautiful lady, whereas we are told that Tolstoy's temptations were gypsy women and the pretty peasant girls, so much so that when he was quite old his wife would disguise herself in peasant clothes and follow him into the forest, just in case . . . Yeats began in the middle class and became more aristocratic, while Tolstoy began as a noble-

man and tried to end as a muzhik. But they were both vision-
aries, they were both strongly sexed, and they were both tormented by their own bodies and tempers. Toward the end of
their lives they were both 'wild old wicked men': like King
Lear, with the storm raging in their own hearts.

Such storms can be calmed only by religion or by philosophy: so we find that, throughout much of his life, Yeats was
occupied by philosophical meditation. In particular, his letters
to Sturge Moore are full of closely argued discussions of complex questions in philosophy. There is one interesting exchange
on a single problem which sounds crazy, but is really valuable.
Yeats explains that Ruskin once picked up a ghost cat and
threw it out of the window; and he says he himself once saw a
real picture and a ghost picture side by side. The problem is
to define in what sense both pictures can be called real. Of
course this problem can scarcely be solved: it is the problem
of *appearance and reality*. But it is fascinating to watch Yeats
grappling with it—since he, much more than most of us, was
aware that there are different orders, or levels, of existence,
and that he (like ourselves) lived in two worlds at the same
time.

In politics also, Yeats lived in one world but belonged to
another. He never, I think, believed that democracy was a
reasonable and admirable way of life. His letters show him
reading Spengler with sympathy, and the English philosopher
Wyndham Lewis with enthusiasm. Wyndham Lewis is not
much read now, partly because his style is so crude, partly because his tone is so repellent, partly because his thought is
terribly uneven; but he is a convinced and bitter critic of many
principles of democracy. Yeats followed him—not as far as
fascism, but certainly toward admiration of the Superman,
and the belief that our world is sustained and made meaning-
ful chiefly by the work of noble families and exclusive groups.
Most of us live in a crowd and the present moment. Yeats was

solitary, gave himself only to a few friends, existed chiefly in the past and the unseen.

But it was neither his philosophical discussions nor his political thinking which really filled his mind and strengthened his poetry. Yeats felt that the many conflicts which beset him, both within his own self and throughout his world, could never be solved by reason alone. And so, it seems, he regarded himself not chiefly as a poet but as a magician. Much of his best poetry is about magic; and some of his best poetry almost *is* magic. If you read his life history, you soon see that he thought far less about the techniques of literature than about the techniques of magic. I don't mean simply mysticism, which is a special kind of meditation upon the nature of the divine and an effort to enter a new relationship with it: I mean actual magic, practices and utterances which evoke and control supernatural forces. Yeats's wife sympathized with him and assisted him, for she was a medium; and it was largely from revelations obtained through her that he wrote the strangest, most consistent, and deepest of all his works, the mysterious panorama of the spiritual world called *A Vision*.

Now, most of us are not magicians, and are not mystically inclined. We find it difficult to take this kind of thing seriously, or at best to tolerate it only because it helps to produce good poetry. But there is another way to understand it and even to approve it. It is to regard Yeats's magical activities through the eyes of the psychologist Carl Jung. In a remarkable analysis of the handbooks of medieval alchemy, Jung points out that the alchemists (and by implication many of the magicians) of the Middle Ages were in fact engaged in a *spiritual* exploration. Their aim was not solely, perhaps not even chiefly, to obtain wealth or any material success; but rather to reduce the conflicts in the human soul to a final harmony. One of the deepest lessons of Jung is that in order to become great one must accept the necessity of suffering. That is what Yeats would never accept; and it is because he rejected the full understanding of tragedy that he never managed to produce a single great work of poetry. Through poetry, Yeats could only express the conflicts that tormented him. It was through *magic* that, for a time at least, he could transcend them.

---

*The Autobiography of William Butler Yeats* (Macmillan, 1953).

*The Collected Plays of W. B. Yeats* (Macmillan, 1953).

*The Collected Poems of W. B. Yeats* (Macmillan, 1951).

*W. B. Yeats and T. Sturge Moore: Their Correspondence 1901–1937* (ed. U. Bridge, Oxford, 1953).

C. G. Jung, *Psychology & Alchemy* (tr. R. F. C. Hull, Bollingen Series xx, Pantheon, 1953).

Vivienne Koch, *W. B. Yeats, The Tragic Phase* (Johns Hopkins, 1952).

## Professor Paradox

O N the wall of my study there hang two portraits of classical scholars. One shows a kindly figure with a huge domed head and peaceful eyes, gazing off into the distance as though he were listening to music. That is Gilbert Murray. From the frame of the other there looks out an unpleasant but intelligent person, who might well be an English country lawyer. Behind him there are a table heaped with books and a packed bookcase. He wears an old-fashioned suit with a single collar and a broad ascot tie. He is a gray-headed man with black eyebrows. A bushy white moustache, trained downward at the ends, curls around and does something to conceal a firm mouth. There is a permanent frown between his eyebrows, and he gazes steadily, not to say rigidly, at the onlooker with an expression of hostility and rejection. This is A. E. Housman.

Housman was a paradox. I have been thinking about him, off and on, for nearly thirty years, and I still cannot understand all his character and all his work. There are some things about him which no one will ever understand now. And yet I have not been able simply to dismiss him from my mind, and to stop wondering what made him tick. His portrait confronts me every day—as unsympathetic and repellent as Gilbert Murray's is attractive and encouraging; there is much to admire in his career as a scholar, for he was at one time the best Latinist in Britain, one of the three best in the world; and then there is his lovely poetry—three tiny volumes, *A Shropshire Lad, Last Poems*, and the posthumous *More Poems*. A distinguished man, but a difficult one.

That long and busy life, 1859 to 1936, produced three small collections of short lyrics, about 150 in all. They are nearly all about youth and love and youthful sorrow; some about soldiering; some about crime and death and suicide— all treated in a manner which breathes youthfulness, which is filled with images of youth (spring flowers, folk music and country dancing, sport and hill-climbing) and empathy with nature; they are not about men and women, but about lads and girls; and their very rhythms are the rhythms of the ballad and the folk song, unsophisticated and uncomplex. They are charming. But is it not a paradox that the man who wrote them was, to the world, a cold, bitter, touchy, taciturn professor, who seemed to have been born elderly, whose best friends were afraid of him, whose brother was accustomed to receiving woundingly cruel letters from him, and who kept a personal notebook full of savage epigrams (with the names of the victims left blank) to be introduced into reviews or conversation whenever he found a suitable opportunity for giving pain?

His work in the classics also was rather paradoxical. If you heard that a professor of the classical languages had written a collection of original poems which made his name famous throughout the English-speaking world, you would expect that he would devote himself to sympathetic literary appreciation in Greek and Latin; that he would use his understanding of poetic creation to penetrate further into the minds of the great classical poets; and that his books would contain elucidations of their artistic technique, their rich vocabulary, their multiple meanings, all the most human but most difficult part of their work. Not so Housman. His chief achievement as a classical scholar was an edition of the five volumes of Manilius, an obscure Latin poet who wrote a poem about astronomy and astrology. Housman spent thirty years on this work, and his major effort was directed toward two things, both unpoetic—explaining the complexities of Greco-Roman astrological theory, and removing the corruptions introduced into the text by medieval scribes.

His poems present a further paradox, particularly when they are read all through from beginning to end. The paradox is this. They are all apparently straightforward and direct, like this:

> Loveliest of trees, the cherry now
> Is hung with bloom along the bough,
> And stands about the woodland ride
> Wearing white for Eastertide.

In this stanza the meter is ordinary ballad rhythm, the rhymes are simple couplets, the words (although charged with poetry) are not unusual, the entire stanza is a single calm sentence, and the thought is simply a description plus a metaphor. And so it is with nearly every stanza, nearly every poem, in Housman's lyrical works.

They are clear and easy to understand—separately. But it is not easy to see what they are about, all together. We can understand one poem by itself; then a second; and then a third. But when we try to understand them as a whole, we fail. Yet Housman published them in carefully arranged groups. The poems were intended to be understood, but they cannot be. They are both explicit and obscure. They are frank, but limited, utterances. They represent both the betrayal and the concealment of a secret. This ambivalence becomes still clearer when we read some of the poems which Housman's brother discovered and published after his death: for these are much more candid than the earlier poems, as though he had grown tired of keeping his secret.

By the way, I hope no one will think that we *ought not* to discuss what lies behind these poems. Anyone who publishes a book is saying something to the world. He wishes to be heard. He wants his words and his thought to be discussed and remembered. Housman was a professor of Latin. He knew well how minutely scholars will examine the models, the techniques, the inspiration, and the philosophy of any poet who is worth reading. He knew this well, for on the title page of one of his prose works he put the phrase from Horace, *nescit uox missa reuerti*, 'a word once spoken cannot return.' If he had not wished to betray something of his own life, he need only have kept his poems unpublished, or circulated them privately among a few friends; and, since he was a distinguished classicist, he would still have made a name for himself in other ways. But he published *A Shropshire Lad* at his own expense, after several publishers had refused it. Therefore his poems and their meaning were meant to be discussed.

Both his poetry and his life were public, and yet secretive. They illuminate each other.

A. E. Housman was born in 1859—not in Shropshire but in

the west of England. At Oxford, where he attended St. John's College, he went out for various university prizes, but won none of them. There are two stages in the degree at which he was aiming. In the first stage (the classical languages and literatures) he got first-class honors. In the second part (philosophy and history) he failed absolutely, and left Oxford with far poorer prospects than he had had when he entered the University. This bitter disappointment darkened his entire life.

He spent the next ten years or so atoning for it. To support himself he got a minor job in the civil service, worked at it daily, and spent the late afternoons and evenings in the British Museum, where he did specialized research on problems of classical poetry, particularly textual criticism. Gradually he made a reputation by publishing learned articles which marked him out as one of the most promising scholars of his day. In 1892, at the age of thirty-three, he became professor of Latin at London University. There he studied hard and taught a little, publishing more and better studies in the technical areas of classical scholarship, until in 1905 he was appointed Kennedy Professor of Latin at Cambridge. There he remained until his death in 1936.

He brought out *A Shropshire Lad* in 1896, when he was thirty-seven. His *Last Poems* appeared when he was sixty-three, in 1922, followed by a still smaller group edited by his brother, Laurence Housman.

One further paradox appears in his poetry. The lyrics in these three volumes are usually melancholy, and sometimes painfully sad. Personally Housman appeared to be a glum and disagreeable man, who seldom smiled. But he also wrote very funny poems, parodies, and squibs. His 'Fragment of a Greek Tragedy' is one of the most brilliant and penetrating poetic parodies ever written. And consider this epigram, which he thought of one morning while shaving. He had just been reading of the election of a new Pope—always a long and oppressive ceremony—and he wrote:

> It is a fearful thing to be
>   The Pope.
> That cross will not be laid on me,
>   I hope.
> The Pope himself must often say,
> Facing the labours of the day,
> 'It is a fearful thing to be
>   Me.'

In fact, Housman was two people, a professor and a poet. As a professor, he wrote a lot and lectured regularly. As a poet, he wrote little and was seldom seen. That second side of him was scarcely known to those who survived to talk about him—including his brother Laurence, his publisher Grant Richards, and Fellows of his own College. They could not understand him fully. They gave differing accounts of his character. But they all knew him later in life, after he had had the experiences which (as he himself declared) created his poetry. These acquaintances (or friends?) speak of him only as he was after the age of thirty-five or so.

Now, nearly all his poems are about youth. Therefore they refer to something that happened to him in his youth. The great public tragedy of his youthful life was his failure to use his brains properly and to make his way directly into a distinguished career as a scholar. It might appear that his debacle in Oxford was the disaster which created most of his poetry— the wish for death, the hatred of the world, the incurable loneliness, all these are the accompaniment of failure.

But, no. It was not that kind of failure. As one reads his poems one sees that the failure had something to do not with ambition but with love. Again and again he speaks of lost love, love misunderstood, love ending in bitter separation,

love ending in death or the wish for death. And so one wonders whether he had been in love with some girl who mis-
treated him: especially when one hears that he usually spoke
of women with hatred, and detested meeting them. But then
one rereads his three volumes of poetry. The love in them is
sometimes, but not always, love for a girl. It is more often love
for a friend, who did not understand or who would not
listen, and who went far away—enlisting in the army, or
dying abruptly, or vanishing in the illimitable distance. This
is such a poem:

> Because I liked you better
>     Than suits a man to say,
> It irked you, and I promised
>     To throw the thought away.
>
> To put the world between us
>     We parted, stiff and dry;
> 'Good-bye,' said you, 'forget me.'
>     'I will, no fear,' said I.

But he did not forget; he could not.

Two or three times we find poems—especially among those
published after Housman's death—in which he says that the
laws of God and man can scarcely be kept and are meaningless to the poet. There is one strange lyric about a youth who
is hanged simply 'for the colour of his hair' although he has
tried to conceal it by dyeing it.

And when we look more closely into Housman's biography,
we see that he had one special friend, from whom he later
parted, and of whom he could never speak without emotion.
This was a young scientist called Moses Jackson. With Jackson
he shared rooms when he was at Oxford; apparently it was
from Jackson that he learned how to be idle and to miss his
first-class honors; even after that, in London, he lived with
Jackson and with Jackson's younger brother. Now, the crisis

which Housman's poems describe happened to him when he was twenty-four or twenty-five. In real life, at the age of twenty-seven, Housman moved away to another house, where he settled down to live alone. A year afterward Jackson got a job in India, and departed.

> Such leagues apart the world's ends are,
> We're like to meet no more.

They seldom did. A few years later the younger Jackson died of typhoid.* But Housman never forgot them. His greatest work, the edition of Manilius, was dedicated 'To M. J. Jackson, who despises these studies,' with an exquisite elegiac poem in Latin by Housman; and among his papers after his death, his brother found Jackson's last letter, written to him when he was about sixty, with every faintly penciled word gone over in ink, to make it last a little longer.

Somewhere in those early years lies the secret which Housman wished both to reveal and to conceal. All that was left to him—after Jackson went to the other side of the world and his young brother died—was a cold heart, filled with bitterness increasing year by year; a memory of friendship, inextricably mixed with suffering and a sense of undeserved guilt; warm emotions which were allowed to appear only now and then, always with embarrassment and constraint and remorse; occasional kindness to a young man with a frank face and an open heart; much cruelty about women, coupled with a certain taste for indecency which appeared now and then in his specialist articles (one of them, sent to the chief British classical periodical, was so revolting that the editors rejected it even though it was in Latin; Housman was furious and had it published in a German magazine); a determinedly selfish gourmandise; an acknowledged preference for Epicureanism over Stoicism, and for Cyrenaicism, the cynical philosophy which teaches

* See 'A. J. J.': *Last Poems* 42.

that nothing matters but the pleasure of the moment, above them both; of course no trace of Christian religious feeling; and, behind it all, what he himself called

> The mortal sickness of a mind
> Too unhappy to be kind.

That was what created the hard, bitter, silent face that looks out from his portrait. If he had not written so well, thought so hard, and sung so sweetly, I should take the picture down. And yet, when I look at those harsh eyes, I seem to see courage, and pain, and a soft heart which was hardened by some evil fortune as well as by its own folly. Although Housman denied that he was a Stoic, there is a Stoical courage in one of the poems he conceived in his worst time: the poem of the spoiled spring and the rain ruining the young flowers which ends

> The troubles of our proud and angry dust
> Are from eternity, and shall not fail.
> Bear them we can, and if we can we must.
> Shoulder the sky, my lad, and drink your ale.

Housman once said that poetry was intended to harmonize our sufferings. Without his poetry, both his sufferings and ours would be more difficult to understand, and far less easy to endure, or to forgive.

----

A. E. Housman, *Collected Poems* (Holt, *c.* 1940).
A. E. Housman, 'Praefanda,' *Hermes* 66 (1931), 402f.

A. S. F. Gow, *A. E. Housman: A Sketch together with a List of His Writings and Indexes to His Classical Papers* (Cambridge University Press, 1936).
L. Housman, *My Brother A. E. Housman* (Scribner, 1938).
Grant Richards, *Housman 1897–1936* (Oxford, 1942).
P. Withers, *A Buried Life* (Cape, London, 1940).

# Imagination and Reality

# The Art of Invective

I N the fall of 1953 a New York publisher issued a book about the Negro cult-leader Father Divine. It was written by two women who had spent a good deal of time and energy on research into Father Divine's unusual character and influence. I suppose it would be called strongly critical. Such books sometimes evoke letters of protest from their subjects: sometimes even lawsuits. This book produced a Curse. Father Divine solemnly cursed the book and all those who read and believed it. Apparently his Curse was delivered at one of his own services, to the accompaniment of shouts from his followers; and then it was printed in his newspaper, *The New Day*. It was headlined on the front page and occupied over two pages inside the paper, most of it printed in large capital letters which gave the effect of thunderous roars. It was really very exciting to read. Lots of people have cursed publishers perfunctorily or casually; but it has not been done so thoroughly and emphatically for a long long time as in Father Divine's Curse upon this particular publisher and this particular book.

Recently I read the Curse to a couple of friends. At first they did not take it too seriously; but as it grew more energetic and more violent, they began to change their expression; they looked grave; they shook their heads and murmured in protest. It wasn't that they particularly loved the publishing firm, and they were not devotees of Father Divine. No, they were simply being overwhelmed by the sheer power of his invective. And suddenly I thought of a similar occasion in a famous novel—a book I don't particularly like but cannot help remembering: *Tristram Shandy*. You probably remember the incident. The obstetrician (or 'man-midwife') is trying to get his bag open; the knots are tied too tight; he tries to cut them and slices his own thumb; then he curses the servant who tied the knots. Tristram Shandy's father says the curse is inadequate: something much more powerful is needed; and he gets out a copy of the formula of excommunication, which is read aloud. It is a most formidable and shattering curse. Tristram's uncle, the old retired officer, listens to it with growing awe and horror, and as it goes on, piling detail upon detail with relentless thoroughness, he cries out, 'Our armies swore terribly in Flanders, but nothing to this!'

Invective is a powerful art. A much neglected art. Or rather it is one of the most neglected parts of that poor misunderstood and mishandled art, rhetoric. Very few of us can make a decent speech nowadays, because we simply don't know the principles of oratory; and still fewer can deliver an effective blast of invective, even against people who are hateful, and who deserve the worst we can say of them. Of course there is always a lot of name-calling, but nothing that really sticks: nothing that really pierces, and wounds. Think of Adolf Hitler: there were many extremely fine cartoons and caricatures which showed both his ridiculous side and his evil side, but nobody ever managed to *say* anything about him that was one tenth as wounding as he deserved. The best that even Churchill could do was to call him 'a bloodthirsty guttersnipe.' Weak, weak.

Invective can be considered simply as a skill, quite apart from the merits or demerits of its unfortunate subject. When we read a good love poem, we need not ask whether the woman was really beautiful or not; we need not even know whether she was kind, and deserved the poet's love. In the same way, when we read a powerful piece of invective, we need not sympathize with the speaker or take sides for or against the sufferer: we need simply judge the skill with which a powerful idea is put into words.

Invective seems to have two purposes, not one. The first is obvious: it is to blacken the reputation of an enemy, to humiliate him, to cast him out of the society of all decent people, to mark him with a stain which he will never be able to erase. (If somebody had been able to say something really effective about Hitler, something that not even his friends and followers could forget or deny, history might have been changed, and changed for the better. Words are weapons.) The second purpose of invective is less obvious: it is to dominate an enemy so that he is left speechless and helpless, so that he cannot retaliate, cannot even defend himself, but stands there as baffled as a bull when the matador has played it to a standstill with the swirling infuriating cape.

A few examples will show how it works. A politician once came up to the Irish wit Curran, and said, 'Have you heard my last speech?' Curran replied, 'I hope I have.' Mark Twain ended an article on the South African statesman Cecil Rhodes by saying, 'I admire him, I frankly confess it; and when his time comes I shall buy a piece of the rope for a keepsake.' Mark Twain once managed to insult an entire city, the city of Chicago. He pictured Satan looking at a newcomer to hell, saying, 'The trouble with you Chicago people is that you think you are the *best* people down here, whereas you are only the *most numerous*.' Oscar Wilde—who made such wonderful epigrams on so many different subjects—made surprisingly few that were really meant to wound (except perhaps in his duel with Whistler); but we cannot forget his terrible description of foxhunting as 'the pursuit of the uneatable by the unspeakable,' and his remark about the climate of London: 'It is impossible to tell whether the people cause the fogs, or the fogs cause the people.' And there is an inimitable remark by Disraeli on his elderly opponent Lord Palmerston. Addressing him in Parliament, he said, 'You owe the Whigs great gratitude, and therefore, I think, you will betray them.' That could be met only with complete silence.

This kind of thing can be done in poetry also. Here is Roy Campbell on some terribly refined novelists:

> You praise the firm restraint with which they write:
>     I'm with you there, of course;
> They use the snaffle and the curb all right,
>     But where's the bloody horse?

The Irish poets are extremely good at it, for they have a tradition of cursing that certainly goes back to the Gaelic bards. The playwright J. M. Synge once put the following curse on a lady critic:

> Lord, confound this surly sister,
> Blight her brow with blotch and blister,
> Cramp her larynx, lung, and liver.
> In her guts a galling give her.
>
> Let her live to earn her dinners
> In Mountjoy with seedy sinners:
> Lord, this judgment quickly bring,
> And I'm
>       Your servant,
>         J. M. Synge.

And here is something rougher but more imaginative by James Stephens:

> The lanky hank of a she in the inn over there
> Nearly killed me for asking the loan of a glass of beer;
> May the devil grip the whey-faced slut by the hair,
> And beat bad manners out of her skin for a year.
>
> That parboiled ape, with the toughest jaw you will see
> On virtue's path, and a voice that would rasp the dead,
> Came roaring and raging the minute she looked at me,
> And threw me out of the house on the back of my head!
>
> If I asked her master he'd give me a cask a day;
> But she, with the beer at hand, not a gill would arrange!
> May she marry a ghost and bear him a kitten, and may
> The High King of Glory permit her to get the mange.

The art of invective resembles the art of boxing. Very few fights are won with the straight left. It is too obvious, and it can be too easily countered. The best punches, like the best pieces of invective in this style, are either short-arm jabs, unexpectedly rapid and deadly; or else one-two blows, where you prepare your opponent with the first hit, and then, as his face comes forward, connect with your other fist: one, two. Both are effective; but they can be administered only by a real artist, with a real wish to knock his enemy out.

But those examples were only short crushing blows. Most famous invective goes on for a long time, and utterly obliterates the opponent. It is not like the single or double punch, but rather like the devastating rain of blows that a really fine boxer will release at the climax of a fight—so that his victim can scarcely even hold up his guard, far less fight back: if the bell does not ring, he is finished.

Here are some examples of this powerful sustained attack. First, the famous description of Gladstone by Disraeli:

A sophistical rhetorician, inebriated with the exuberance of his own verbosity, and gifted with an egotistical imagination that can at all times command an interminable and inconsistent series of arguments to malign an opponent and glorify himself.

Next, the satirist Dryden's portrait of his despicable rival, the fat, coarse poet Shadwell, disguised under the Biblical name of Og:

Now stop your noses, readers, all and some,
For here's a tun of midnight work to come,
Og, from a treason-tavern rolling home.
Round as a globe, and liquored every chink,
Goodly and great he sails behind his link.
With all this bulk there's nothing lost in Og,
For every inch that is not fool is rogue,
A monstrous mass of foul corrupted matter,
As all the devils had spewed to make the batter.
When wine has given him courage to blaspheme,
He curses God, but God before cursed him;
And if man could have reason, none has more,
That made his paunch so rich, and him so poor . . .
But though Heaven made him poor (with reverence speaking),
He never was a poet of God's making.
The midwife laid her hand on his thick skull,
With this prophetic blessing: *Be thou dull.*

In 1688, by the bye, Shadwell succeeded Dryden as Poet Laureate.

Here is another single-sentence explosion, aimed at Oliver Cromwell by a republican opponent called Saxby (who vainly tried to have Cromwell assassinated as a dictator): he calls Cromwell His Highness, as though he were another Caesar:

Had not His Highness had a Faculty to be fluent in his
Tears and eloquent in his Execrations; Had he not had

spongy Eyes, and a supple Conscience; and besides, to do with a People of great Faith but little Wit; his Courage and the rest of his Moral Virtues with the help of his Janizaries had never been able so far to advance him out of the reach of Justice, that we should have need for any other Hand to remove him, but that of the Hangman.

And now, the master of English, Shakespeare. There is one single curse, only forty lines long, in his *Timon of Athens*. It covers all misanthropy, the entire hatred of mankind, and ends with a tremendous description of the whole of civilized life as corrupt and ready for destruction by an epidemic:

> Plagues incident to men,
> Your potent and infectious fevers heap
> On Athens, ripe for stroke! Thou cold sciatica,
> Cripple our senators, that their limbs may halt
> As lamely as their manners! Lust and liberty
> Creep in the minds and marrows of our youth,
> That 'gainst the stream of virtue they may strive
> And drown themselves in riot! Itches, blains,
> Sow all the Athenian bosoms, and their crop
> Be general leprosy! Breath infect breath,
> That their society, as their friendship, may
> Be merely poison!

You notice two things about these marvelous pieces of invective. First, they are all coherent, and highly elaborated. Sentence follows sentence, building on its predecessor, higher and higher, until they all crash down on the head of the victim. Complete *control* is essential to good invective. Of course, it is not quite so simple as to say, 'The man who first loses his temper is finished'—for the finest invective is written or spoken by people who *have been* in a foul and outrageous temper. No, it is much more like Wordsworth's prescription for writing poetry: *emotion recollected in tranquillity*. If you want to write invective and have found a subject who thoroughly deserves it, first, get mad; while furious, boil up the ideas and the crushing descriptions and the lava-flow of invective. Then calm down. Cool off. Reduce them to some form which will overwhelm your opponent: either a single phrase, or a double blast of heat, or an overpowering flow of rhetoric which will shrivel him to a cinder.

But also, in most masterpieces of rhetorical abuse, we notice one other quality. Although they are very offensive, most of them are based on the assumption that both the attacker and the victim are intelligent and educated (perhaps that was the reason why Hitler never got his real comeuppance in invective) and they usually assume that both parties and the audience will recognize elaborate words and difficult allusions. For example, Whistler could attack Ruskin by comparing him to the donkey in the Bible which suddenly spoke to the prophet Balaam because it had seen an angel in the road. He said that Ruskin's criticism would

> give Titian the same shock of surprise that was Balaam's, when the first great critic proffered his opinion.

But how many of us would now catch the allusion?

Much art is the product of tension. It looks as though the art of invective was at its best when it combined two opposing factors: savage hatred and delicate control of language; primitive rage and the cool appraisal of strategy; crude and shocking ideas together with rich, cultured, even graceful expression. Some of the finest invective is very nearly unprintable, and yet its sumptuous style makes it tolerable. Here is Swinburne, denouncing poor Ralph Waldo Emerson. Emerson had accused Swinburne of writing immoral poetry: Swinburne didn't know Emerson, and did not even know he was clean-shaven, but his reply is an elaborate assertion that Emerson and the journalists who quoted him are all a set of dirty monkeys.

Put like that, it is cheap. But how powerful it is when couched in these tremendous cadences:

> A foul mouth is so ill-matched with a white beard that I would gladly believe the newspaper scribes alone responsible for the bestial utterances which they declare to have dropped from a teacher whom such disciples as these exhibit to our disgust and compassion as performing on their obscene platform the last tricks of tongue now possible to a gap-toothed and hoary-headed ape, carried at first into notice on the shoulders of Carlyle, and who now in his dotage spits and chatters from a dirtier perch of his own finding and fouling: coryphaeus or choragus of his Bulgarian tribe of autocoprophagous baboons, who make the filth they feed on.

Perhaps such an overpowering blast is too much for us nowadays. Yet I can think of men of our own generation who have deserved it a great deal more than poor Emerson; and they have lived out their lives in comparative tranquillity. Is invective to become another of the many arts we have lost?

Roy Campbell, 'On Some South African Novelists,' *Adamastor* (Faber and Faber, London, 1930), 104.

M. J. Herzberg, *Insults, a Practical Anthology* (Greystone Press, 1941).

H. Kingsmill, *An Anthology of Invective and Abuse* (Eyre and Spottiswoode, London, 1929).

H. Read and B. Dobree, *The London Book of English Prose* (Eyre and Spottiswoode, London, 1931).

N. Slonimsky, *A Lexicon of Musical Invective* (Coleman-Ross, 1953).

James Stephens, *Collected Poems* (Macmillan, London, 1926).

J. M. Synge, *Collected Poems* (Random House, 1935).

L. Untermeyer, *A Treasury of Laughter* (Simon & Schuster, 1946).

S. Vines, *Whips and Scorpions* (Wishart, London, 1932).

# The Witches and Their God

WE still remember the witches—as we remember the nursery rhymes we heard when we were children, and the fairy stories we were told. They seem to belong to the far past, to the childhood of our world. They come out of it once a year, on Hallowe'en: on that evening ghosts also appear—cut out of pumpkins or cardboard, but still looking like skulls glowing with an unnatural inner life; our own children turn into evil spirits with strange clothes and blackened faces, to run about after sunset doing mischief; and the decorations for Hallowe'en parties always include pictures of witches, thin women with peaked hats, in black clothes, talking to a sinister black cat or riding a broomstick through the air. After that night (the night of the Dead, All Souls' Night), the witches vanish for another year. In other countries, they have other festivals. In

Germany the night before May Day is a witches' sabbath, the Walpurgis-Nacht which Dr. Faust attended; and all over western Europe there is something uncanny about St. John's Eve, the 21st of June, the night before Midsummer: you remember the spirit of confusion and witchery which spreads over the darkling town of Nuremberg, in Wagner's *Mastersingers*, on that same enchanted night.

But apart from one or two dates in the year and one or two vestigial memories like hex marks, we have almost forgotten the witches. We think of them as a delusion typical of the Middle Ages, when people thought the sun went round the earth.

Yet, if we think over it, we shall begin to see that we are a little vague about the whole question. What *was* witchcraft? Mumbo-jumbo, hocus-pocus . . . no doubt. A delusion . . . yes, but who was deluded? The witches? Or the people who believed they were witches and persecuted them? Or both the witches and the public? Or neither, but only a few witch-hunting officials? Whenever you read the straight historical evidence, you find that it is more and more difficult to find a single, rational explanation of the witches, their power, their punishment, and their beliefs.

Take the first, the simplest explanation. There never was any such thing as witchcraft. Nobody can do magic. Nobody can fly through the air on a broomstick or conjure up the devil or cast spells on a neighbor. Anyone who *believed* that he or she could do such things was simply a crackpot. Even today we see many people who might well have been thought to be witches a few hundred years ago. Nobody can walk through the streets of a big city without seeing three or four really sinister-looking men and women, their faces distorted by savage inner pressures and conflicts, their pace irregular as though they were engaged in some hideous secret rite, their gestures fierce and unnatural, their mouths moving with half-audible words, usually malevolent, always repellent and pitiful. They seem to wish evil to the surrounding world. Perhaps the witches of whom we hear in the past were only mentally disturbed people who thought they were talking with unseen spirits (produced by their own troubled minds), and who did practice complicated ceremonies meant by them to hurt other people, although in fact the ceremonies did have and could have no objective effect whatever. If that is the true explanation of witchcraft, then the witches were only mental sufferers, and their mistreatment was one aspect of the long-standing failure of society to look after the insane.

That could well be a partial explanation; but it cannot be the complete explanation. Many of the people charged with witchcraft were outwardly sane and sensible: in Europe, they included eminent statesmen and scholars, and professional soldiers with long records of competent behavior; in America, one of the accused was a dignified Bostonian, son of the famous John Alden and his wife Priscilla.

Therefore there must be another solution. The first was that the accused witches were mad and the public was sane. The second possible explanation is that the accused were sane and the public was mad. Hysterical exhibitions took place at some of the trials, and it is often said nowadays that the men and women who stood in court to watch a witch trial were suffering from 'collective hysteria,' and that the judges were simply swept along on the irresistible tide of their emotion—in fact, that the whole thing was like a riot, or a lynching where the entire mob was wildly excited, and drunk, and virtually insane. This is the theme of a recent comedy, Christopher Fry's *The Lady's Not for Burning*, and of a still more recent tragedy, Arthur Miller's *The Crucible*.

Yet it is not easy to accept this solution either. For one thing, the hysteria was usually manifested not by the general public but by the people accused of being witches or said to have been bewitched—usually the latter. At most of the witch trials the public was kept in the background, and was quiet, passive, and gloomy, the reverse of a lynching mob. For instance, at the Salem trials and at the examination of the nuns of Loudun, it was the so-called victims who screamed and twitched and had rigors, not their relatives or the audience. And furthermore, in many trials nobody got excited at all: the whole thing was as sober and gloomy as a modern prosecution for income-tax evasion.

But what is most disturbing is that large numbers of accused witches confessed; that some of them at least seem to have confessed without torture (for instance, Major Weir, in Scotland in 1670); and that they confessed the same sort of thing in widely different and far distant countries such as southern France and Sweden and eastern England; and that some of them refused to withdraw their confessions but defied their accusers and died laughing, proclaiming that they were right and renouncing the Christian religion. One of the slogans which they are said to have repeated is 'Out, out of my house all Crosses and cares!' Yes, but what did they really confess?

I could never see my way into this problem until I looked up the article on witchcraft in the *Encyclopædia Britannica,* and later went on to read several books on primitive religion. One of these is essential for everyone interested in the subject: *The God of the Witches,* by an eminent anthropologist of London University, Margaret Murray. Then there are valuable sidelights on primitive religion today in a book on the voodoo religion of Haiti, called *Divine Horsemen,* by Maya Deren: not a pleasant book, but a powerful and thoughtful book. It is filled with stories of performances which you and I would call magical, actually seen by the authoress, and of powerful spirits, which a Puritan would call devils and which Miss Deren calls non-Christian elemental gods, possessing men and women at voodoo ceremonies, and once at least possessing Miss Deren herself.

There is one reasonable and systematic explanation of witchcraft which does not assume that the witches or the public were mad. It is that witchcraft was simply a religion—a non-Christian religion, an anti-Christian religion, which was practiced in Europe and elsewhere before the introduction of Christianity, which survived as it were 'underground,' and which is fundamentally opposed to Christianity, as to Judaism and Islam also. It was a religion of this world: of pleasure and carnal satisfaction; it was a cult of the animal element in man. When people confessed that they were witches, they sometimes meant that they were not Christians but adherents of this religion. When they said that the devil had appeared to them and made a pact with them, they meant that they had seen and talked to the god of this religion, renounced Christianity, and been baptized and accepted by this other god into his own cult. The devil, the god of the witches, was not a disembodied spirit from heaven or hell. He was simply a man, a human being, wearing a disguise, very often an animal disguise such as a horned mask so that he would appear as half-man and half-goat, or half-man and half-bull: sometimes also in special shoes that looked like cloven hooves. He was a man, but —as in most primitive religions—in this costume he was a god incarnate.

The worship of the beast-man-god was an old, old religion, going back to the Stone Age hunters and the cattle breeders for whom the horned animals were vitally important and sacred. There are many traces of it as a genuine cult, throughout history: paintings on the walls of the caves where our ancestors lived; legends of sacred monsters like the Minotaur and the satyrs and the god Pan; festival dances, still surviving, where the dancers wore animal masks; even the name of the devil in Scotland, Auld Hornie. From this perspective, witchcraft begins to be understandable. It was apparently an organized underground religion far older and far more carnally enjoyable than Christianity. And it was persecuted because its creed and its practices were diametrically opposed to Christianity: its rites were not sober meetings to sing hymns and hear sermons and attend Mass, but festivals often held at night, with eating and drinking and wild dancing and sexual adventure—both because sexual adventure was forbidden in the Christian church and because the religion of the witches was a fertility cult.

But how about magic? Did the witches really fly, on broomsticks? Dr. Murray explains: according to their own evidence, they often rubbed themselves with a flying ointment which would produce effects like those of marihuana today. (Sometimes, in New York, you can see a marihuana-smoker in the condition described as 'floating': doped up, he thinks he is flying, and he walks across the street with huge strides, as though he were leaping or soaring over the cars which just miss him.) And did witches cause illness and death to others by magic, simply by casting spells? Dr. Murray does not go fully into this, but it seems clear that the old religion carried with it a considerable knowledge of powerful drugs—remedies and poisons: if you wanted to cure a sick child or to produce abortion or to kill your neighbor's cows, the old woman in the tumble-down cottage would give you a brew of herbs which (although administered with a lot of hocus-pocus) would have the same effect as an efficient prescription today. The use either of drugs or of carefully directed hatred is implied in the remarkable Danish film about witchcraft, *Day of Wrath*. Some of the trials of the so-called witches might have contained more convincing evidence if a medical examiner had dissected the cattle they were supposed to have bewitched; and probably some of the scoundrels who peddle marihuana to school children today would, in the sixteenth century, have thought of themselves as witches—opening the way into a new and forbidden universe of sensual satisfaction with its own secret language, persecuted by the God-fearing world outside.

This looks reasonable. Many witches were unjustly accused; but others appear to have been adherents of a primitive, anti-Christian religion with quite different conceptions of morality and family life and the laws of thought. We can understand this more easily because on this continent, no further away than New Mexico and Guatemala and Haiti, such primitive religions survive actively and energetically, today. (All the authorities on the witch trials of Salem agree in saying that the thing started with a woman called Tituba, part Indian and part Negro, who taught the little girls something—something like voodoo?)

But the thing which is left out of most rational explanations is the hysteria suffered by the girls in the Salem trials and by the nuns at Loudun. Why did they squirm and scream and stiffen and become apparently deaf and blind and start acting wickedly and unnaturally? And why did this happen most often in the presence, or at the mention, of the persons accused of enchanting them? Here Miss Maya Deren's book on Haiti will help us. She says again and again that one of the essences of the primitive religion of voodoo is possession; the climactic experience of that cult is that its devotees are 'mounted' by spirits who ride them and dominate them. 'The self must leave if the loa is to enter; one cannot be man and god at once.' She describes how, after much drumming and ritual and prayer and singing and dreaming and dancing, a man will suddenly fall down as though dead, and then jerk violently, catapulted from side to side, mastered by the spirit Ogoun—to be left afterward, exhausted and limp. She says she herself was possessed by the charming female spirit Erzulie, and she prints photographs of several worshipers possessed by spirits and transfigured.

You and I probably do not believe in the Haitian god Ogoun, or in Baron Saturday and The Siren and Marinette-Congo and such elementals; but we can easily believe that there are powerful subliminal psychical forces which Christianity and other reasonable spiritual religions help us to keep under control, and which a really irrational cult, calling on the historic forces of sex, and blood, and the night, and the animal ancestors, would set free within us. In Haiti the man who knows how to preside over the rites which evoke such forces is entitled a *houngan* (chief of the spirits); in the sixteenth and seventeenth centuries he was called a chief wizard, or a priest of the devil; and twenty or fifty centuries before that, he was himself the priest, and the chief dancer, and the chief male, and the king, and the bull, the stag, the goat, the life of the herd and of the primitive human beings who followed it and depended on it; and so, himself personifying all that life, he was divine.

------

Maya Deren, *Divine Horsemen: The Living Gods of Haiti* (Thames and Hudson, 1953).

Christopher Fry, *The Lady's Not for Burning* (Oxford, 1949).

Pennethorne Hughes, *Witchcraft* (Longmans, Green, 1952).

Aldous Huxley, *The Devils of Loudun* (Harper, 1952).

Arthur Miller, *The Crucible* (Viking, 1953).

Margaret Murray, *The Witch-Cult in Western Europe* (Oxford, 1921).

Margaret Murray, *The God of the Witches* (Oxford, 1953).

W. S. Nevins, *Witchcraft in Salem Village in 1692* (North Shore Publishing Company, 1892).

M. L. Starkey, *The Devil in Massachusetts* (Knopf, 1949).

C. W. Upham, *Salem Witchcraft* (Wiggin & Lunt, 1867).

*I to the Hills Will Lift Mine Eyes*

---

THERE are many marvelous experiences which life—at some time—presents to most of us: getting married, having a child, seeing the sun rise, watching a thunderstorm. There are other grand experiences which are fully human and yet unusual, difficult, often dangerous: outside the normal lives of most people. Poets collect some of these, but they do not know them all. Artists miss many, though they immortalize a few. Philosophers seldom fit such events into their systems of thought. They are left for others to enjoy, and occasionally to write about.

One of these experiences is climbing a mountain.

Many are the wonders of the world (says the poet Sophocles), but none more wonderful than man—who conceives and carries out such plans. And of them all, the ascent of almost impossible mountains is surely the most poetic.

A mountain itself, with its forested approaches, its bare, hard shoulders, and its snow-clothed, heaven-lit crest, is an epic thing. A long climb—in its extent, its variety, its magnificence, and its daring—is a complete epic, lacking only the wealth of speech. Not all of us can be epic heroes; but all of us should be able to appreciate the power and intensity of the kind of life which can be called epic. That is the real value of books about mountains. They describe a rare and splendid experience, which can illuminate the ordinary routine of our lives in the same way as a powerful drama or a heroic symphony.

Mountain climbing is a new idea. It began in Switzerland about a century ago, and it has spread to almost every civilized country where there are mountains. There is a valuable description of its history in James Ramsey Ullman's *High Conquest*, which goes back to the first ascent of Mont Blanc and forward to 1941, but still can scarcely cover all the achievements of that short epoch. In the last few years, too, there have been many good books about climbing, and one or two fine movies: it would be a splendid theme for a young poet to attempt. But, the ordinary man, with his feet firmly on the flat ground, is likely to ask, but—why bother?

Why climb, through infinite discomfort, painful exhaustion, and deliberately incurred danger, to reach . . . nothing?— the rocky or snowy tip of a mountain on which there is nothing?

The central answer to this question is easy. It is the Faustian answer. We live in the age named after Dr. Faust: we feel that like him we *must* struggle outward toward infinity. Suppose you had a car which would do 100 miles an hour. Suppose you were on a clear highway, with no special reason for reaching the next stopping place at any fixed time. Now would you stick to 45? or 60? or would you push the car up as far and fast as she would go, even if it meant arriving at nowhere, for no special purpose? You would? That is the impulse which makes men climb mountains. It is also the impulse which makes young men try to run a hundred yards in nine seconds. It is the impulse which stirs in those who are eager to visit the the moon and the planets, against all odds, and for no particular purpose. It is the instinct which compels men to try to to be better, to be stronger, to achieve more. So, when you see a group of horses running freely, and when one of them moves out ahead of the others with a clear and joyful rhythm, your heart goes with it, shouting 'Go on, win, win!' Or when two or three dancers have each done a little solo, and the prima ballerina enters the stage, taking up the rhythm and melody of the orchestra, to leap and pirouette and soar more gracefully than all the others, more delicately than seems possible, your admiration is assisted by the fact that she is excelling, exceeding the ordinary. Or when you watch a solo skater; or when you hear a violinist like Heifetz tackling something fiendishly and inhumanly difficult (like the Bartók concerto), you exult in his daring as much as in his skill. Only human beings, and only heroic human beings, attempt the impossible.

There is the first motive: the extreme impulse, the effort to achieve heroism, without witnesses and usually without applause.

Next to that is a simple and central motive which we all understand. Mountaineers love nature. They tolerate cities and towns as places where they have to earn their living; but —even more intensely than the rest of us—they love the rest of the world, the soft grass and the hard rock and the running water, the rain and the sun, the clouds and the sky. It is not only fun for us, it is a necessity for us to live with nature—*in* nature—for a certain time every year. The mountain-men know that.

Think of the different ways in which they experience the world. They feel its weather in varieties and strengths which we seldom see. They labor under the rain, they shiver in the freezing wind, they cower like hibernating animals when it snows. Then, in the fair weather, they drink in the air and light with every pore of their being. You and I sometimes feel glum when the barometer falls, or complain about the inconvenience of a storm, but unless we live far out in the real country, it is all somehow external to us.

Apart from weather, the climber sees nature as few others do. In front of me are two pictures taken by one of the finest and subtlest mountaineers of modern times, the late Frank Smythe: they appear in his book, *The Valley of Flowers*. One of them shows a spring morning; the other, a sunset. One shows a flat valley, high in the Himalayas: it is covered with delightful flowers—a long plain of cool green and rose balsam, running toward a majestic valley (tree-clad) between three huge walls of rock and snow. The other—a picture only six inches by four—takes us high into the sunset sky, gold and blue and red and silver, a world made for celestial spirits, seen across the red and gold snows of a mountain, nearly four miles up in the sky.

But God made the creatures to be our companions; and the climber is constantly reminded that they share the world with us. My wife and I were once making our way painfully around the steep side of a mountain in Austria. There was hardly any trail, only precarious slopes, and the angle on which we were walking was gradually tending toward the vertical. Far beneath us we could hear the torrent roaring—out of sight, but loud and deep; we could see the tops of the highest trees, for we were above timberline: it felt lonely. And suddenly in the midst of this solitude and distance, we heard a sharp noise, a rattle of stones. With a single leap, a large animal, the size of a mule-deer, landed on the mountainside ahead of us. It looked at us with an expression of disgust mingled with horror; then, with two more swift leaps, it disappeared, downward, into the chasm. It was perfectly safe. It was a chamois; and the mountainside which seemed like a precipice to us was, for its nimble feet, a thoroughfare. Again, I recall how my son and I once got to the top of a ridge in the Big Horn mountains in Wyoming. We sat down to enjoy the fifty-mile view. Uncounted miles of air stretched before us. Gradually, high above, there came into view a speck which became a spot and grew into a double curve and approached and was visible as an eagle: without moving his wings, he sailed along an invisible current two miles high: he had seen us; he slanted slowly down to look at us a little more closely; and then, with an infinitely calm nobility, he swam onward another mile or so along the crest, another mile or two, until he was out of our sight (but we not out of his). We knew, we knew then whose world we had entered, and ventured to share. So Frank Smythe constantly appreciated the presence and companionship of even small birds and animals. He records one evening after a long hot upward march, when, after he had made camp, dusk fell; and then, in the profound peace of twilight,

> a small bird in a tree above my tent broke suddenly into song, a queer little song, plaintive, very sad and very sweet. It was an unhurried little song, a tweet-tweet or two, then silence, then a sudden trill, then a slow sad note. For a full half-hour this bird sang its evening hymn, until darkness had thickened in the valley and the sky filled with stars.

The life of nature, and its voices . . . Even apart from that vital sympathy, the sheer aesthetic beauty of mountains is as great as anything on this earth. It can be equaled only by the sea at its grandest, by the cloud-filled air and a wide landscape, seen from an airplane; it can be surpassed only by the starry sky. Clean snow is nearly always beautiful. In the high altitudes, where there is more blue in the light, it is almost heavenly. Forests and rivers and rocks vary from one region to another. And mountains, individual mountains, differ in their forms and characters as radically as the ancient gods. One is Jupiter. One is Venus. There are many types. Each has its own special kind of beauty. Some are male. Some are female. The most famous of all masculine mountains is the bold, arrogant, energetic Matterhorn. The greatest of all feminine mountains is Mont Blanc, a rich, amply proportioned, splendidly dressed queen. Among American mountains, too, there are some beautiful princesses: the loveliest that I know is Taos Mountain in New Mexico—a tranquil and exquisite presence, wearing a blue lake like a jewel above her heart. Then again, some mountains are restful: sleeping gods. Others vibrate with the passion of the fire which threw them up still molten, or tremble with the impact of the ice that carved them into sheer ridges and slender spikes. Some are malevolent, murderous: they have a long, long list of deaths, to which they are constantly adding: such is Everest. Others, though difficult, are kindly disposed; and even if they humiliate the climber, they will indulgently spare his life. Some even welcome the visitor, guide him up their valleys, give him resting places on their high ridges, and seem to stoop (as he reaches their crest) so that he can look around and laugh, like a child raised on his father's shoulders.

Yet, some climbers seem to feel very little of the aesthetic beauty of the high mountains. They talk much more about the problems involved in climbing. And there is another kind of fascination. To get up a tough mountain is an intellectual effort. All through *Annapurna* you can see how the French expedition which climbed that savage peak planned, and mapped, and reconnoitered, and discussed, with an intensity that reminds us sometimes of chess players studying a difficult game, and sometimes, more often, of a group of officers workout a tactical problem in warfare. Once you have tried that kind of climbing, you find it practically impossible to see a mountain close by, without starting to plan routes to the summit. And the most complex kind of climbing involves two quite different sets of problems: one, the problem of getting up complicated and treacherous formations of rock; the other, that of crossing and climbing ice and snow—only water, frozen in various states, but water capable of killing you in a hundred different ways, by dropping a single spike of ice on your head, for instance, or by burying you beneath a mile-long avalanche. Mr. Ullman's book contains many fine descriptions of such problems. Describing the adventures of the 1929 Bavarian expedition to Kanchenjunga, he says that on the eastern spur of the north ridge

> there were no rocks anywhere, no bare straightaway slopes of ice or snow, such as mountaineers ordinarily encounter on every peak. Instead, the spur climbed skyward for thousands of feet in one unending spine of broken, twisted ice. There were towers piled upon towers, cliff upon cliff, huge vertical columns which tapered like church-spires, and shining curtains, festooned with icicles, hanging down the precipices from cornices above. There were great bulges and chasms, wrenched by the wind and cold into fantastic . . . shapes. Gigantic blocks and bergs of solid ice, breaking off high above, swept down the chutes and spirals of the spur in two-mile drops of thundering destruction.

Most of us have never been on ice like that. Most of us have never climbed difficult rocks. But once we have known anything of the dangers and problems and beauties of the heights, we begin to feel the fascination of the sport. Even when we are too old to attempt any really interesting climbs, there are still many fine books which can broaden and deepen our experience. I have lately found a reminiscent pleasure in reading one of the classics of climbing, Whymper's *Scrambles amongst the Alps*, and I am looking forward to passing a week with Frank Smythe, one of the best climbers and finest stylists and biggest snobs who ever swung from a rope.

That is the electric current in mountain climbing, in the books and in the expeditions and in the pervasive ideal: courage and individuality. We are often told that this is an age of anxiety and hysteria and inadequacy and meager pessimism. This is bosh. Far more brave things have been done in the last thirty years than in many a quiet century. This is an age of courage and enterprise, an epoch of conflict, ambition, adventure, victory. Its real personification is not the underground plotter or the spineless neurotic, but the eager mountain climber and the bold inventor. Perhaps you remember a fat boy who stayed shut up in a cellar for five years, because his mother wanted to keep him safely away from the army? Suppose he wrote a book in the manner of Kafka, exquisitely enwombed in a Proustian style—would that truly express our feelings and our age? Or should we rather feel that our hopes and energies were embodied in the quiet, balanced, cool, comradely, slightly mad, but infinitely courageous men who have just done something which could bring them no personal profit, which hazarded their lives, and which asserted something of the highest in humanity, by climbing the peak of the world and conquering Everest?

C. E. Engel, *They Came to the Hills* (Allen and Unwin, London, 1953).

M. Herzog, *Annapurna* (Dutton, 1953).

F. S. Smythe, *The Valley of Flowers* (Norton, 1949).

J. R. Ullman, *High Conquest* (Lippincott, 1941).

J. R. Ullman, *The White Tower* (Lippincott, 1945).

E. Whymper, *Scrambles amongst the Alps in the Years 1860–1869* (fifth edition, Murray, London, 1900).

*Kitsch*

———————————

I F you have ever passed an hour wandering through an antique shop (not looking for anything exactly, but simply looking), you must have noticed how your taste gradually grows numb, and then—if you stay—becomes perverted. You begin to see unsuspected charm in those hideous pictures of plump girls fondling pigeons, you develop a psychopathic desire for spinning wheels and cobblers' benches, you are apt to pay out good money for a bronze statuette of Otto von Bismarck, with a metal hand inside a metal frock coat and metal pouches under his metallic eyes. As soon as you take the things home, you realize that they are revolting. And yet they have a sort of horrible authority; you don't like them; you know how awful they are; but it is a tremendous effort to drop them in the garbage, where they belong.

To walk along a whole street of antique shops—that is an

experience which shakes the very soul. Here is a window full of bulbous Chinese deities; here is another littered with Zulu assegais, Indian canoe paddles, and horse pistols which won't fire; the next shopfront is stuffed with gaudy Italian majolica vases, and the next, even worse, with Austrian pottery—tiny ladies and gentlemen sitting on lace cushions and wearing lace ruffles, with every frill, every wrinkle and reticulation translated into porcelain: pink; stiff; but fortunately not unbreakable. The nineteenth century produced an appalling amount of junky art like this, and sometimes I imagine that clandestine underground factories are continuing to pour it out like illicit drugs.

There is a name for such stuff in the trade, a word apparently of Russian origin, kitsch*: it means vulgar showoff, and it is applied to anything that took a lot of trouble to make and is quite hideous.

It is paradoxical stuff, kitsch. It is obviously bad: so bad that you can scarcely understand how any human being would spend days and weeks making it, and how anybody else would buy it and take it home and keep it and dust it and leave it to her heirs. It is terribly ingenious, and terribly ugly, and utterly useless; and yet it has one of the qualities of good art—which is that, once seen, it is not easily forgotten. Of course it is found in all the arts: think of Milan Cathedral, or the statues in Westminster Abbey, or Liszt's settings of Schubert songs. There is a lot of it in the United States—for instance, the architecture of Miami, Florida, and Forest Lawn Cemetery in Los Angeles. Many of Hollywood's most ambitious historical films are superb kitsch. Most Tin Pan Alley love songs are perfect 100 per cent kitsch.

There is kitsch in the world of books also. I collect it. It is horrible, but I enjoy it.

* The Russian verb *keetcheetsya* means 'to be haughty and puffed up.'

The gem of my collection is the work of the Irish novelist Mrs. Amanda McKittrick Ros, whose masterpiece, *Delina Delaney*, was published about 1900. It is a stirringly romantic tale, telling how Delina, a fisherman's daughter from Erin Cottage, was beloved by Lord Gifford, the heir of Columba Castle, and—after many trials and even imprisonment—married him. The story is dramatic, not to say impossible; but it is almost lost to view under the luxuriant style. Here, for example, is a sentence in which Mrs. Ros explains that her heroine used to earn extra cash by doing needlework.

> She tried hard to assist in keeping herself a stranger to her poor old father's slight income by the use of the finest production of steel, whose blunt edge eyed the reely covering with marked greed, and offered its sharp dart to faultless fabrics of flaxen fineness.

Revolting, but distinctive: what Mr. Polly called 'rockockyo' in manner. For the baroque vein, here is Lord Gifford saying goodby to his sweetheart:

> My darling virgin! my queen! my Delina! I am just in time to hear the toll of a parting bell strike its heavy weight of appalling softness against the weakest fibers of a heart of love, arousing and tickling its dormant action, thrusting the dart of evident separation deeper into its tubes of tenderness, and fanning the flame, already unextinguishable, into volumes of blaze.

Mrs. Ros had a remarkable command of rhetoric, and could coin an unforgettable phrase. She described her hero's black eyes as 'glittering jet revolvers.' When he became ill, she said he fell 'into a state of lofty fever'—doubtless because commoners have high fever, but lords have lofty fever. And her reflections on the moral degeneracy of society have rarely been equaled, in power and penetration:

Days of humanity, whither hast thou fled? When bows
of compulsion, smiles for the deceitful, handshakes for
the dogmatic, and welcome for the tool of power live
under your objectionable, unambitious beat, not daring
to be checked by the tongue of candour because the
selfish world refuses to dispense with her rotten policies.
The legacy of your forefathers, which involved equity,
charity, reason, and godliness, is beyond the reach of
their frivolous, mushroom offspring—deceit, injustice,
malice, and unkindness—and is not likely to be codi-
ciled with traits of harmony so long as these degrading
vices of mock ambition fester the human heart.

Perhaps one reason I enjoy this stuff is because it so closely
resembles a typical undergraduate translation of one of Cicero's
finest perorations: sound and fury, signifying nothing. I regret
only that I have never seen Mrs. Ros's poetry. One volume
was called *Poems of Puncture* and another *Bayonets of Bastard
Sheen*: alas, jewels now almost unprocurable. But at least I
know the opening of her lyric written on first visiting St.
Paul's Cathedral:

> Holy Moses, take a look,
> Brain and brawn in every nook!

Such genius is indestructible. Soon, soon now, some earnest
researcher will be writing a Ph.D. thesis on Mrs. Amanda
McKittrick Ros, and thus (as she herself might put it) con-
ferring upon her dewy brow the laurels of concrete immortality.

Next to Mrs. Ros in my collection of kitsch is the work of
the Scottish poet William McGonagall. This genius was born
in 1830, but did not find his vocation until 1877. Poor and
inadequate poets pullulate in every tongue, but (as the *Times
Literary Supplement* observes) McGonagall 'is the only truly
memorable bad poet in our language.' In his command of

platitude and his disregard of melody, he was the true heir of William Wordsworth as a descriptive poet.

In one way his talents, or at least his aspirations, exceeded those of Wordsworth. He was at his best in describing events he had never witnessed, such as train disasters, shipwrecks, and sanguinary battles, and in picturing magnificent scenery he had never beheld except with the eye of the imagination. Here is his unforgettable Arctic landscape:

Greenland's icy mountains are fascinating and grand,
And wondrously created by the Almighty's command;
And the works of the Almighty there's few can understand:
Who knows but it might be a part of Fairyland?

Because there are churches of ice, and houses glittering like glass,
And for scenic grandeur there's nothing can it surpass,
Besides there's monuments and spires, also ruins,
Which serve for a safe retreat from the wild bruins.

The icy mountains they're higher than a brig's topmast,
And the stranger in amazement stands aghast
As he beholds the water flowing off the melted ice
Adown the mountain sides, that he cries out, Oh! how nice!

McGonagall also had a strong dramatic sense. He loved to tell of agonizing adventures, more drastic perhaps but not less moving than that related in Wordsworth's 'Vaudracour and Julia.' The happy ending of one of his 'Gothic' ballads is surely unforgettable:

So thus ends the story of Hanchen, a heroine brave,
That tried hard her master's gold to save,
And for her bravery she got married to the miller's eldest son,
And Hanchen on her marriage night cried Heaven's will be done.

These scanty selections do not do justice to McGonagall's ingenuity as a rhymester. His sound effects show unusual talent. Most poets would be baffled by the problem of producing rhymes for the proper names *General Graham* and *Osman*

*Digna*, but McGonagall gets them into a single stanza, with dazzling effect:

> Ye sons of Great Britain, I think no shame
> To write in praise of brave General Graham!
> Whose name will be handed down to posterity without any
>     stigma,
> Because, at the battle of El-Tab, he defeated Osman Digna.

One of McGonagall's most intense personal experiences was his visit to New York. Financially, it was not a success. In one of his vivid autobiographical sketches, he says, 'I tried occasionally to get an engagement from theatrical proprietors and music-hall proprietors, but alas! 'twas all in vain, for they all told me they didn't encourage rivalry.' However, he was deeply impressed by the architecture of Manhattan. In eloquent verses he expressed what many others have felt, although without adequate words to voice their emotion:

> Oh! Mighty City of New York, you are wonderful to behold,
> Your buildings are magnificent, the truth be it told;
> They were the only thing that seemed to arrest my eye,
> Because many of them are thirteen stories high.
>
> And the tops of the houses are all flat,
> And in the warm weather the people gather to chat;
> Besides on the house-tops they dry their clothes,
> And also many people all night on the house-tops repose.

Yet McGonagall felt himself a stranger in the United States. And here again his close kinship with Wordsworth appears. The Poet Laureate, in a powerful sonnet written at Calais, once reproached the English Channel for delaying his return by one of those too frequent storms in which (reckless tyrant!) it will indulge itself:

> Why cast ye back upon the Gallic shore,
> Ye furious waves! a patriotic Son
> Of England?

In the same vein McGonagall sings with rapture of his return to his 'ain countree':

> And with regard to New York, and the sights I did see,
> One street in Dundee is more worth to me,
> And, believe me, the morning I sailed from New York,
> For bonnie Dundee—my heart it felt as light as a cork.

Indeed, New York is a challenging subject for ambitious poets. Here, from the same shelf, is a delicious poem on the same theme, by Ezra Pound:

> My City, my beloved,
> Thou art a maid with no breasts
> Thou art slender as a silver reed.
> Listen to me, attend me!
> And I will breathe into thee a soul,
> And thou shalt live for ever.

The essence of this kind of trash is incongruity. The kitsch writer is always sincere. He really means to say something important. He feels he has a lofty spiritual message to bring to an unawakened world, or else he has had a powerful experience which he must communicate to the public. But either his message turns out to be a majestic platitude, or else he chooses the wrong form in which to convey it—or, most delightful of all, there is a fundamental discrepancy between the writer and his subject, as when Ezra Pound, born in Idaho, addresses the largest city in the world as a maid with no breasts, and enjoins it to achieve inspiration and immortality by listening to him. This is like climbing Mount Everest in order to carve a head of Mickey Mouse in the east face.

Bad love poetry, bad religious poetry, bad mystical prose, bad novels both autobiographical and historical—one can form a superb collection of kitsch simply by reading with a lively and awakened eye. College songs bristle with it. The works of Father Divine are full of it—all the more delightful because in him it is usually incomprehensible. One of the Indian mystics, Sri Ramakrishna, charmed connoisseurs by describing the Indian scriptures (in a phrase which almost sets itself to kitsch-music) as

> fried in the butter of knowledge and steeped in the honey of love.

Bad funeral poetry is a rich mine of the stuff. Here, for example, is the opening of a jolly little lament, 'The Funeral' by Stephen Spender, apparently written during his pink period:

Death is another milestone on their way.
With laughter on their lips and with winds blowing round them
They record simply
How this one excelled all others in making driving belts.

Observe the change from humanism to communism. Spender simply took Browning's 'Grammarian's Funeral,' threw away the humor and the marching rhythm, and substituted wind and the Stakhanovist speed-up. Such also is a delicious couplet from Archibald MacLeish's elegy on the late Harry Crosby:

> He walks with Ernest in the streets in Saragossa
> They are drunk their mouths are hard they say *qué cosa*.

From an earlier romantic period, here is a splendid specimen. Coleridge attempted to express the profound truth that men and animals are neighbors in a hard world; but he made the fundamental mistake of putting it into a monologue address to a donkey:

> Poor Ass! Thy master should have learnt to show
> Pity—best taught by fellowship of Woe!
> Innocent foal! thou poor despised forlorn!
> I hail thee brother . . .

Once you get the taste for this kind of thing it is possible to find pleasure in hundreds of experiences which you might otherwise have thought either anesthetic or tedious: bad translations, abstract painting, grand opera . . . Dr. Johnson, with his strong sense of humor, had a fancy for kitsch, and used to repeat a poem in celebration of the marriage of the Duke of Leeds, composed by 'an inferiour domestick . . . in such homely rhimes as he could make':

> When the Duke of Leeds shall married be
> To a fine young lady of high quality,
> How happy will that gentlewoman be
> In his Grace of Leed's good company.

> She shall have all that's fine and fair,
> And the best of silk and sattin shall wear;
> And ride in a coach to take the air,
> And have a house in St. James's Square.

Folk poetry is full of such jewels. Here is the epitaph on an old gentleman from Vermont who died in a sawmill accident:

> How shocking to the human mind
> The log did him to powder grind.
> God did command his soul away
> His summings we must all obey.

Kitsch is well known in drama, although (except for motion pictures) it does not usually last long. One palmary instance was a play extolling the virtues of the Boy Scout movement, called *Young England*. It ran for a matter of years during the 1930's, to audiences almost wholly composed of kitsch-fanciers, who eventually came to know the text quite as well as the unfortunate actors. I can still remember the opening of one magnificent episode. Scene: a woodland glade. Enter the hero, a Scoutmaster, riding a bicycle, and followed by the youthful members of his troop. They pile bicycles in silence. Then the Scoutmaster raises his finger, and says (accompanied fortissimo by most of the members of the audience):

> Fresh water must be our first consideration!

In the decorative arts kitsch flourishes, and is particularly widespread in sculpture. One of my favorite pieces of bad art is a statue in Rockefeller Center, New York. It is supposed to represent Atlas, the Titan condemned to carry the sky on his shoulders. That is an ideal of somber, massive tragedy: greatness and suffering combined as in Hercules or Prometheus. But this version displays Atlas as a powerful moron, with a tiny little head, rather like the pan-fried young men who appear in the health magazines. Instead of supporting the heavens, he is lifting a spherical metal balloon: it is transparent, and quite empty; yet he is balancing insecurely on one foot like a furniture mover walking upstairs with a beach ball; and he is scowling like a mad baboon. If he ever gets the thing up, he will drop it; or else heave it onto a Fifth Avenue bus. It is a supremely ridiculous statue, and delights me every time I see it.

Perhaps you think this is a depraved taste. But really it is an extension of experience. At one end, Homer. At the other, Amanda McKittrick Ros. At one end, *Hamlet*. At the other, McGonagall, who is best praised in his own inimitable words:

> The poetry is moral and sublime
> And in my opinion nothing could be more fine.
> True genius there does shine so bright
> Like unto the stars of night.

---

D. B. Wyndham Lewis and C. Lee, *The Stuffed Owl: an Anthology of Bad Verse* (Dent, London, 1930).

W. McGonagall, *Select Poems* (ed. L. Macartney, Burnside, Glasgow, undated).

*Poetic Gems Selected from the Works of William McGonagall, Poet and Tragedian, with Biographical Sketch and Reminiscences by the Author, and Portrait* (Macmillan, 1954).

W. Reynolds, *Young England* (Gollancz, London, c.1930).

Amanda McKittrick Ros, *Delina Delaney* (Chatto and Windus, London, 1935).

*A New Pleasure*

———————

THEY say that an Eastern monarch once offered a huge reward to anyone—anyone in the world—who could invent for him a new pleasure; but that he died disappointed. That must have been long before the machine age. Although machinery has brought us many new anxieties and dangers, although it certainly cannot produce anything like happiness, still, it has created many kinds of comfort for us, and it has even shown us the way to certain new, qualitatively new, types of pleasure. All that most of us lack is the sense of continuous wonder required to appreciate them.

One of these new pleasures was only invented in our lifetime, although three or four eccentrics had experimented with it in earlier centuries. It is still quite fresh. There have been one or two short movies about it; there are devotees of it in southern Europe and in California and elsewhere; one or two magazine articles have explained it; during the Second World War it was, like almost everything else, converted into a means of destruction; but some of us have never heard of it and few of us have ever tried it. Fortunately, a pretty good introduction to it has recently been published, with pictures which show us something of its fascination and its uniqueness. This is the pleasure of living under the sea.

I do not mean surface swimming, delightful as it is; or diving from a height; or going down in a submarine—which (as Dr. Johnson said about sea voyages in general) is just like going to prison. I mean the hitherto impossible pleasure of swimming about quite freely, a hundred or two hundred feet beneath the surface of the sea, at depths where men without the aid of machinery have never been able to penetrate before, except with tremendous effort and danger, for profit and not for pleasure.

I should not venture to discuss this at all if I had not experienced something like it—not the real thing, but something close enough to convince me that the genuine experience must be delightful.

It was in Bermuda. We heard of a man who had diving equipment and would guide people on a trip to the bottom of the sea. We sought him out and prepared to go down with him. He himself was a merman: a tremendous swimmer and goggle-diver, who seemed to live more in the sea than on land; trustworthy. In his motorboat we chugged away from the harbor toward the ocean. We could not go down in the deepest water, but we went out about half a mile, well away from the shore, and anchored at a place where the pilot told us there were coral reefs below us. Coral will not grow lower down than 150 feet, so that we were really lying above a submarine hill. We gazed into the water, but we could see no coral, nothing: it looked blue, deep, and dark.

Then the pilot started a little engine which was to pump air down to us. He coupled two helmets to it by stout rubber air tubes, fitted one into his own shoulders, and the other onto the shoulders of the first adventurer. We wore nothing else, only bathing trunks and sneakers. When my turn came, I put on the helmet with some uneasiness, because it felt so wobbly and clumsy. As I walked to the side of the motorboat and climbed overside, I felt topheavy. Then I started down the ladder into the sea.

Down, down, down. The ladder hung far below the keel of the launch, stretching downward. As soon as I got beneath the surface, I scarcely felt the weight of the helmet any more. Instead, I began to hear a deafening noise, *hammer, hammer, hammer.* This was the air coming in through the airpipe at the top. The water rose up beneath the helmet and lapped round my chin; but as long as the pump kept working above, and forcing the air down the tube, I could still breathe perfectly well, inside a sort of metal and glass bubble.

The pilot was waiting for me. As I got off the ladder, he took my hand, and we started to walk along the bottom of the sea. Beneath our feet was fresh firm sand; all round were rocks, fantastically pitted and hollowed, with bouquets of coral growing on them; light came down in a vertical funnel from the sunshine above. After a few steps, we stopped; and I had my first adventure, a delightful one. Dozens of tiny fish, about the size of a finger, came up to visit us. They had grotesque shapes, like small children dressing up as funny men, and they were exquisitely colored, like tropical birds. The pilot had some shellfish ready for them; he and I shredded the meat, and they came and picked it daintily out of our fingers.

After feeding these pretty creatures, these bird-fish, the pilot and I moved on. We could walk only slowly, and all our balance was different: we could not stride out, scarcely even stand upright, but rolled from side to side without falling, and thrust onward through the clear invisible water, like walking in a dream. We envied the fish which whisked back and forward and upward and downward around us, like butterflies round a heavy tractor. Slowly, with the air hammering in our helmets and the cone of sunshine following us like a searchlight, we walked along the reef. It was like a tiny mountain range, all alive. Here was a forest of delicately filigreed pink and golden branches of coral, all waving gently and seeming to change their tints with every flutter. A forest, yes, but a forest which lived and felt and fed like a crowd of tiny animals or a hive of bees; and indeed corals are called *anthozoa*, which means flower-animals. Here again the rock was all overgrown with another kind of coral which looked like living moss. It was more reposeful than the waving branches; but as we stooped near it we could see it was full of myriads of tiny mouths opening and closing and taking in minute particles of drifting food. When I touched it, the mouths vanished and the whole thing became hard rock. When I moved my hand away, the little mouths reopened. One of the finest phrases in Greek poetry is Aeschylus' description of the sunlit sea, κυμάτων ἀνήριθμον γέλασμα, *kumaton anerithmon gelasma,* 'the innumerable laughter of the waves'; and I remembered it then, when I saw the very rock, beneath the sea, laughing and praying.

Then there were fish, too, quite big ones, waiting and watching in cavities of the rock. When we threw them food, they came out and then went back, like a bird returning to its home in the branches. Then, suddenly, as we came round a bend of the reef, I looked up, and saw a monster directly above us: a huge body, almost blotting out the sunlight, twenty or thirty feet long, far above our heads. I clutched the pilot's arm and pointed up. I could see him smiling behind his glass visor. He pointed to one end of the monster, where a peculiar organ jutted out; then he tapped himself on the chest; then me; then he imitated the act of climbing; and suddenly I saw. The monster was the keel of our own motorboat, with its propeller protruding; we were seeing it from a new angle: in fact, I had become so absorbed in the underwater garden with its fishbirds that I had forgotten all about the surface. I had, for the moment, become an inhabitant of the water. That is the new pleasure; and, like all pleasures, it carries its dangers with it. For a time I had felt the perpetual sense of danger that haunts the people of the sea. And, just at that moment, before we turned back, I saw the sand sloping away downward beyond the plateau, into a depth where there was no coral and no sunlight. Among these dark waters, faint shapes seemed to be moving. The strange thing is that I felt like groping my way downward toward them, into the dreamlike gloom . . . until the pilot gripped my arm and steered me back to the boat and the light and the air.

It was wonderful though. After my son came up he said he felt it, too; and so, when the next divers were down, he and I both went off the side, and then, holding our breath like ordinary divers, tried to penetrate once again to those mysterious depths. We held onto the anchor chain and endeavored to pull ourselves down toward them. But we could not. We could not even see the men who we knew were walking about on the sea floor: only the air tubes disappearing down into that delightful world which we had briefly visited, and which had vanished like a dream.

Even that short visit to the bottom of the sea was a memorable experience; but we were only walking about, not far down. The essential pleasure of underwater life is kept for swimmers. It is this. Instead of diving into the water and holding your breath until you are forced to return to the surface, or climbing down while attached to an air pipe coming from the surface (and wearing either a heavy helmet or a complete diving suit), it is now possible to carry your air with you, in tanks on your back which weigh nothing under water; to wear a small almost weightless helmet; and, with flippers on your feet, to swim freely beneath the sea at any depth down to fifty fathoms. It is like flying. It is like an atavistic dream of soaring through the aerial pinnacles of a forest, surrounded only by birds and waving branches and delicate winged creatures.

Several remarkable books and motion pictures about this experience have come out in the past few years: Captain J. Y. Cousteau's *The Silent World*; Dr. Hans Hass's *Manta*, as well as a film taken by its author; and Philippe Diolé's *4,000 Years under the Sea*, with a valuable bibliography. These and other books on the subject all describe very strange experiences. But all these experiences are extensions of two of the oldest human activities: exploring, and hunting. Some, and the most vulgar, of these 'skin-divers' go down merely so that they can shoot an unsuspecting fish, and bring it up, writhing and bleeding, to the surface. (I have very little admiration for this particular feat ever since, in Bermuda, I saw a proud skin-diver bring in his bloody prize from the offshore reef, and then observed a leash of swift and deadly barracuda following the blood trail among the swimmers on the very edge of that quiet sea.) Some go down so that they can hunt for treasure. They explore the past. As M. Diolé says, it is much easier to visit some of the cities sunk beneath the Mediterranean Sea than to approach the Central American and Southeast Asian cities lost in dangerous jungle; and there are, often quite near the surface, innumerable wrecks that still contain the treasures with which (or for which) they sank to the bottom: coins, and statues, and sculptures, and lost inscriptions, still speaking to those who can understand.

But the strangest thing in these books is the half-playful, half-terrifying association of frail, swimming men with large or frightening fish. Captain Cousteau says he found none of them really dangerous, except perhaps the shark. The horrid octopus (he says) is really a shy creature—as I suppose we should be if we had no bones and no hard skull and looked so repulsive. He and his friends used to tease the octopuses which they met: he prints a fearful picture of a diver carrying an octopus on his back, a group out of a ballet designed by Poe; but he says his men were never in danger. The moray, a giant eel with a fiendishly disagreeable expression, would bite them if they entered its house, but never deliberately attacked them. And the shark itself . . . Consider its profile: obviously a strong, greedy, stupid, single-minded beast. Cousteau says it will attack anything that floats or swims on the surface; but whenever he and his friends were down below, the sharks would look at them with a puzzled interest, which apparently never grew into the idea that they were good to eat. Naturally enough. The sharks have been swimming about since the Cretaceous period (and you know how long that is); it is safe to say that never, since they came into existence, have they seen one of their human kinsmen swimming placidly about far beneath the surface of the sea, wearing a helmet, carrying a camera, and voiding bubbles. Captain Cousteau has four astonishing pictures of a large shark approaching to investigate him. It comes closer and closer, without change of expression, looking often like a large fat bird, and certes often like the late Marshal Goering, until (at the distance of two feet) Cousteau bangs him on the nose with the camera—and the shark retreats, still endeavoring to assimilate this astounding new experience, one of the very few novelties that have confronted his family in the last five hundred million years. In Dr. Hass's book and film, the strangest things are the beasts sometimes called devil-fish, the manta rays, which, from above, look so dark and menacing. Yet, although they have a poisonous sting in their tails, they do not attack divers. Underwater they have a primitive and monstrous beauty—as though God, in a cubist mood, had decided to create a simple and stylized fish, a big, calm, flexible rhomboid which would swim just by waving its own angles. As the mantas pass the camera and disappear, they seem as though they needed only an Oriental prince sitting upon them to complete the old picture from the *Arabian Nights*, the dream of the Flying Carpet.

That is the charm of the world under the sea. It is a world of magic; a world of the remote past; a world of naked hunters and explorers. Stripped, helmeted, carrying his little pouch of air, his claws, and his spear, the diver becomes a man of almost inconceivably distant antiquity: his kinsman of the Age of Stone, hunting the fourteen-foot-high elephant among the jungles of primitive America; or our ancestral hero the Baltic prince Beowulf, who plunged into a haunted lake to fight a monster, and there found a mighty treasure.

---

J. Y. Cousteau, *The Silent World* (Harper, 1953).

P. Diolé, *4,000 Years under the Sea* (tr. G. Hopkins, Messner, 1954).

H. Hass, *Manta: Under the Red Sea with Spear and Camera* (Rand McNally, 1953).

## The Philosopher of the Atom

_____

IN English, the word 'epicure' means (to quote Webster) 'a person who is especially fond of luxury and sensuous pleasure.' In Hebrew, the word 'apikoros' means a renegade, an abominable person. Both words come from the simple Greek word *epikouros*, which means 'helper,' 'supporter,' 'ally.' But they have taken their new meaning from the fact that the word was also the name of a quiet little man who taught philosophy, a particular system of philosophy which has often been misinterpreted. This was Epicurus, who lived, talked, and wrote in Athens for over thirty years (between 306 and 270 B.C.). He founded a school that survived for seven centuries, inspired at least one magnificent poem, and—this is the strangest thing about it—anticipated many of the most remarkable discoveries of modern science.

The first big book in English about Epicurus appeared not long ago. It is called *Epicurus and His Philosophy*. The author, Norman DeWitt, is a veteran Canadian scholar who is a passionate partisan of Epicurus. He says his aim is to 'rescue Epicurus from the injustice of centuries'—an injustice which is partly reflected in the two by-meanings given to the philosopher's name, 'voluptuary' and 'renegade.' Mr. DeWitt's book is full of information which he has gathered from many sources over many years, and is little known even to students of philosophy. For instance, most of us do not know that St. Paul started the long crusade of the Christian Church against the Epicureans by quoting one of their slogans and exposing its hollowness. (This is in the First Letter to the Thessalonians, chapter 5: 'For when they shall say *Peace and Safety*; then sudden destruction cometh upon them, as travail upon a woman with child; and they shall not escape.') Mr. DeWitt's book is a valuable one, because it is the most complete in our language; but it is too violently partisan, so that it will not expose the real weaknesses, moral and physical, in the theories of Epicurus; and it exaggerates the connections between his thought and the Christian religion. However, it is impossible to read it without taking Epicurus seriously. Most of it is given up to discussing his moral rules—which sound simple and sensible, though impossible for most people to practice.

Yet there is something else about Epicurus which would interest most of us much more today. This is the fact that he either thought out, or passed on, many of the fundamentals of atomic physics. He was not the originator of most of these ideas, although he did introduce at least one important one; but he did systematize them. (Before him was a very great scientific thinker called Democritus, but all his books are lost —so we must rely on the adaptations of his work which we find in Epicurus and in the poem of Epicurus' pupil, Lucretius.)

Most of us do not much care about the theories of a Greek philosopher who lived twenty-five centuries ago. Yet those theories become much more urgent and important if it can be shown that they were true; that the world forgot their truth, or denied it, for many, many centuries; and that the most recent researches of our most advanced scientists seem to coincide with them.

The first point which Epicurus makes is the most important of all. He says that the world is built up of tiny particles, called atoms, moving with inconceivable speed, limited in number, and forming an enormous variety of combinations. He and his pupils give various proofs of this. The most astonishing to us is one which was forgotten throughout the Middle Ages and the Renaissance. It was rediscovered by the Scottish botanist Robert Brown, less than 150 years ago. Here is how Lucretius describes it (2.113–23):

> Watch carefully and see how, when the light of the sun
> pierces a darkened room in a house, and spreads its rays:
> then you will see a multitude of tiny bodies
> mingling in many ways and moving within the light,
> as though in perpetual conflict, battling eternally,
> struggling with one another in crowds and never
>
> > stopping,
> incessantly exercised in contact and disjunction.
> From this you can infer how the invisible atoms
> are being tossed and driven throughout the infinite void.

This is the phenomenon which you can see for yourself in any dark room where the windows are closed, the air is undisturbed, and a beam of sunlight is entering through a single window. Within the beam of sunlight, the motes of dust dance, dance, dance, and never stop. They are not moved by heat, or else they would go upward. They are not moved by the currents of air, because they stay in the same relative position and the atmosphere is still. They are moved by something else.

The botanist Brown devised a finer test for the phenomenon. It is this. Put a light powder into a jar of water. Seal the jar. Put the jar on a perfectly motionless table, in a room kept at the same temperature, without vibration coming in from outside. The powder, if it is of the right weight, will be distributed all through the water, and will appear to be quite stationary. But put the microscope on it, and you will see that every particle is moving, not regularly, not swinging in an orbit, but rising and sinking and oscillating and rotating, incessantly exercised in contact and disjunction. And this is perpetual motion. It never stops. Almost all other motions we know come to an end. If you drop a stone or shake a liquid, after you stop intervening the motion finishes. But the Brownian motion of these tiny particles never ends, is never exhausted. Unlike the almost perpetual motion of the planets round the sun, this particular (yes, particular) motion does not slow down. The water is still. The powder is not capable of moving itself. Therefore the particles of powder are moved by some other force, which we cannot see. That is the incessant movement of the invisible atoms: the movement which Epicurus and his master saw must lie beneath the changes that take place in our world, beyond the frontiers of touch, sight, sense perception.

The universe, which appears so solid and stable to us, is made of infinite number of tiny bodies, in infinitely rapid movement. So said Epicurus, and so say modern scientists—except that they have got down to a further stage at which those atomic bodies themselves dissolve into energy in movement, or into an entity for which most of our poor human languages have as yet no name.

A universe infinite in extent, with an infinite space of void, an infinite numbers of atoms. Surely the atoms must be infinite in variety as well as in number? No. Epicurus taught that they were not. He said that the generic distinctions between physical things would tend to disappear if there were an endless variation in the kinds and shapes of atoms. And here again, he anticipated one of our own discoveries. Throughout the known universe, there are only a few types of primary substances combined in a limited variety of inorganic structures: less than one hundred elements make up the entire visible cosmos.

After Epicurus formulated his philosophy, he was bitterly criticized for one peculiar idea which seemed to be so wildly inconsistent as to make his theories into nonsense. The atoms move perpetually in fixed patterns and combinations. This world, the planets, the sun, the stars, are all structures of atoms, like the eddies in a gigantic waterfall. But if that is so, surely the whole of history and of human and animal life is an enormous machine, moving endlessly and inevitably? And yet we know that it is not. We know that some of our own actions are inevitable and compulsory, but we also know that others are free and spontaneous. When a bright light shines in our eyes, our pupils *must* contract; but when we hear a shout, we can decide freely whether or not to look up. The human will is free, in a manner unlike the physiological mechanism to which it is attached. Now, Epicurus wished to explain everything through the combination and movements of the atoms. How could he explain free will? Here is his explanation, as reported by his pupil Lucretius (2.284–93). First, he describes the unmistakable difference between involuntary and voluntary action, and then goes on:

> Therefore among the atoms we must admit that some-
> how,
> apart from weight and impact, there is some other cause
> which moves them: that is the source of our inborn
> power of will:
> because we see that nothing can be produced by nothing.
> Inertia means that actions are not all produced by
> impacts—
> that is, by external force. The mind has no inborn
> necessity, that drives it to every single action
> and makes it into a slave, an object not a subject:
> this is ensured by a tiny swerve of the moving atoms,
> beginning at no fixed place, and at no definite time.

The atoms, said Epicurus, did not move in a regular and steady flow forever. At times, irrationally, unpredictably, they *swerved*; and that swerve accounted both for the interposition of chance in the pattern of events, and for the existence and activity of our will power.

For many centuries this swerve of the atoms was laughed at. The critics of Epicurus pointed out that it destroyed his own theory of rigid physical causation, by introducing one important event which had no cause whatever. The atoms move according to complex but logical rules. Why should they suddenly depart from those rules? So said the ancients; so said the moderns. But within the last generation our own physicists have been making discoveries which appear to be strikingly parallel to Epicurus' theory. The researches of Max Planck and others into what is known as the quantum phenomenon show that, when a particle emits energy, it does so not in a steady and calculable stream but in irregular jets or jerks; or, to put it from another point of view, the scientist can always predict what a large number of moving particles will do, but never what any individual particle will do. Looked at from the atomic point of view, the universe combines mechanical determinism with something very like freedom of will. Max Planck verified the swerve of the atoms of Epicurus.

Epicurus was a thoroughgoing materialist. For him, nothing existed, nothing, except the atoms and empty space. The soul (he said) was merely a complex of uniquely fine atoms; thought and sensation were both atomic movements, inconceivably rapid. Going further, he explained that the delicate atoms of the soul actually were the atoms of air (in two states, rest and motion), of fire, and of another substance even more subtle and moving even more rapidly. This also was scoffed at by some of his critics, and of course it is a pretty primitive way of describing a complex set of functions. And yet, if we look at it sympathetically, does it not seem as though Epicurus was trying to say that thought and sensation were electrical processes? The force, or substance, which is like air and fire and yet is finer and moves more rapidly, surely that is electricity? And physiologists tell us that when a muscle contracts it sets free a charge of heat; that nervous and muscular action is always accompanied by an electrical discharge of ions accumulated and stored within the nerve fiber; and that the activity of the brain is accompanied by measurable pulsations of electrical energy. It is a long way from saying that sensation and thought are accompanied by electrical pulsations to saying that they actually *are* the movements of atoms; and that is where most of us would part company with Epicurus. But he was an absolutely convinced and determined materialist: nothing existed, he held, and nothing could exist except the atoms and the void.

We have been considering him chiefly as a scientific speculator. He himself based his system on physics; but he thought its physical aspects the least important. What mattered most, for Epicurus, was his ethical principles. Most of his teaching was concerned not with the structure of the world and of our bodies but with the way to live happily—which, for him, was the same thing as living well. His moral code now seems to be rather empty and selfish, and to neglect many of man's deepest instincts and needs; but Epicurus himself still remains a provocative and original thinker who, by the power of sheer thought, penetrated farther into the secrets of the physical universe than mankind was to succeed in doing for more than two thousand years.

Lucretius, *De Rerum Natura* (ed. and tr. C. Bailey, Oxford, 1947).

Lucretius, *On the Nature of the Universe* (tr. by R. Latham, Penguin, 1952).

N. DeWitt, *Epicurus and His Philosophy* (University of Minnesota, 1954).

K. Heim, *The Transformation of the Scientific World-View* (Harper, 1954).

# The Small Flat World

M OST of us live in a world arranged according to the rules of Euclid. A straight line is the shortest distance between two points (at least on the ground) and parallel lines never meet (even on the Long Island Railroad). And yet it is possible to construct other worlds run on different principles: it is fascinating to work out their principles and to inhabit them mentally—for a time.

Now, apart from geometry, we all know of such special universes: they are like life, and yet unlike life: they are a projection of life on different sets of co-ordinates.

One of these special worlds is inhabited by many thousands of extremely intelligent men. It is two-dimensional in space, but it extends something like thirteen centuries in time. On an average it measures something between two and four square feet. It is a neat regular pattern of sixty-four squares, alternately black and white. Thirty-two of the squares are empty at all times; the other thirty-two are occupied by symbolic figures representing types of force. This universe contains a competition for power: but it involves logic, mathematics, geometry, will, imagination, history, memory, and other still unnamed qualities. It is the game of chess.

There are many different ways of entering this universe. In spite of the stern logic that governs it (or perhaps because of the stern logic that governs it) aesthetes would say that chess is a beautiful game, surrounded by tangents of beauty. I remember an exhibition of chess sets sponsored by the Metropolitan Museum of New York in 1944, which evoked more imaginative and original designs from many different societies and periods than even the most dreamy chess player would have conceived. And a number of books show photographs of enviable collections: chessmen from India and China, carved with fabulous intricacy, and too delicate for real play (at least the way most people play); twelfth-century chessmen found in the sandy shores of the remote Scottish Hebrides, carved from the ivory of the walrus, showing medieval kings, queens, bishops, and knights, in their very habit as they lived (they have the gloom of the Middle Ages, not the confident swagger of the Renaissance, as we see it on the kings and queens and courtiers of playing cards); there are also modern chessmen made of metals and plastics, starkly geometrical like a Mondrian painting. There is a handsome ballet, called *Checkmate*, which many of us have seen, and whose music we still enjoy: Arthur Bliss composed it, and it was first produced in 1937. Even more beautiful, there has sometimes been a chess game with living pieces. E. M. Forster saw it played in the courtyard of the Wawel Castle in Poland, with music and torchlight. What style the Poles have, and how uselessly they sometimes apply it!

Then there are many people who love chess because of its long and wonderful history. It is hardly possible to play the game without hearing echoes. In its vocabulary there are Persian words which go back to the Middle Ages. The second strongest piece is called rook, which is *rukh*, or chariot, the strength of a medieval army (perhaps we should change it to 'tank'); the name of the game itself is *shah*, or king, and its end is checkmate, *shah mat*, the king is dead. Like the history of costume, the history of games is a marvelous insight into the growth of civilization: chess itself has been constantly changing with the development of society. There is a superb *History of Chess*, by F. J. R. Murray. Most of it is concerned with the medieval origins and Renaissance development of chess; there is not much about the nineteenth century and nothing about the twentieth; but it is a fascinating piece of scholarship, packed with romantic pictures and unimaginable tales of the past. For instance, the church lawyers held that if a clerk (which I think means anyone holding the degree of M.A.) quarreled with his opponent at chess and killed him, the verdict was not murder but accidental homicide, because the clerk was engaged in a lawful occupation. And there is the strange story that Napoleon played against the miraculous chess machine—this was a mechanical figure of a Turk, a malignant and a turbaned Turk, apparently empty of everything but wheels and cylinders, which beat nearly all opponents: Napoleon played it and lost, because it contained the distinguished Austrian chess player Allgaier. The book is full of such tales.

But the game has another kind of attraction. Its history contains many unique personalities and names. Some of them are as romantic as though invented by Dumas: the French master Philidor, the Spanish priest Ruy Lopez, the Man in the White Cloak from Cuba, called Capablanca. Some sound harsh and cruel: Botvinnik, Steinitz, and Tarrasch. Some are eccentric, almost surrealist. My favorite is a brilliant doctor, pianist, and linguist, called Sugar Tart, Zukertort; there is also a former champion of Britain who sounds like an unknown but magnificent piece, Mir Sultan Khan. There is a master who sounds like a pawn's move—Gilg; there is a master who sounds like a king castling—Böök. Even apart from their names, the famous players are often striking in appearance and personality. The American Paul Morphy, from New Orleans—who became virtual champion of the world at the age of twenty-one, offered odds to the entire human race, and then withdrew into something very like insanity—must have closely resembled Edgar Allan Poe and Charles Baudelaire, proud, taciturn, brilliant, self-doomed. In World War II there was a Greek champion who escaped execution by the Germans simply because he could play chess blindfolded against a German guard. There was a Polish player who compared his own game to Mary Queen of Scots, because it was 'beautiful but unlucky.' There was an eminent but acrimonious historian, Buckle, who was also a fine player: once when waiting for his opponent to move, he burst out, 'The slowness of genius is hard to bear, but the slowness of mediocrity is insufferable.'

With all this history, with all these picturesque individuals associated with its development, surely it is surprising that there is so little literature about chess. There are hundreds of technical treatises, but there are few books for non-specialists to read about the game. There is nothing that does for chess what Hemingway's *Death in the Afternoon* did for bull fighting. Much of the best of what exists has been assembled in an anthology by Jerome Salzmann, *The Chess Reader*.

There are many remarkable things in it: for instance, a painting of Shakespeare playing chess with Ben Jonson, by a contemporary Dutch artist, Carel Van Mander; and a delightful short story by Lord Dunsany called 'The Three Sailors' Gambit.' This is about three sailors who came to England during a tournament and began to challenge distinguished players at so much a side (only they had to play by consultation, putting their heads together), and, although they appeared scarcely to understand the right moves, always won. How? Because they had inherited (from a damned messmate) a crystal which always showed the right move; a little board with all the pieces was inside the crystal and the moves were worked out within it, clearly under the devil's direction as all good opposing games are. They kept playing (always in consultation), and they were never beaten, until finally, when drunk, they played the best available player with only a king and a row of pawns. They won, but the crystal blew up with a horrible smell. Even the devil cannot distort that orderly little universe.

Probably the best thing ever written on chess is a long short story by the late Stefan Zweig. Zweig, born in Vienna of a Jewish family, talented and tasteful and fragile, produced not long before his death one of the best recent autobiographies I know, *The World of Yesterday*; it was dictated partly by despair and the sense of loss, and these same feelings created his wonderful story 'The Royal Game.' In this a quiet intellectual, who has been saved from madness during a long period of solitary confinement under a totalitarian government by learning to play chess and mastering 150 championship games, first challenges and then temporarily conquers a formidable, silent, almost mechanical world champion; but at the crucial move he crumples up (as Zweig himself was to crumple up). Chess is a war game, and one cannot win it without having the will to conquer.

Besides this there is a chess game in *Alice through the Looking-Glass*, by Lewis Carroll; but whenever I try to work out that game, I forget it, and become absorbed once again in the marvelous fantasy and the wonderful epigrams. There are also poems, from the baroque age chiefly, and stories from the Arabian Nights and the medieval romances. But no more. There are, in chess, the elements of many interesting dramas and exciting stories; so far, they have not been written.

But most of the best chess players are above all that. They approach the universe of chess with a different point of view. They see it as pure strategy; the interplay of forces within the mind; something like fencing with invisible but deadly blades; something like the formidable musical feat of improvising a fugue on a theme suggested by someone else. In fact, I once met a distinguished musician who would entertain his friends by playing Bach's preludes and fugues straight through, from memory, of course, while conducting a game of chess against a good opponent: I suppose he dictated his moves between fugues, and tried, like Cyrano, to announce mate after the 24th, in B minor . . . And again, the good players see chess as something like the activity of the astrophysicist or the metamathematician who—using symbols for forces that cannot possibly be visualized—works out complex and elegant groupings in a system as big as a nebula or as small as an atom. They see it resembling diplomacy; and metaphysics; and abstract art. It is a wonderful activity. It is the stratosphere of games.

That is the point at which I cannot live in the chess world. Its atmosphere is pure, but too thin for me. It is all cloudless and clean, but it gives me the bends. Its subtleties are beyond me. But they do not make me dislike the game. On the contrary: their difficulty is like the difficulty of El Greco's pictures; or the prose of Proust; or the later Beethoven quartets. Strange how chess and music are allied: some of Capablanca's finest games remind me of the compositions of De Falla in their blend of intricacy, elusiveness, dignity, and basic simplicity.

That graceful stylist, E. M. Forster, has explained how duffers like me feel about chess. He says:

> I play the Evans.
> The invention of a naval officer, the Evans Gambit is noted for its liquidity. A heavy current rapidly sets in from the southwest and laps against the foundations of Black's King's Bishop's Pawn. The whole surface of the board breaks into whirlpools. But sooner or later out of this marine display there rises a familiar corpse. It is mine. Oh, what have I been doing, what have I been doing? The usual thing. Premature attack, followed by timidity. Oh, why didn't I move out my Rook's Pawn? Because as always I was misled by superficial emotions. No, not as always. It must be that the Evans doesn't suit my style. Henceforward I play Old Stodge.
> I do so. There is nothing liquid about Old Stodge. He smacks of the soil. On either side runs a dreary ridge of Knights and Bishops. Between them is a plain (whence the term Giuoco Piano) where the Pawns butt one another like rams. The powers of earth move slowly to the shock, then topple over with alternate and uninspiring thuds. It's supposed to be an exchange. But when the lines of the new landscape emerge from the dust, what familiar corpse is disclosed? Mine. Oh, what have I been doing? The usual thing. My character has come out. If I go down to the depths of the sea, it is there; if I seek the heart of the hills it is there also. Chess, which severely eliminates accident, is a forcing house where the fruits of character can ripen more fully than in Life.

That is the world of chess, and that is why people love to inhabit it, for a short time at least: it is more logical and more satisfactory than life, a great deal neater, but less hazardous, and, on the whole, not *quite* so difficult.

-------

Gerald Abrams, *The Chess Mind* (Pellegrini & Cudahy, 1952).

Assiac, *The Pleasures of Chess* (with built-in chessboard, Simon & Schuster, 1952).

I. Chernev, *The Bright Side of Chess* (McKay, 1948).

A. Hammond, *The Book of Chessmen* (with interesting pictures, Morrow, 1950).

K. Matthews, *British Chess* (also well illustrated, Collins, London, 1948).

H. J. R. Murray, *A History of Chess* (Oxford, 1913).

H. J. R. Murray, *A History of Board-Games other than Chess* (Oxford, 1952).

F. Reinfeld, *The Human Side of Chess* (Pellegrini & Cudahy, 1952).

F. Reinfeld, *The Complete Chessplayer* (Prentice-Hall, 1953).

Jerome Salzmann, *The Chess Reader* (Greenberg, 1949).

## A Bouquet of Poison Ivy

———

THE Preacher says, 'Of making many books there is no end'; and then goes on to talk about weariness, weariness of the flesh—which sounds as though he had been trying to read a set of galley proofs in the bus. But he was elderly, and discouraged. Most of us still enjoy the idea that there are lots of fine books waiting to be written; and we look forward to enjoying them.

For a long time I have been dreaming about one book which ought to be put together. Everytime I think of it, it grows larger and more expensive. It would be an anthology of parody. Most of us love reading good parodies. In the first place, they are funny. Their drollery is the best kind, a skillful distortion of something solemn and systematic into something almost wholly illogical. And they are always intelligent: for parody is a form of criticism, sometimes the most effective form. One might believe that Ezra Pound was a silly poseur and a third-rate poet, but in straight prose discussion one would have to spend a hundred pages on proving it, whereas with half a dozen pages of parody, one might thrust the point deep home, and twist the blade.

A really satisfying anthology of parody would cover a tremendous field of literature past and present. There is no reason why it should not begin at the beginning and come right down to the present day. In fact, it would be a rather attractive way of introducing readers to some of the best books of earlier ages: like approaching Parnassus on a butter-slide.

Western literature begins with Homer: grand, complex, heroic, stylized, and therefore easy to burlesque. The Greek comedians and Cynic philosophers loved to make fun of Homer, although nowadays only scholars can catch most of the jokes. Still, there is at least one modern parody of Homer that goes down well—Fielding's *Tom Jones*: it is really very amusing to see a scrap between Somersetshire villagers in a country churchyard described in the same lofty phrases as the battles of Greek princes and Trojan paladins.

Following Homer, and building on him, came the Greek tragedians. And following them, making rude noises, came the comedian Aristophanes. It must have been pretty discouraging for an Athenian tragic poet to think, while he was composing his profoundest visions of sin and destiny, that a few months after the production of his new play, a bitterly brilliant and uproariously irreverent travesty of it would be shown on the same stage to the same audience. Do you think a modern playwright could endure that? Or would it perhaps stimulate him and strengthen his conviction and sharpen the wits of his audience, as happened in Greece? In modern times one of the finest parodies in the world has been written about

Greek tragedy. It is not possible to enjoy it fully unless you know the conventions of the original. It sounds funny, but merely absurd, instead of pointed and witty: like watching Bert Lahr imitating a heroic scene from Wagner's *Ring* without having sat through a performance of the *Ring* itself. This masterpiece of parody is a *Fragment of a Greek Tragedy*, by the famous poet and scholar, A. E. Housman. Practically every phrase in it is taken directly from the greatest Greek plays, the plot and the management of the characters are all respectably Greek; and yet the conventions all crowded together are irresistibly ridiculous.

One short passage will show this. In Greek tragedy (as in modern opera) the chorus seldom takes any action. It expresses deep feeling, and voices the excitement of the audience (thereby enhancing it), but it does not interfere with the major characters. So sometimes it merely sings without moving while some ferocious crime is being planned and committed. Usually such a scene is moving to watch, but rather unsympathetic to read. Here then is Housman's parody of that typical climactic scene. A mother is being chopped to pieces by her own son inside the palace; the chorus comments: the phrases are full of Greek restraint.

| | |
|---|---|
| *Eriphyla:* | O, I am smitten with a hatchet's jaw; |
| | And that in deed and not in word alone. |
| *Chorus:* | I thought I heard a sound within the house |
| | Unlike the voice of one that jumps for joy. |
| *Eriphyla:* | He splits my skull, not in a friendly way; |
| | One more: he purposes to kill me dead. |
| *Chorus:* | I would not be reputed rash, but yet |
| | I doubt if all be gay within the house. |
| *Eriphyla:* | O! O! Another stroke! That makes the third. |
| | He stabs me to the heart against my wish. |
| *Chorus:* | If that be so, thy state of health is poor; |
| | But thine arithmetic is quite correct. |

Parodies of the Bible, of the Christian liturgy, and of sermons were common in the Middle Ages; and parodies of heroic romance naturally occurred, too. *Reynard the Fox* is really a set of mock-chivalrous adventures whose heroes are animals behaving like both animals and men. The whole of Rabelais is one long parody of romance, ending with the Quest for the Oracle of the Holy Bottle, which I am afraid is a burlesque of the search for the Holy Grail. The seventeenth-century English author Samuel Butler wrote a parody of knighthood crossed with an attack on bigotry, called *Hudibras*. The hero is a Puritan, of a type we have met in other creeds both religious and political:

> Such as do build their faith upon
> The holy text of pike and gun;
> Decide all controversy by
> Infallible artillery;
> And prove their doctrine orthodox
> By apostolic blows and knocks;
> Call fire, and sword, and desolation
> A godly-thorough Reformation.

In the Renaissance the dramatists loved parody. There is a lot of it in Shakespeare. Irrepressible joker, he even took one of Marlowe's heroes and made him into a clown: his swashbuckling soldier Pistol speaks splendid meaningless lines just like Tamburlaine:

> A foutra for the world and worldlings base!
> I speak of Africa and golden joys . . .
> Under which king, Bezonian? Speak, or die.

A little later, the baroque playwrights were burlesquing heroic drama even more systematically. Buckingham's *Rehearsal*, Fielding's *Tom Thumb the Great*, and a terrific tragicomedy by Carey called *Chrononhotonthologos*—these are only a few of the masterpieces produced in the age of periwigs. Here are the first two lines from Carey's play, in splendid blank verse: a courtier addresses another courtier:

> Aldiborontiphoscophornio!
> Where left you Chrononhotonthologos?

(Magnificent. You can almost hear Purcell's trumpets in the distance.) In fact the baroque age was full of fine parodies. Philips did a burlesque of Milton called *The Splendid Shilling*; Pope's *Rape of the Lock* parodied his own forthcoming translation of Homer; and Swift, one of our greatest satirists, was also one of our cruelest parodists.

Next comes one of the most successful single enterprises in this field. In 1812 the managers of Drury Lane offered a prize for the best poetic welcome to be recited at the reopening of their theater after a fire. Two London wits named Smith then published a volume called *Rejected Addresses*, supposed to be unsuccessful attempts by Byron, Wordsworth, Scott, and a dozen or so others. They are absolutely brilliant. Here is the opening of one of them:

> Sated with home, of wife, of children tired,
> The restless soul is driven abroad to roam;
> Sated abroad, all seen yet nought admired,
> The restless soul is driven to ramble home . . .

You recognize at once the misanthropic ennui of Lord Byron. And compare this fine sentence by the ghost of the Grand Panjandrum, Dr. Johnson himself:

> Parturient mountains have ere now produced muscipular abortions, and the auditor who compares incipient grandeur with final vulgarity, is reminded of the pious hawkers of Constantinople, who solemnly perambulate her streets, exclaiming 'In the name of the Prophet— figs!'

The nineteenth century produced many brilliant parodists.

Sometimes their work is so good that one scarcely needs to know the original. When I was a youngster I got hold of a book called *Condensed Novels* by Bret Harte, and used to laugh myself sick over it, without realizing that it was a set of burlesques of novels by Victor Hugo and Charlotte Brontë and others whom I had not read. About a generation later Max Beerbohm wrote a collection which is not so famous as it ought to be, describing Christmas in the styles of distinguished contemporary novelists. It is so trenchant that they say Arnold Bennett, after reading Beerbohm's 'Five Towns' tale of a pudding filled with broken pottery by a masterful woman and chewed up by her lover, was unable to write for several days. The book is called *A Christmas Garland*, and really reads rather better nowadays than the original novelists whom it burlesques.

And we should not forget Gilbert and Sullivan. Much of Gilbert is parody of contemporary melodrama, and Sullivan kept parodying composers such as Donizetti and Verdi. This element of their work is not given quite enough emphasis in the new book on their partnership by Audrey Williamson. In *Princess Ida*, Gilbert has one of the most startling parodic puns in literature. You remember how Macbeth, after murdering his king, says that the drugged attendants cried out, 'God bless us,' and he should have said 'Amen,' but '*Amen* stuck in my throat.' So in *Princess Ida*, when Melissa is about to denounce male intruders in a women's college,

> 'Why, these
> Are men,' she would have added, but *Are Men*
> Stuck in her throat.

But we are even better off today. There are more parodists writing effectively in our own time than in any comparable period for generations past, and most of them are American humorists. It is as though they recognized that ambitious authors sometimes distort reality by making it too complex or too tragic, and were determined to restore the balance. There are some deft correctives by Corey Ford and Frank Sullivan; some crazy parodies by Benchley, dear Benchley; don't forget the eccentric Englishmen J. C. Squire and A. P. Herbert; and really there is almost nothing to choose between the four most consistently successful parodists of today: Wolcott Gibbs, S. J. Perelman, James Thurber, and E. B. White. You see why we need a collection of their work: it is nearly all scattered, and the only single book I know which tries to bring some of these masterpieces together is a *poetic* anthology called *What Cheer*, by David McCord. One of these modern parodies is already becoming a classic, for it is being reprinted in college manuals of creative writing, heaven save us! It is Mr. White's travesty of the typical *Vogue* article, called 'Dusk in Fierce Pyjamas.' Listen—

> It is the magic hour before cocktails. I am in the modern penthouse of Monsieur Charles de Beistegui. The staircase is entirely of cement, spreading at the hemline and trimmed with padded satin tubing caught at the neck with a bar of milk chocolate. It is dusk . . .

Or try this, from Gibbs's 'Death in the Rumble Seat,' a burlesque of Hemingway slinging the bull:

> If you don't know anything about driving cars you are apt to think a driver is good just because he goes fast. This may be very exciting at first, but afterwards there is a bad taste in the mouth and feeling of dishonesty. Ann Bender, the American, drove as fast on the Merrick Road as anybody I have ever seen, but when cars came the other way she always worked out of their terrain and over in the ditch, so that you never had the hard, clean feeling of danger, but only bumping up and down in the ditch, and sometimes hitting your head on the top of the car.

Thurber is famous; yet few of us realize, until we read his parodies, how many different styles he can travesty. Here is a brief specimen, in the energetic manner of James Cain:

> I walked close to her. It was like dying and going to Heaven . . . I reached over and let her have one on the chin and she went down like a tray of dishes. I knew then I would be beating her up the rest of my life. It made me feel like it was April and I was a kid again and had got up on a warm morning and it was all misty outdoors and the birds were singing.

Frankly, my own favorite of these four is S. J. Perelman, partly because he is more fantastic than the others and partly because he works much closer to the bull. He can achieve a parody in only one or two sentences. For instance, he once dreamed up a highbrow quarterly magazine called *Spindrift,* in which he said he was following a serial called 'Mysticism in the Rationalist Cosmogony, or John Dewey Rides Again.'

> In the previous number, the cattle rustlers (post-Hegelian dogma) had dropped Dewey in an abandoned mine-shaft (Jamesian pragmatism) and had ignited the fuse leading to a keg of dynamite (neo-Newtonian empiricism).

In the same volume Perelman outlined a modern ballet called 'Six Who Pass While the Concrete Boils,' in which

> half a dozen stocky Bryn Mawr girls in grey jersey stride convulsively from one end of the stage to the other tugging at a veil. This symbolizes the forces of water, sand, and Portland cement at first refusing to work harmoniously, then uniting for the common good.

The ideal anthology of parody would contain all these and many more, together with the work of many almost unknown writers. I remember a brilliant parody of *John Peel,* published in *Punch* some years ago: here are two stanzas:

D'ye ken Mrs. Twickenham-Dalrymple-Spruce-Jones at
                                    the break of day,
When she wakens the dead with her laugh so gay?
D'ye ken Mrs. Twickenham-Dalrymple-Spruce-Jones,
                                    who can't keep away
From a Meet of the Hounds in the morning?

I can see her now on her large flat feet,
In a coat of a style long obsolete,
Singing ho-tally-ho in the blinding sleet,
        At the Meet of the Hounds in the morning.

Finally, an intelligent and wealthy publisher (all publishers
ought to be wealthy and most are intelligent) would actually
commission new parodies in order to fill out the list. For
example, we need a parody of MacLeish; and a parody of
Thomas Mann, doubtless called *Mann and Obermann*; and
one of Sartre, entitled *Sartre Resartus*; and one of André Gide,
which would surely be called *La Nature Déteste le Gide*, or
perhaps *Gide the Obscene*. And then we could find some
eminent authors who appear to be parodying themselves:
dare I mention Mr. Faulkner's *Absalom, Absalom*? But
enough of this. As the Irish judge said when he was passing
sentence on a local criminal, 'If this pig-stealing continues,
none of us will be safe!'

---

Max Beerbohm, *A Christmas Garland* (Heinemann, London,
    1912).

Bret Harte, *Condensed Novels* (Osgood, 1871).

Bret Harte, *Condensed Novels, Second Series* (Houghton Mifflin,
    1902).

H. J. Owens, *The Scandalous Adventures of Reynard the Fox,
    a Modern American Version* (Knopf, 1945).

David McCord, *What Cheer* (Coward-McCann, 1945).

S. J. Perelman, *The Dream Department* (Random House, 1943).

E. B. White and K. S. White (editors), *A Subtreasury of Amer-
    ican Humor* (Coward-McCann, 1941).

D<small>ON'T</small> you think that everyone ought to know something about science? Doesn't it seem ridiculous that we should live seventy or eighty years in the world without understanding how it is constructed, how our neighbors the animals live, and how our own bodies work? Of course it is. Most of us have actually had some smatterings of science at school or in college. But few, very few of us, have been able to keep it up. We may read an occasional scientific article in a newspaper or magazine, and wonder for a while; but we do not have any continuous picture of scientific advance in our minds, and we have enormous areas of ignorance even about important new discoveries. How many of us could explain what happens during an atomic explosion, or say what the achievements of the last scientific Nobel Prize winners really meant?

There are three reasons for this.

The first is that many of the fields in which science is busiest are terribly difficult to understand. That is, even the experts find them difficult, and for the average man they are almost utterly unintelligible. Some of the latest thinking about the atomic structure of matter, and in particular about the relationship between matter and energy, requires extremely hard and complex intellectual work: some of it must be carried on without visualization, some of it is scarcely expressible in the crude language of words and sentences which we use everyday, and some of it seems to operate in regions outside our accustomed framework of time, and space, and even logic. The British scientist J. B. S. Haldane says, 'The universe is not only queerer than we suppose, but queerer than we can suppose.'

Then there is the second difficulty that much science seems to have nothing to do with daily life, and often to contradict ordinary common sense. It takes a tremendous effort to convince oneself that the stationary walls and floor of one's own home are spinning through space in a dizzy combination of three movements all at once (the earth rotating, the planet revolving round the sun, and the whole box of tricks rushing madly toward a spot somewhere near the star Vega). It takes still more of an effort to assimilate the idea that the walls and the floor, and in fact one's own body, are composed of uncountable myriads of tiny atomic systems all engaged in complex relationships which involve inconceivably rapid movement and the emission of intermittent spurts of electrical energy. Much of science does not appeal to the average man because he cannot see that it matters. This is a variation on the principle well known to schoolteachers, that human beings are *able* to learn almost anything, but *willing* to learn almost nothing unless they can make what they learn into part of their own lives.

The third difficulty is the one which interests me chiefly. This is that many of the sciences are now operating in areas which cannot be understood without a considerable amount of introductory work. They use concepts which the average man never encounters, and terms of measurement which are beyond him. Probably this is why there are not enough, not nearly enough, good scientific books for the ordinary reader, who is at best a scientific amateur, and more usually wholly untrained. Yet they are badly needed. Whenever one is produced it is a most valuable stimulus: as valuable as a good new poem or a penetrating novel.

Fortunately, several excellent scientific books for the ordinary man have come out recently. I enjoyed them all, and can recommend them. The first is *The Scientific American Reader*: about sixty articles on twelve different aspects of science, by experts nearly all of whom write clearly and interestingly. Then there is *Science in Progress, 8th Series*, a group of lectures edited by George Baitsell. Let me also praise a delightful set of essays called *The Itinerant Ivory Tower* by G. E. Hutchinson.

While reading these books, I was struck by the amazing diversity and novelty of scientific discovery; but also, more forcibly, by something which is not explicitly pointed out in any of them. This is the fact that there are at least two different kinds of science: two different types of exploration of the universe. Not long ago, in the era when some of us were introduced to the subject, there was one predominant type of science. But in the past thirty or forty years the other type has come on with increasing vigor, and is gaining strength all the time.

The first type of science is *descriptive*. It takes a certain field, and investigates it on the strict assumption that it will be intricate and subtle, but that it will not change. That is, changes and processes will occur within the field, but they will occur again and again and again and again uniformly; the field itself will not alter. There are several good examples of this in *The Scientific American Reader*. For instance, an article on the language of bees: this is a report on the experiments made by the Austrian naturalist Karl von Frisch, who has spent forty years working with bees and in that time, using the experimental method and modern equipment, has found out as much as hundreds of generations of earlier bee-keepers managed to learn, observant as they were.

The problem is simple. It is this. Bees live collectively, but they operate singly. They do not fly in schools or move in swarms, like driver ants or some kinds of fish. How then do they communicate with one another? We know that they do: for when one bee, working alone, finds a good new source of food, other bees from the same hive soon come and visit it, too. Somehow the discoverer must have told the other bees *what* he has found and *where* it is. He does *not* guide them to it, and he has nothing like our own verbal language; he can't even point. How does he do it? The answer was discovered (as far as we know, for the first time in history) by von Frisch. He put out some concentrated sugar solution, waited until an exploring bee found it, and then observed what it did inside the dark hive. (He used photographic red light, which the bees cannot see.) It was fantastic. The result was always the same. The bee fed, and then flew back and entered the hive. Inside the hive it performed an elaborate dance, or rather one of two different types of dance. The other bees watched it, became excited, imitated the dance, and then— this is the vital point—flew out and went straight to the sugar solution. When they returned, they, too, danced, and so encouraged any unemployed bees to join in the feast. Von Frisch noticed two kinds of dance: one, a circular movement followed by a reverse circle, means that the bee has found a source of food quite close to the hive (within fifty yards or so); the other, a run forward and backward, accompanied by a switching movement of the abdomen, means that the source is some distance away. Not only is this a fine piece of scientific discovery, but, like much scientific discovery, it contains elements of poetry. We have all enjoyed the brilliant dances of the butterflies, which remind us of a classical ballet; isn't it delightful to know that the hard-working bees, whenever they strike it rich, rush back home and execute either a waltz or a rumba?

This is descriptive science. It assumes that the object of investigation will not change. As long as there are hive-bees, they will behave in that way when they find a new source of food. As long as there is the substance which we know as ammonia, it will be composed of three atoms of hydrogen and one atom of nitrogen, arranged in a pyramid with the nitrogen atom at its apex, oscillating from one side to the other under radiation at 24,000 megacycles per second. Time does not alter the bees: they have apparently completed their evolution; time does not alter the structure of $NH_3$, ammonia.

But there is another way of approaching the universe. It can be seen as a chain of events in time, it can be investigated as a process, and usually as an irreversible process. This is one of the fundamental distinctions in science. If you boil a kettle of water and allow it to cool again, you have made it pass through a reversible process. It is just the same water at the end of the experiment as it was at the beginning (allowing for the escape of a little in the form of steam). But every day we pass through phases of life which will never be reversed and never be exactly repeated. The history of our lives cannot be run backward, like a film reversed or like water cooling in a kettle. Now, there are many similar processes in nature, which scientists are exploring with growing interest and success.

For instance, in biochemistry, scientists have been forced to become historians, and to expect constant changes in their field. Some of the most damaging diseases are transmitted by organisms which are too small to be seen, except with the electron microscope: these are called viruses. Influenza, measles, and polio are all virus diseases. Now, it is not possible to study a virus and the disease it produces as though they were going to remain constant until the end of time. Viruses are alive; they breed; they change by mutation; they evolve. A virus that produces a disease of no particular importance may suddenly be transformed, and may become lethal. On the other hand, a virus which inhabits a certain human population may in time lose much of its kick: not because it is not inherently dangerous to mankind, but because that particular group of people has become immune to its effects.

In the same way scientists must study the life of mankind *as a species*; that is, they must explain a time-process which produced us as we now are. Most of us find it pretty difficult to imagine how such a fundamental change as that from animal to man could ever take place, also how changes in the physical structure of complex living things could occur. We think of ourselves as static, not as changing. But several good articles in *The Scientific American Reader* stress the idea that nearly all living types have the power of producing almost limitless variations. Insects and birds and animals and people have thousands of genes, which in combination can easily form new patterns running into many millions. In a changing environment a *new* pattern, produced by this combination of genes, may be the best fitted to survive and reproduce; and so a *new variety* will be formed, and ultimately a new species. Thinking along the same lines, scientists have dropped the idea that modern man must have had *one* single chain of ancestors leading back to the lower primates. On the contrary, there were many different branches on the trunk from which we grew. The Scottish anthropologist Broom, working in South Africa, explains how he and others have found many remains of different types, not of our ancestors but of their cousins: some are erect people with delicate hands but with brains markedly smaller than ours; and others are giants far bigger than the average of mankind today. Widen the range of possible variation, and the entire story of evolution becomes easier to understand and accept.

But the most enthralling aspect of this—what we might call historical science—is the study of astronomy. There are five admirable articles upon it in *The Scientific American Reader,* and two more in *Science in Progress.* They all stress the same point: that the life of the stars must be viewed as a historical process. Yet in this particular field we come closer than anywhere else to the God's-eye view. In other studies we see the present, and remember the past, and try to predict the future. In astronomy the present and the past and even the future are all observable at once. We live on a planet revolving round a medium-sized star. By observing other such stars we can reconstruct the career of our own. Our star is part of an island universe: we can see the rest of our island any clear night; it is the Milky Way, the Galaxy, 100,000 light years in breadth. But away in the distance we can see other galaxies, other island-universes. By studying them and comparing their structure and behavior with the galaxy we ourselves inhabit, we can determine the past of our own and begin to see its future. We can observe young stars, mature stars, and old stars; there are even some which are dead but yet speak—they are the remnants of huge exploded supernovae which are invisible, but still emit radio waves: the ghosts of space.

All this is difficult to understand. One clear truth, however, emerges from it. This is that time is an essential component of our universe, and that no explanation which omits time can possibly claim to be valid. It was Bergson who first emphasized this strongly enough. He said that most philosophical systems failed because they were static: collections of equations; timeless metaphysical theorems; what Bradley called 'a ballet of bloodless categories.' Philosophers have neglected the essential fact not only of human existence but of the life of the universe: its constant change, its marvelous, unpredictable novelty. Science, too, has sometimes seemed to paralyze and deaden our world, to make it unreal by fitting it into neat, timeless schemes; but now it is endeavoring to understand the eternal process of change and development. It is almost impossible, therefore, to read its most recent discoveries without feeling two of the most important and valuable human emotions: wonder, and hope.

G. E. Hutchinson, *The Itinerant Ivory Tower* (Yale, 1953).

*Science in Progress, 8th Series* (ed. George A. Baitsell, Yale, 1953).

*The Scientific American Reader* (Simon & Schuster, 1953).

C. R. Ribbands, *The Behaviour and Social Life of Honeybees* (Hale Publishing Co., 1954).

*Escape*

---

ONE of the horrifying things about this twentieth century is its tremendous concentration on exile and imprisonment. Perhaps there have been as many displaced persons in other epochs; but there have rarely, if ever, been so many people behind fences or bars or stone walls in the history of the world. Hundreds of thousands of people in Europe, who, when they were at school or in college, would have shrunk with horror from the idea of even visiting a prison, later found themselves inhabitants of prison camps, and spent years there, or died, or were murdered. In our grandfathers' time there were some thousands of prisoners in the Asiatic territories of Russia; now the number is a huge multitude, running into millions. And during the last big war, from East to West all over the world, an unprecedentedly large number of soldiers and civilians were swept into prisons of various types —some to be released in time, some to languish there until the end, and some to escape.

There are a number of fine books about escaping from prison—some of them about recent adventures, others ranging through a great part of history. As one reads them, one begins to see that, in order to escape from prison successfully, special physical and mental qualities are required. What is the character of the ideal escaper?

First and foremost the man who is to escape successfully needs sublime self-confidence. The odds are so heavily against him that he will never, never win by behaving as he would in ordinary life, by thinking of himself as an average man. He must believe that he is exceptional: uniquely lucky, phenomenally clever, something of a hero. Usually it is easy enough to acquire this strengthening confidence, because when one is alone in a cell, one can concentrate on one's own personality; and when one is imprisoned with others, there are comparatively few who are determined to escape, so that one can legitimately feel superior.

The most famous of all escapers was the Venetian crook, profligate, confidence man, and lone wolf: Casanova. He was imprisoned by the Inquisition in a peculiarly difficult kind of jail: a cell in the attics of the Ducal Palace in Venice. His escape was not to be made upward or outward, like those of so many other prisoners; but downward. He began, therefore, by making a hole in the floor under his bed. He got through a double layer of planks; beneath that there was a sub-floor of terrazzo—a sort of concrete made of cement and marble chips. Casanova got through that, too. Just as he was about to make a rope of bedsheets and lower himself down to the room below, he was taken out of his cell and moved to a larger one because it was more comfortable.

All Casanova's work had to begin over again; and what was worse, the guards discovered the hole in the floor in the old cell, and searched every part of his new cell every day, so that (although he had kept the iron bar he used for digging) he could dig no more. At this point most of us would have given up. Casanova merely became more determined than ever. Anger increased his self-confidence. He could not make his own way out. Therefore he had to get someone else to do the digging. He began to exchange books with a prisoner in a neighboring cell, a monk called Balbi. On the blank fly-leaves of these books he wrote messages in invisible ink (it was mulberry juice, and he wrote with a pointed fingernail). The messages persuaded Balbi to dig through the ceiling of his own cell, then move along the rafters and break down into Casanova's cell. To help him, Casanova sent him the iron bar, concealed inside a dish of macaroni; for inducement, he promised to lead Balbi and his cellmate safely out of the prison. Sublime confidence! A further complication was the fact that an informer was put in to share Casanova's cell. Casanova took care of that by playing on the informer's religious sensibilities, and getting him to believe that an angel from heaven was coming to break through the roof. If this sounds improbable, remember that in the First World War a British officer persuaded a Turkish jailer that he was in communication with the occult, and could discover huge hidden treasures; while the Russian nihilist Nechayev converted not only his guard but the commandant of his prison.

Casanova still had to get out on the roof of the palace, work his way painfully and dangerously along it, and down into a window of a room away from the prison block, then walk downstairs through the palace, out into the courtyard, across the public square, into a gondola, and at last across the frontier. The miserable accomplice Balbi never ceased to cry and complain and declare the whole enterprise impossible. Casanova dominated him and sustained himself and won freedom through his matchless self-confidence. In later life he would never tell the story, even to a duke, unless he could be assured of a clear hour or more, uninterrupted; and it was that same belief in his own powers that made him a brilliantly adventurous confidence trickster, and a terrifyingly daring gambler.

In every escape there seems to be at least one crisis when the escaper has to risk everything without flinching. Self-confidence is then the only thing he can trust. Young Winston Churchill, a prisoner of the Boers, hopped over the wall of his pen and hid in a garden. But he still had to pass a sentry.

> Failure being almost certain, no odds against success affected me. All risks were less than the certainty . . . I said to myself 'Toujours de l'audace,' put my hat on my head, strode into the middle of the garden, walked past the windows . . . without any concealment, and so went through the gate . . . I passed the sentry at less than five yards . . . Whether he looked at me or not, I do not know, for I never turned my head. I restrained with the utmost difficulty an impulse to run. But after walking a hundred yards and hearing no challenge, I knew that the . . . obstacle had been surmounted. I was at large.

There, then, is the first quality you need in order to escape from prison: supreme trust in yourself.

The second quality (which dovetails into the first) is that you must despise or hate your jailers. Hence all the practical jokes that American and British prisoners used to play on the Germans, simply to keep from being dominated. But such things were virtually impossible with captors who did not observe the Geneva Convention: for instance, the Japanese, and more recently the Chinese and North Korean Communists, and the Germans in concentration camps as opposed to military prison camps. (One of the saddest things in Dr. Cohen's book about the concentration camps is his description of what he calls 'regression': the process by which prisoners were reduced not to animals but to something like children, both in their habits and in their morals, and, worst of all, in their attitude to their jailers. He says, with emphasis, that most prisoners did not hate the SS, even after their liberation. And in the camps they could not think of escape, because they were dominated.)

The third quality which we might think necessary for escapers turns out (judging by the statements of those who have succeeded) not to be vital. This is a knowledge of the language of one's jailers and of the surrounding country. It is a help, but many men have escaped without it. Brigadier Hargest, who was in a special camp in Italy, got out disguised as an elderly artisan and jumped onto a train for Milan. The man next to him was an Italian military policeman, who began to talk to him. Hargest had already thought of this, and had learned a single Italian sentence: in a whisper he said, 'I am sorry, but I am very deaf.' This worked. Other escapers, faced with the same difficulty, have pretended to be drunk, or half-witted. Several of them say this was rather hard to do— not because it was difficult to make the pretense, but because it was difficult to accept the contempt of the other side, even while deceiving them.

Then there are four or five technical requisites. They are nearly always listed in the same order. First of all is clothes. Military prisoners are always in uniform: they have to get out of uniform. Other prisoners are in prison dress, ugly and easily identifiable, like those dismal stripes of the concentration camps, or else in very poor clothes, sloppy and repulsive. To escape, they must have clothes which will look like those of the ordinary population outside. But it is sometimes difficult to get out of the immediate danger zone wearing such clothes, and two suits are sometimes needed. Often in the First World War and occasionally in the Second, Allied prisoners managed to fake German uniforms and walk out of German camps, relying on the ordinary German soldier's reverence for anything that even looked like an officer. The ingenuity which they used was unbelievable. For instance, H. A. Cartwright and his friend Harrison made German uniforms by taking British greatcoats, changing the buttons, adding stars and numerals, weaving silken shoulder straps, forging cap badges with buttons and silver paper, to be added to suitable caps, buying boots on the pretext that their own were worn out, and finally carving swords and scabbards out of pieces of a wooden packing case. Then, fully uniformed and loaded with concealed packages of food, they walked through the camp and approached the gate. The sentry did nothing; he simply stared. They probably looked a bit strange; but he could not believe that anything which looked like a German officer might not be a German officer, so he stood still. In desperation, Cartwright raised a finger, as though returning a salute. The sentry sprang to the gate, threw it open, clicked his heels, and froze. The two disguised escapers walked slowly out, acknowledging some more salutes on the way, and strolled off down the road . . . their pace made slower by the fact that one of them was lame and rattling clang-clang-clang, because a can of crackers had come adrift inside his trouser leg. Yet they made it. Five minutes later they were in a garden, changing into their second disguise, workmen's clothes; and in a couple of hours they had sunk their fake uniforms deep in a canal.

Clothes first, not forgetting the all-important boots, fit to travel many miles. Then a map, plus a compass, or else the ability to travel by the sun and stars. Usually this is extremely hard for city-bred people, who simply follow streets or ride in subways; on the other hand, they have less chance of getting lost when they reach a big town and have to make their way through it surrounded by the enemy. And then, obviously, food: even small packages of something to chew will keep the escaper from feeling he is going to starve to death in the next few hours; almost every prisoner who has got away reports that he thought incessantly about food; and we know now that eating is not only a source of physical energy but a method of calming the nerves.

Another helpful quality for the escaper is a sense of humor. Ridiculous things are apt to happen to him. He will march in a circle all night and find himself at dawn back in the same field he left seven hours before; or he will jump onto the wrong train, to be carried far away from the frontier. If he can laugh at such things, even inwardly, it may be valuable for him. But that is not always true. Some prisoners, like Richard Pape, actually gave themselves away by getting excited and clowning; others, like the Poles who escaped from both the Germans and the Russians, saw so much barbarity that they could laugh no more.

One rather rare innate gift that is often a tremendous help in escaping is to have a way with women. Women don't make wars. Secretly or openly, nearly every woman in every country hates fighting, and rejects the constant hostility which smolders in the hearts of so many men. Again and again, escaping prisoners report that while they passed through hostile territory, or else neutral territory, men would hunt them, or at best ignore them, but women would pity them, feed them and nurse them, even offer them love. Richard Pape would have died if he had not been nursed back to life in a Polish convent. A German girl fell in love with Sergeant Dowd, and got him civilian clothes, to help him to escape, which meant leaving her: because 'she was a woman first and a German second.' A prisoner in a Jap camp got out and made his way to a native village, and there was so beloved by a beautiful Chinese-Javanese girl that he married her and settled down, while her father took his two buddies across the straits to Sumatra. The funniest of all these stories is the tale of Roy Farran's escape from a prison hospital just outside Athens. He seized an unguarded moment, and bolted. Within a few minutes, an old peasant woman had taken charge of him and shown him where to change his clothes: then he was led into a 'safe house.' Visitors began to pour in, carrying presents. They filled his pockets with cigarettes. They gave him a huge plate of food. They kissed him. They danced a sort of jig around him. Finally they brought in a pretty girl, pointed out her various charms, explained that she had lost her husband in Albania, and suggested that he should consider himself married right away. He was English, so he said it was rather too quick work (besides, she had only one eye); still, it made him feel he was human again.

There is one ultimate possession which every escaper, and in fact every prisoner, should command. He must have something to think about. He must have a sense of purpose. That was the very worst thing about the concentration camps. The few who survived them without major spiritual damage were people with a profound belief in something, people who did not live day to day or meal to meal, but lived for something else. The sense of purpose need not be lofty and other-worldly: with Casanova it was not much more than an assertion of his own individual importance and perhaps of his powerful sexual drive; sometimes it is the wish for revenge; often it is party feeling, or nationalism, or a sense of military obligation; but some sense of purpose is utterly necessary. This is the deepest meaning of existentialism, and of most good philosophies: the will to live, the will to survive, not to *escape*, but to conquer the jailers and the tormentors, to make defeat into victory, helplessness into freedom. Only the brave and the wise are free.

---

Paul Brickhill, *Escape or Die* (Norton, 1952).

Elie Cohen, *Human Behavior in the Concentration Camp* (tr. M. H. Braaksma, Norton, 1953).

Basil Davenport, *Great Escapes* (Sloane, 1952).

Heinrich Harrer, *Seven Years in Tibet* (tr. Richard Graves, Dutton, 1954).

Richard Pape, *Boldness Be My Friend* (Houghton Mifflin, 1954).

Eric Williams, *The Book of Famous Escapes* (Norton, 1954).

# Index